Palgrave Macmillan Studies in Family and Intimate Life

Series Editors

Lynn Jamieson
University of Edinburgh
Edinburgh, UK

Jacqui Gabb
Faculty of Arts & Social Sciences
Open University
Milton Keynes, UK

Sara Eldén
Lund University
Lund, Sweden

Chiara Bertone
University of Eastern Piedmont
Alessandria, Italy

Vida Česnuitytė
Mykolas Romeris University
Vilnius, Lithuania

'The *Palgrave Macmillan Studies in Family and Intimate Life* series is impressive and contemporary in its themes and approaches'
– Professor Deborah Chambers, Newcastle University, UK, and author of *New Social Ties.*

The remit of the *Palgrave Macmillan Studies in Family and Intimate Life* series is to publish major texts, monographs and edited collections focusing broadly on the sociological exploration of intimate relationships and family life. The series encourages robust theoretical and methodologically diverse approaches. Publications cover a wide range of topics, spanning micro, meso and macro analyses, to investigate the ways that people live, love and care in diverse contexts. The series includes works by early career scholars and leading internationally acknowledged figures in the field while featuring influential and prize-winning research.

This series was originally edited by David H.J. Morgan and Graham Allan.

Jenny Björklund
Dovilė Kuzminskaitė • Julie Rodgers
Editors

Negotiating Non-Motherhood

Representations, Perceptions, and Experiences

Editors
Jenny Björklund
Uppsala University
Uppsala, Sweden

Dovilė Kuzminskaitė
Vilnius University
Vilnius, Lithuania

Julie Rodgers
Maynooth University
Maynooth, Ireland

This work was supported by Vilnius University, European Union's Horizon 2020 research and innovation programme (952366), National University of Ireland Maynooth and Uppsala University.

ISSN 2731-6440   ISSN 2731-6459   (electronic)
Palgrave Macmillan Studies in Family and Intimate Life
ISBN 978-3-031-66696-4   ISBN 978-3-031-66697-1   (eBook)
https://doi.org/10.1007/978-3-031-66697-1

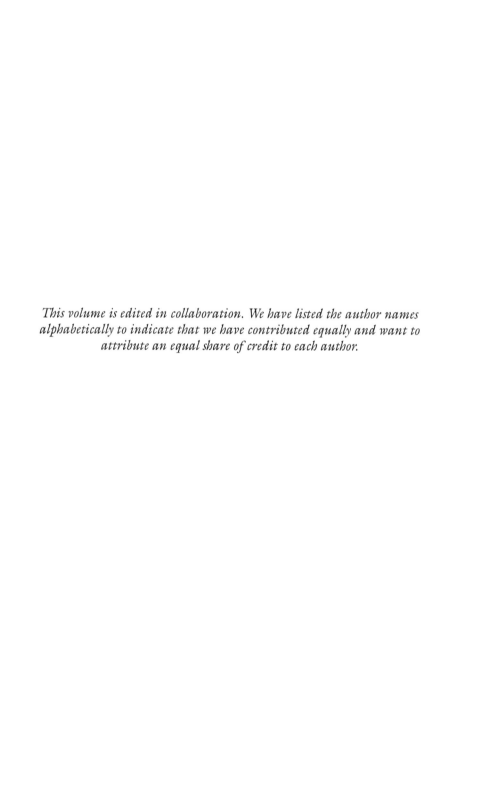

This volume is edited in collaboration. We have listed the author names alphabetically to indicate that we have contributed equally and want to attribute an equal share of credit to each author.

ACKNOWLEDGEMENTS

This volume has grown out of a collaboration between researchers from Vilnius University (Lithuania), Uppsala University (Sweden), and Maynooth University (Ireland). Together, these researchers are part of MotherNet, a network that has received funding from the EU Horizon 2020 TWINNING research and innovation programme to carry out collaborative and interdisciplinary cutting-edge research on contemporary motherhood (grant agreement No 952366). We would like to thank all MotherNet participants for the engaging and thought-provoking discussions on non-motherhood—and motherhood—that we have had since the network commenced at the beginning of 2021. We would particularly like to thank the contributors of this volume, which also includes authors from outside the network, for their hard work and for the discussions that we had during a five-day workshop at the Faberllull Residency in Olot, Spain, in March 2022. We are extremely grateful to the Faberllull Residency in Olot for hosting us during this extraordinary visit—we were really fortunate to have peace and quiet to work on the volume in such a beautiful place. Finally, we would like to thank line editor Rebecca Ahlfeldt, who language-edited some of the chapters, and Madelon Nanninga, who did the index.

Praise for *Negotiating Non-Motherhood*

"With the volume *Negotiating Non-Motherhood: Representations, Perceptions, and Experiences* editors Jenny Björklund, Dovilė Kuzminskaitė, and Julie Rodgers bring together a unique and rich tapestry of voices exploring non-motherhood well beyond the conventional, but simplistic, distinction between voluntary and involuntary childlessness. It offers an engaging, thought-provoking and deeply inspiring read with each chapter adding another layer to our understanding of the many dimensions of non-motherhood."
—Helen Peterson, *Professor in Sociology, Örebro University, Sweden*

"This is a highly welcome entry into scholarship on the maternal. The volume brings together a range of international researchers who together interrogate this important topic. It makes an important contribution to the field of non-motherhood by theorising the wide range of forms non-motherhood can take."
—Natalie Edwards, *Professor of Literature in French, University of Bristol, author of Voicing Voluntary Childlessness (2016)*

"An exhaustive collection of writing on 'non-motherhood' that moves beyond seeing motherhood as a monolithic state. From academic research in different cultural contexts to analysing other writing, this takes a hybrid and intersectional approach to tell a different kind of story than what media would like us to believe in. We all need to read this so we build a better understanding of womanhood and motherhood, and the spaces in between, and move beyond polarised discussions."
—Professor Pragya Agarwal, *author of (M)otherhood: On the choices of being a woman (2021) and Hysterical: Exploding the myth of gendered emotions (2023)*

NOTES ON CONTRIBUTORS

Anna Morero Beltrán is an associate professor in the Department of Sociology at the University of Barcelona, Spain. Her research interests are mainly related to the study of the social construction of reproductive technologies, family diversity, sexist violence, and sexuality. She has participated in several competitive research projects and in research agreements with public administrative bodies. She has written numerous scientific articles and is a member of the Interuniversity Research Group Copolis 'Wellbeing, Community and Social Control'.

Jenny Björklund is Professor of Gender Studies at Uppsala University, Sweden. Her current research deals with cultural representations of in/voluntary childlessness, reproductive decision-making and climate change, and queer readings of literature. Her books include *Maternal Abandonment and Queer Resistance in Twenty-First-Century Swedish Literature* (2021) and *Lesbianism in Swedish Literature: An Ambiguous Affair* (2014). She is the co-editor of *New Dimensions of Diversity in Nordic Culture and Society* (2016).

Mercedes Carbayo-Abengózar is Lecturer in Spanish and Latin American Studies at Maynooth University, Ireland. Her research falls under the umbrella of Hispanic cultural studies and she publishes mainly on the relationship between gender and class, focusing on writers such as Carmen Martín Gaite, singers like Concha Piquer, and painters like Frida Kahlo. For the last ten years, the focus of her research has moved towards issues of intersectionality in relation to motherhood and mothering.

Jasmine D. Cooper is the Fairlie-Hutchinson Research Fellow in French at Girton College, Cambridge, UK. Her current research explores intersectional rage in contemporary Francophone women's writing and visual arts, focusing on the revolutionary and decolonial potential of women's anger in the last decade. Her doctoral thesis, 'An End in Herself: Non-Motherhood in Contemporary French Women's Writing', examined literary representations of non-motherhood by French and Francophone authors. She is currently preparing this project as a monograph with Liverpool University Press (forthcoming 2025).

Valerie Heffernan is Professor of Literary and Cultural Studies in the School of Modern Languages, Literatures and Cultures at Maynooth University, Ireland. Her research interests include literary and cultural portrayals of mothers, mothering, and motherhood; her recent work has focussed on cultural expressions of maternal regret. Heffernan is also the co-editor (with Gay Wilgus) of *Imagining Motherhood in the Twenty-First Century* (Routledge, 2021).

Dovilė Kuzminskaitė is an associate professor at the Faculty of Philology, Institute for Literary, Cultural and Translation Studies, Vilnius University, Lithuania. She holds a PhD in Latin American Literature. Her main research interests are contemporary Latin American and Spanish literature, experimental literature, gender studies, and identity issues, as depicted in literary works and media.

Laura Lazzari holds a PhD from the University of Lausanne and a Master of Studies from the University of Oxford. She is a Scientific Collaborator at the Sasso Corbaro Foundation for the Medical Humanities, Switzerland, an Affiliate Scholar at the Department of Italian Studies and an Affiliate Faculty at the Medical Humanities Initiative at Georgetown University, USA. She specializes in Motherhood Studies and the Medical Humanities and has published extensively on women's writing in the Italian-speaking world.

Julie Rodgers is Associate Professor of French and Francophone Studies at Maynooth University, Ireland. She has written extensively on the depiction of motherhood in contemporary women's writing and film in French, most notably on topics such as maternal ambivalence, pregnancy denial, single motherhood, teenage pregnancy, and voluntary childlessness. Along with Helene Cummins and Judith Wouk, she is the co-editor of *The Truth About (M)Otherhood: Choosing to be Childfree* (Demeter, 2021).

Elisabet Almeda Samaranch is Professor of Sociology at the University of Barcelona, Spain. She is a member of the Interuniversity Research Group COPOLIS 'Welfare, Community and Social Control' and of the CEFOCID-COPOLIS teaching innovation group. Her research and teaching have developed in three main areas: systems of criminal justice (female criminality and women's prisons), changes and family policies (family diversity, one-parent families, and welfare policies and gender), and memory and identity (gender and sociology of memory).

María Sebastià-Sáez is an assistant professor at the Institute of Literary, Cultural and Translation Studies, Vilnius University, and researcher at the Institute of English, Romance and Classical Studies, Vilnius University, and at the Centre for Studies in Comparative Literature, Vilnius University, Lithuania. Her main research areas are classical reception, comparative literature, gender studies, and motherhood, more specifically non-motherhood and non-traditional models of motherhood in classical reception.

Lina Šumskaitė is Associate Professor of Sociology at Vilnius University, Lithuania. She teaches in the Social Policy Department for Social Policy and Social Work programmes. Her doctoral thesis (2014) focused on men's fathering practices. Her research field is reproductive intent (men and women), experiences of not having children, and qualitative research on mothering and fathering issues.

Orlagh Woods has recently completed her PhD in English Literature at Maynooth University, Ireland. Her dissertation explores representations of motherhood across a range of twenty-first-century adaptations of Shakespeare by prominent female authors including Anne Enright and Jeanette Winterson. While her current work focuses specifically on literary adaptation, her wider research interests include stage performance and cinematic adaptation as well as women's life writing.

LIST OF FIGURES

CHAPTER 1

Conceptualising Non-Motherhood

Jenny Björklund and Julie Rodgers

Selfish, unfeminine, unfulfilled, crazy, and desperate are some of the qualities that have been erroneously and indiscriminately applied to women who do not have children. Parenthood is often viewed as the

This chapter is written in collaboration. We have listed the author names alphabetically to indicate that we have contributed equally and want to attribute an equal share of credit to each author. The authors would like to thank Dovilė Kuzminskaitė who has given valuable feedback on earlier versions of this text.

This project has received funding from the European Union's Horizon 2020 research and innovation programme under grant agreement No 952366.

J. Björklund (✉)
Uppsala University, Uppsala, Sweden
e-mail: jenny.bjorklund@gender.uu.se

J. Rodgers
Maynooth University, Maynooth, Ireland
e-mail: julie.rodgers@mu.ie

© The Author(s) 2025   1
J. Björklund et al. (eds.), *Negotiating Non-Motherhood*,
Palgrave Macmillan Studies in Family and Intimate Life,
https://Doi.org/10.1007/978-3-031-66697-1_1

ultimate life goal and the expected trajectory, especially for women, since motherhood is positioned at the core of femininity. While feminist theory has paid close attention to motherhood and mothering, there has been a much less rigorous focus on non-motherhood. This failure on the part of feminist thinking amounts to a double sense of marginalisation for non-mothers. In the first instance, they are excluded by mainstream society which continues to assume that all women will or at the very least want to become mothers. In the second instance, non-mothers are overlooked by the very structure that one would expect to support them, namely, feminism. Thankfully, however, the first two decades of the twenty-first century have witnessed a marked surge in the number of publications on the topic of non-motherhood to the extent that a clear theory of non-motherhood is evolving and, moreover, becoming established as an integral component of academic scholarship on the maternal. This volume contributes to this effort and is committed to both overturning the negative connotations that are frequently aligned with non-motherhood as well as working to find new descriptions that are respectful of and empathic towards the diverse range of forms that non-motherhood may take.

At first sight, it may seem contradictory for feminist motherhood studies to devote its attention to women who are not, in fact, mothers. However, as this volume demonstrates, motherhood and non-motherhood are more closely intertwined than one might realise, with non-mothers often having spent substantial time questioning and examining their relationship with motherhood than actual mothers themselves. For example, the voluntary non-mother often engages in deep reflection on the institution itself and the ongoing prevalence of pronatalism in culture and society. Similarly, the involuntary non-mother observes and yearns for an experience that she cannot be part of. Being outside of motherhood, whether through choice or not, does not, therefore, necessarily imply a lack of interrogation of and interaction with both the experience and the institution. Indeed, it is through the figure of the non-mother that we can gain a better appreciation of motherhood as it is defined in culture and society as well as the central role that it continues to play in assumptions and expectations of womanhood.

The title that we have chosen for this volume is *Negotiating Non-Motherhood: Representations, Perceptions, and Experiences*. To explain our rationale for this title, it is important to first reflect on the range of alternative terms that currently exist to designate women who are not mothers for one reason or another. As has previously been noted in numerous scholarly publications, the terms that are commonly used to refer to those women who do not have children remain largely problematic and indicative of negative social attitudes. The main ones in current usage include 'non-mother' (also seen as 'nomo'), 'unchilded', 'without child', 'childless', and 'childfree', not to mention the now outdated but still iterated 'barren'. It is unfortunate that so many of these terms insist on lack and deviance, with the inclusion of suffixes such as 'less' or prefixes such as 'un' and 'non'. Even the term 'childfree', coined as a more positive alternative to the negative labels listed above carries the potential to aggravate the tension between the childless and the child-bearing majority. The term 'childfree' came into circulation to distinguish voluntary non-parenthood from involuntary non-parenthood. Although the term is useful in this respect, it is not without its critics as it seems the addition of 'free' implies a desire to get rid of children. What is clear from the ongoing debate concerning the terminology then is that non-motherhood continues to be a contested identity and, to a certain extent, one which language has failed to adequately capture.

While we acknowledge that there may not be any one, ideal term to designate the woman without children and that all terms may in fact contain fault-lines, in this volume, we have opted for non-mother and non-motherhood. We have deliberately retained the hyphen in the terms non-mother and non-motherhood as it denotes, we feel, a specific theoretical position. The hyphen very importantly indicates both separation from but also involvement with ideologies of motherhood. Given that both the choice not to mother and the inability to do so are often bound up with careful reflection on the practice and experience of mothering itself, it is essential that the terms used to signify those who are not mothers effectively convey the double-coded nature of this particular identity, an identity which is at once outside but also connected to maternal discourse. And yet, those women who choose not to have children are also keen to articulate their distance from the societal expectation to mother. To remove the hyphen from the terms non-motherhood and non-mother would collapse the non-mother into the dominant figure of the mother, whereas the hyphen, on the other hand, preserves the destabilising potential of the non-mother with regard to normative constructions of womanhood. Following a similar logic, the woman who is involuntarily childless has no doubt devoted immense psychological and physical energy to the endeavour of one day becoming a mother. The term non-mother as hyphenated, therefore, comprehensively conveys a sense of connection to maternal identity, the pain of being excluded but also the deliberate decision to stand outside of motherhood. Finally, the hyphen is suggestive of an identity in transit or in flux, an identity that is still evolving, establishing its own voice and gradually claiming its own space.

This is where the choice of the word 'negotiate' comes into play. Given that non-motherhood continues to be poorly understood by society at large and that the experience itself can manifest in different ways, sometimes shifting from one position to another within the spectrum of non-mother, we felt that 'negotiate' was the verb that best conveyed the individual experiences of the range of non-mothers who appear in this volume. For some, it is about negotiating ostracisation, for others it is about negotiating pain and suffering. It is about negotiating the right to speak and tell their own story, the right to language and the right to legitimacy. It is also about negotiating their position with societies that continue to consider motherhood as the norm, thereby relegating the non-mother to a status of invisibility.

Finally, the non-mother is a subversive figure who has the potential to derail traditional genealogical structures and essentialised ideas of womanhood. As some of the chapters in this volume demonstrate, the non-mother can force us to think about alternative forms of care and relationality beyond reproduction and the heteronormative family. There is a power within non-motherhood in its rupture with hegemonic norms. As the chapters unfold in this volume, this power becomes increasingly evident and the figure of the non-mother gradually asserts herself and claims her identity on her terms through a process of writing back, talking back— enacting a negotiation of her own non-motherhood as well as telling stories about a life experience that has been rendered invisible in mainstream culture and society.

Motherhood Studies and Non-Motherhood

During the last century, feminist researchers have paid close attention to motherhood and mothering and analysed them as social constructions. In her ground-breaking work *The Second Sex*, Simone de Beauvoir (1949/2010) argues that motherhood should not be seen as women's sole life purpose and, moreover, the key to women's happiness. Motherhood, as it was understood in post-war France, limits women's possibilities for self-realisation; women should be able to combine motherhood and professional life, and society needs to take greater responsibility for child-rearing. Motherhood and mothering were also key issues for second-wave feminists, such as Adrienne Rich (1976), who analyses motherhood as socially, culturally, and historically constructed and an institution in which patriarchal power is maintained and sustained. In the decades that followed, feminist motherhood studies were primarily concerned with how cultural ideals of motherhood limited women and confined them to their homes (e.g. see DiQuinzio 1999; Hays 1996), but some researchers also highlighted how the care work that mothers do should be upgraded and seen as an important force in society (e.g. see Ruddick 1989). Motherhood studies have flourished since the emergence of the canonical texts in the mid-to-late twentieth century and, moreover, expanded into new domains such as single motherhood and queer motherhood. Lately, there has been a notable surge in scholarly interest in motherhood. This scholarship represents a variety of new perspectives on motherhood and often dives into its more complex and darker sides, such as ambivalence, rage, and regret (e.g. see Björklund 2021; Bodin 2023; Bourdeau 2019; Donath 2017; Heffernan and Stone 2021). It also acknowledges diverse experiences and representations of motherhood by focusing, for instance, on migrant mothers (Kačkutė 2023; Lombard 2022), mothers with disabilities (Gevorgianienė et al. 2022), single mothers (Åström and Bergnehr 2021; Bergnehr and Henriksson 2021), LGBTQ+ mothers (Goldberg and Allen 2020; Park 2013), teenage mothers (Rodgers and Gorman 2023), and motherhood in different geopolitical contexts (Akujobi 2011; Henriksson et al. 2023; Herrera and Sanmartín 2015; Rye et al. 2018).

Less scholarly interest has been devoted to non-motherhood. Furthermore, existing research has typically focused on either involuntary or voluntary non-motherhood, disregarding Gayle Letherby's work from the turn of the twenty-first century which states that the boundary between involuntary and voluntary childlessness is not clear-cut: "It is perhaps more appropriate to refer to a continuum of childlessness with some individuals being definite in their place at each end of the continuum and a group in the middle whose position is likely to change over time" (2002b, 8; see also 1999, 2002a; Letherby and Williams 1999). Other researchers have pointed out that reproductive 'choices' are not always conscious (Engwall 2010), or that the decision-making process is complex; it may not be seen as a one-time decision but rather as decisions that are made and remade across the life course (Blackstone and Stewart 2016; Morell 2000; Shaw 2011).

Such deconstructive approaches to the rigid categorisation of non-motherhood and childlessness, however, remain uncommon and research on childlessness continues to be polarised into involuntary and voluntary and separated out into different disciplines. Involuntary childlessness is often linked to infertility and infertility treatments and is studied primarily in medicine or psychology (e.g. see Buhr and Huinink 2017; Gameiro et al. 2014; Rotkirch 2013; Volgsten et al. 2010; Wirtberg et al. 2006), although some work has been done from humanities and social science perspectives. Rebecca Feasey (2019) analyses media representations of infertility and non-traditional family building and finds that these tend to promote miracle-baby-in-the-end narratives that contrast with the medical reality, where infertility treatments often fail and the chances for women over 40 to become pregnant are small. Other scholars have studied representations of involuntary childlessness in film, literature, social media, reality TV, and print media (e.g. see Archetti 2019; Björklund 2023; de Boer et al. 2022; Edge 2015; Graham and Rich 2014; Striff 2005). Cristina Archetti (2020) and Melanie Notkin (2014) have done ethnographic work on women who move on with their lives after failing to have children.

If involuntary childlessness has more often been studied in the medical sciences, voluntary childlessness has caught more scholarly interest in the humanities and social sciences. In fact, in the last two decades, there has been a surge of publications on women who choose not to have children (Clarke et al. 2021). While research from the twentieth century tended to focus on definitions and reasons for being childless (e.g. see Gillespie 1999; Houseknecht 1987), twenty-first-century research often has a more critical perspective. It has shown how women who choose not to have children are still viewed as suspects by society and are victims of various stereotypes, and these analyses are sometimes empowering as they suggest various possibilities and trajectories for women that do not include motherhood (Rodgers 2021). Feminist researchers have analysed societal structures, such as pronatalism, that marginalise and stigmatise women who have chosen not to have children, as well as their impact on their everyday lives (e.g. see Addie and Brownlow 2014; Cummins et al. 2021; Doyle et al. 2012; Fjell 2008; Gillespie 2000, 2003; Kelly 2009; Morison et al. 2016; Park 2002; Peterson and Engwall 2013; Peterson and Fjell 2010; Rich et al. 2011; Turnbull et al. 2016; Vinson et al. 2010).

Unlike the majority of texts on non-motherhood which choose to focus on the experience as either voluntary or involuntary, this volume seeks to deconstruct the barriers between these two positions and, instead, allow them to enter into dialogue with each other. Rather than pitting the voluntary non-mother against the involuntary non-mother, we believe it is more fruitful to consider the experience of non-motherhood in a more processual and interconnected way. As highlighted by Ruby Warrington (2023), for too long, non-motherhood has been approached through a binary lens. Warrington writes, "Non-Moms tend to exist in the two-dimensional either/or space: we are either grieving something we never had the chance to hold OR we are cold-hearted, delusional and self-obsessed" (72). Warrington argues that non-motherhood should, however, be seen as a "full spectrum of opinions, projections and conflicted states" (72) as it is experienced in a multitude of ways and subject to fluctuations. This volume, therefore, adopts a non-binary approach and works to expand the definition of non-motherhood by including representations and experiences that are not usually discussed as part of the research field on non-motherhood, such as secondary infertility, miscarriage, and perinatal loss. It unites scholars from different disciplines and national contexts in the study of non-motherhood across a variety of materials and from many different perspectives. Existing scholarship has tended to focus on either representations or experiences, and this volume includes the use of different methods to study a diverse material in order to give wide-ranging new knowledge on non-motherhood.

This Volume

In 2020, a group of researchers from Vilnius University (Lithuania), Uppsala University (Sweden), and Maynooth University (Ireland) were awarded funding from the EU Horizon 2020 Twinning research and innovation programme to carry out collaborative and interdisciplinary cutting-edge research on contemporary motherhood (grant agreement No 952366). The project has since become known as MotherNet and has promoted the establishment of research clusters, publications, summer schools, mentoring, scientific missions, knowledge dissemination, and public outreach activities, all in connection with the theme of motherhood. One of the specific research collaborations that was established within MotherNet was the Negotiating Non-Motherhood research cluster. Over the course of various meetings and discussions, it became evident to us that any comprehensive research project on motherhood should also attend to the issue of non-motherhood, both voluntary and involuntary, hence the incentive for this edited volume.

The contributions in this volume are diverse and innovative in their exploration of the concept of non-motherhood. Not only does the volume bring different disciplinary perspectives, such as literary studies and sociology, into dialogue with each other, the contributions also carefully engage in the probing and widening of the term 'non-motherhood' itself which, of course, is the central aim of this volume. The various chapters gathered here present detailed analyses of a range of 'non-motherhood' narratives across a spectrum of European cultures and societies. It is crucial, however, to bear in mind that non-motherhood, just like motherhood, intersects with a multitude of other factors that can impact on how it is negotiated, such as race and class. Pragya Agarwal's (2021) astute observation in relation to motherhood can also apply to the experience of non-motherhood. Agarwal notes that while there is no single narrative of motherhood and what it means for women, more often than not we only hear one kind of story. She emphasises the importance, therefore, of paying attention to differences "across race and class [...], social and historical differences [...], oppression, diversity and inequality amongst women" (8). If we think of non-motherhood, the ability to choose voluntarily to remain childfree is not necessarily a choice that all women have, depending on their social and cultural background. Additionally, the stigma and suffering attached to experience of infertility can equally vary widely across different contexts. This volume attempts to tease out some of these complexities but it is true that, as stated by Agarwal, close attention to intersectionality needs to infuse future studies of both motherhood and non-motherhood (8).

While there are national differences in how non-motherhood is understood and experienced, there are also similarities. One of the overriding features shared by all chapters is the importance placed on the negotiation of the experience of non-motherhood via story-telling from a first-person perspective. There is a clear desire on the part of the narrators/non-mothers (both fictional and real) to articulate either their deliberate life-choices or their encounters with loss. It is evident from the chapters that there is an urgent need on the part of these women to take ownership of their individual narratives and, by doing so, to challenge the reductive stereotypes of non-motherhood that continue to exist in contemporary culture and society. The articulation of their experiences is both personally therapeutic but also educational, in that these stories show us that the nature of non-motherhood is by no means homogenous, but, rather, complex, layered, and expansive. While some chapters focus on women for whom non-motherhood tends to be a stable identity, other chapters depict shifting figures of non-motherhood who embody a certain fluidity in relation to their status. What emerges then, from this collection, is that any definition of 'non-motherhood' must be inclusive and flexible if it is to capture the heterogeneity of the experience.

The multifarious nature of non-motherhood comes to the fore in Jenny Björklund's chapter which approaches the experience from a multitude of angles: involuntary childlessness and infertility; childlessness by choice; childlessness by circumstance. Employing an angle that aims to revalorise non-motherhood as a life position, Björklund tackles a broad span of contemporary literary texts, including fiction, autofiction, and personal essay and carefully contextualises these within Swedish culture and society. What emerges from this chapter is that Swedish women writers are keen to challenge the negativity that is regularly associated with non-motherhood and one of the ways that this is achieved in their writing, Björklund argues, is through the use of laughter. At the same time, Björklund is aware of the marginalisation that non-mothers are subjected to and deftly employs Kristevan theory to demonstrate the way in which they are abjected from society and labelled aberrant. In the texts selected for analysis in this chapter, Björklund notes a tone of defiance throughout the various narratives of non-motherhood whose purpose is to deconstruct society's reductive image of the women without children and reposition non-motherhood as an actual liveable life.

Remaining in the domain of literature but moving to a Spanish backdrop, Dovilė Kuzminskaitė's contribution approaches non-motherhood, like Björklund's chapter, from a multidirectional perspective. Kuzminskaitė introduces us to a woman who already has two children but decides to abort the third as she does not want more children. Furthermore, it is important to note that the character concerned used IVF to conceive the first two children. In this respect, Kuzminskaitė presents us with a character who fluctuates between non-motherhood (involuntary), motherhood, and then back to non-motherhood (voluntary). Kuzminskaitė's chapter, therefore, shows us that it is impossible to polarise mother and non-mother given that both experiences can exist within the one person. Kuzminskaitė also draws our attention to falling fertility rates in Spain and increased awareness of feminism and bodily autonomy among Spanish women, factors which, she suggests, are intertwined with the protagonist's choice to abort her third child.

The rapidly decreasing birth rate in Spain is the focal point of the following chapter which engages with the emerging phenomenon of non-motherhood as an active and desired life choice. Anna Morero Beltrán and Elisabet Almeda Samaranch carefully examine the factors that have led to such a cultural mutation in Spain, a country which, up until the 1980s, was traditionally associated with high birth rates and large families. In comparison to Kuzminskaitė, they acknowledge the influence of feminism on the increase of women who are choosing to be childfree. However, they also list other reasons for voluntary non-motherhood such as personal circumstances, finances, and lack of public services/support systems. Based on a series on interviews with women who have chosen not to have children and employing a qualitative method, Beltrán and Samaranch, in comparison with many of the chapters in this volume, point to the importance of listening to the voices of women whose stories have previously been silenced and allowing them to articulate their experience in their own words. Beltrán and Samaranch adeptly show us that having a space for talking about and reflecting openly on non-motherhood is undeniably essential in today's society. It is restorative for the women concerned, provides recognition of their identity, and is something that, unfortunately, is not found in public policy or popular opinion. Indeed, as previously mentioned, this is one of the central aims of this particular volume, that is, to create a text where different experiences of non-motherhood can be freely expressed and then potentially better understood by society, and moreover, accepted as valid life-paths.

Lina Šumskaitė's chapter adopts a similar approach to Beltrán and Samaranch but situates it within the Lithuanian context where pronatalist norms and pressures continue to prevail. Like Beltrán and Samaranch, Šumskaitė works with a series of interviews conducted among women without children and employs a qualitative method. However, unlike Beltrán and Samaranch who focus only on voluntary childlessness, Šumskaitė considers non-mothers who are both voluntarily and involuntarily childless. Through close analysis of the interviews, Šumskaitė endeavours to unpick both the micro and macro factors that are embedded in a woman's choice not to have children as well as a woman's experience of being involuntarily without children. As we read these autobiographical reflections, we become aware of the myriad of issues, circumstances, feelings, and reactions that are bound up in the experience of non-motherhood. Taking all of these mixed and sometimes ambivalent attitudes and responses into account, Šumskaitė, like many of the other in this volume, questions the possibility of rigidly defining ...otnerhood, instead promoting a more hybrid interpretation. Similar to Beltrán and Samaranch, Šumskaitė highlights the importance of allowing non-mothers to narrate their personal experiences in their own words.

Story-telling is also a central trope in the following chapter where we move into a discussion of non-motherhood from a more unconventional perspective. Tackling the poorly understood phenomenon of secondary infertility and the idea of the incomplete mother, Julie Rodgers's contribution adds further subtlety and refinement to our understanding of the non-mother. Focussing on British author Helen Davies' *More Love to Give* (2017), this chapter highlights the silence that exists around experiences of secondary infertility and reveals the way in which women suffering from the condition often feel unauthorised to recount their story due to the fact that they are caught between motherhood and non-motherhood. However, as this chapter demonstrates, not only does the woman who suffers from secondary infertility share much of the same pain and sense of loss as the involuntary non-mother, the fact that she is displaced and discounted from discussions of non-motherhood further heightens her sense of nothingness and non-existence. Rodgers makes a strong case, therefore, for validity of secondary infertility as a form of non-motherhood. Furthermore, in line with the other contributors to this volume, Rodgers argues that secondary infertility shows us that defining non-motherhood as a singular and absolute state is both impossible and counterproductive. On the contrary, as exemplified by non-motherhood, becoming and being a non-mother can present as a much more labyrinthine state, assume many shapes and, what is more, has the potential to shift and fluctuate.

Another chapter that nuances our interpretation of the non-mother is Laura Lazzari's exploration of narratives of miscarriage and perinatal loss in contemporary Italophone women's writing. Like secondary infertility, there is little empathy in society for the anguish caused by this specific reproductive trauma and, as a result, those experiencing it feel that their stories and suffering have been ignored and silenced. Lazzari selects a wide corpus of texts and examines the role played by writing and journaling in the recovery of the women concerned and once again, as observed by several other contributors, the therapeutic qualities of simply being able to speak. In line with Rodgers's position, Lazzari also argues that non-motherhood must become more inclusive and encompass women who have either not had children or not had the desired number of alive children due to episodes of miscarriage and stillbirth. Similar to women suffering from secondary infertility, women who experience pregnancy loss find themselves in a liminal position where they are caught between motherhood and non-motherhood and without any language to articulate their identity. This volume, therefore, aims to open up the definition of non-motherhood so as to incorporate all of these disparate and dislocated subjects.

The contribution by María Sebastià-Sáez introduces a further angle to the complex negotiation of non-motherhood through her discussion of surrogacy as a response to infertility. The focus of her analysis is the novella-play *Dos madres* (1920) by Spanish author Miguel de Unamuno. The social, political, and historical context of the text is the early twentieth century in Spain, a time of great change and transformation, particularly in relation to women's rights. Sebastià-Sáez interrogates the good and bad dichotomy that exists in relation to fertility/infertility with the infertile non-mother viewed as incomplete and lacking. Infertility in the text causes pain and suffering and gives rise to feelings of 'otherness' and exclusion. Subsequently, desperate measures are pursued in the quest to transition out of non-motherhood and into motherhood, with the pathway chosen in this instance being surrogacy. Although the text may appear to promote a normative trajectory for women through the use of surrogacy as an entry point to motherhood and out of abject non-motherhood, Sebastià-Sáez argues that the unusual family model that emerges from this form of reproduction can, in fact, be viewed as progressive and innovative. The women involved in the surrogacy establish what might be described as a 'queer' family based on shared motherhood, whereby mothering together becomes the response to non-motherhood more so than the actual surrogacy itself.

Jasmine D. Cooper's chapter shifts the cultural context to France through her analysis of Amandine Gay's personal essay in book form, *Une poupée en chocolat* (2021). If Sebastià-Sáez touches on the idea of an alternative family unit through surrogacy and shared mothering, Cooper's contribution expands the possibilities for alternative forms of relationality even further. A staunch rejection of pronatalism, the essentialised female body, and the traditional family model underpins the text examined in this chapter. Cooper explains that this determined choice not to become a mother is closely linked to Gay's experiences as a transracial adoptee in France, her quest for bodily autonomy and the fact that she herself was conceived through rape. Her own mother then becomes the original figure of the non-mother as she bore a child involuntarily and Gay's non-motherhood becomes a product of this. As well as reflecting on the personal experiences that have led to her decision not to mother, Gay's essay also engages in careful reflection of the heteronormative family at large and tackles important issues such as sterilisation, adoption, and more radical and subversive forms of kinship which would allow the figure of the non-mother to be recognised as legitimate.

Staying with the trope of radical resistance to motherhood, Orlagh Woods' chapter engages in a thoughtful discussion of *We That Are Young* (2017), the debut novel by British-Indian writer, Preti Taneja. The central narrative, Woods informs us, is based on a postcolonial adaptation of Shakespeare's *King Lear*, which the author has very effectively recast in modern-day India. Against this backdrop of a fervently pronatalist society which presents motherhood as the highest criterion of female success and disdainfully disregards those who fail to achieve this goal, Woods focuses on the subversive figure of the childfree woman by choice and the way in which her very existence challenges the heteropatriarchal structures of Indian society and, what is more, calls into question the very foundations of the nation itself. Woods examines the tensions that emerge when women assert control over their reproductive capacity within a culture that reifies motherhood and expects them to have children, thereby preserving the nation. The voluntary non-mother, Woods argues, becomes representative, therefore, of insubordination to and defiance of a maternormative society that tries to deprive her of bodily autonomy.

The final two chapters in this volume move into the realm of the visual and explore the role of the image, both still and moving, in the negotiation of non-motherhood. The chapter authored by Mercedes Carbayo-Abengózar tackles the topic of voluntary childlessness through the lens of the contemporary graphic novel, in particular Irene Olmo's *No quiero ser mama* (2020). The argument is structured around the unique potential of graphic autobiography to offer a robust response to the taboo of a freely chosen childless life. Via clever manipulation of colour space and the fantastic, *No quiero ser mama* transports the reader into the imagination of the protagonist and, as a result, this facilitates readerly appreciation of the various pressures to which non-mothers are subjected both from society at large and close friends and family. Like other chapters in this volume, Carbayo-Abengózar draws our attention to the specific pronatalist context of Spain where motherhood is expected of women and those who do not conform are cast as outsiders. Against this backdrop, therefore, the non-mother is positioned as a kind of 'killjoy' by refusing to adhere to the normative conception of 'natural female fulfilment' and instead exposing the institution of motherhood as a form of imprisonment for women when it is enforced. While most of this chapter concentrates on the isolation and marginalisation of the protagonist once her decision not to have children is assumed and made known, in the final section, there is a discussion of the possibility of a collective of non-mothers that can emerge once the silencing of their individual experiences has been overcome, an act to which the graphic novel in question strives to contribute.

From the static image on the page, we transition to the moving screen in Valerie Heffernan's chapter which closes the volume. In her discussion of the adaptation of a German language short story by Swiss writer Peter Stamm ("The Natural Way of Things") into film by Austrian film-maker Ulrike Kofler entitled *What We Want* (2020), Heffernan examines the representation of a couple who have been struggling with infertility. What is perhaps most interesting in this chapter (and also pertinent to the overall aim of the volume) is the shift that occurs within the filmic narrative from one of being childless due to infertility to a reconciliation of sorts with this status which almost presents as a choice to be childfree, or, at the very least, a decision to move forwards as couple and assume their identity as non-parents. By highlighting this particular plot development, Heffernan's chapter works to deconstruct the polarised the more traditional opposition of voluntary and involuntary non-motherhood, instead pointing to the feelings of ambivalence that are often inherent to the experience. In conjunction with this, Heffernan also carefully explores the differences that exist between the textual and screen versions of this couple's life-story and alerts us to a further shift which requires unpacking. While the textual version presents a couple who are childfree by choice, the film complicates this by introducing the tropes of infertility and regret before allowing the husband and wife to move into a state of acceptance. Heffernan suggests that the occurrence of such a digression from the original genre of the short story to the screen adaptation no doubt signals an ongoing discomfort in popular culture with voluntary childlessness, a point that is also emphasised in Carbayo-Abengózar's analysis of the same topic in the graphic novel.

When approached collectively, it is clear that, in spite of the inherent diversity of the range of narratives and experiences of non-motherhood recounted, there are, nonetheless, a number of common threads binding together all of the chapters included here. In turn, these common threads can be said to constitute the core aims of this volume. First and foremost, the volume seeks to draw attention to the fact that non-motherhood cannot be defined as a singular experience. On the contrary, as is evident in the volume, it manifests in multiple figurations and can present as contradictory, unpredictable, and changeable for the non-mother concerned. Secondly, the contributions in this volume demonstrate the fact that the contextual factors involved in non-motherhood are often just as hybrid as the experience itself, and range from the macro (social, cultural, historic) to the micro (biology, trauma, choice, circumstance). However, regardless of the differences between each separate narrative and each individual experience presented in this volume, there are similarities and connections between the diverse narratives of non-motherhood. One underlying trope is the sense of isolation, marginalisation, silencing, and judgement that many non-mothers feel, whether they are voluntarily childless or childfree through choice. This points to a third aim of the volume, on the part of both the contributors and the authors of the material selected for analysis, that is, the deconstruction of the harmful stereotypes that are often associated with the non-mother and a reconfiguration of this identity in more affirmative terms. In conjunction with this, the volume interrogates the norms and expectations of cultures and societies across Europe that continue to conflate motherhood with womanhood, thereby causing the non-mother to feel like an outcast and an aberration. Finally, this volume highlights the necessity of creating a space where the silenced stories of non-mothers can be both articulated and heard and where they can claim an identity that is legitimate. The volume is concerned with promoting a form of non-motherhood that is inclusive and which does not create a hierarchy of suffering or pit different versions of the non-mother against one another. Perhaps then, as is reiterated throughout the volume, the key to fully unravelling non-motherhood is to first accept that it cannot be rigidly defined. Subsequently, the reader of this volume should expect to find their preconceptions challenged and their understanding of non-motherhood expanded well beyond one static and homogenous model.

References

Addie, Elizabeth, and Charlotte Brownlow. 2014. Deficit and Asset Identity Constructions of Single Women Without Children Living in Australia: An Analysis of Discourse. *Feminism and Psychology* 24 (4): 423–439. https://doi.org/10.1177/0959353514539463.

Agarwal, Pragya. 2021. *Motherhood: On the Choices of Being a Woman*. London: Canongate.

Akujobi, Remi. 2011. Motherhood in African Literature and Culture. *CLCWeb: Comparative Literature and Culture* 13 (1). https://doi.org/10.7771/1481-4374.1706.

Archetti, Cristina. 2019. No Life Without Family: Film Representations of Involuntary Childlessness, Silence and Exclusion. *International Journal of Media & Cultural Politics* 15 (2): 175–196. https://doi.org/10.1386/macp.15.2.175_1.

———. 2020. *Childlessness in the Age of Communication: Deconstructing Silence*. London and New York: Routledge.

Åström, Berit, and Disa Bergnehr, eds. 2021. *Single Parents: Representations and Resistance in an International Context*. Cham: Palgrave Macmillan.

Bergnehr, Disa, and Helena Wahlström Henriksson. 2021. Hardworking Women: Representations of Lone Mothers in the Swedish Daily Press. *Feminist Media Studies* 21 (1): 132–146. https://doi.org/10.1080/14680777.2019.1704815.

Björklund, Jenny. 2021. *Maternal Abandonment and Queer Resistance in Twenty-First-Century Swedish Literature*. Cham: Palgrave Macmillan.

———. 2023. Struggling to Become a Mother: Literary Representations of Involuntary Childlessness. In *Narratives of Motherhood and Mothering in Fiction and Life Writing*, ed. Helena Wahlström Henriksson, Anna Williams, and Margaretha Fahlgren, 55–75. Cham: Palgrave Macmillan.

Blackstone, Amy, and Mahala D. Stewart. 2016. 'There's More Thinking to Decide': How the Childfree Decide Not to Parent. *The Family Journal* 24 (3): 296–303. https://doi.org/10.1177/10664807166486.

Bodin, Maja. 2023. Regretting Parenthood in a Family Friendly, 'Gender Equal' Society: Accounts from Swedish Online Forums. *Journal of Family Studies* 29 (5): 2195–2212. https://doi.org/10.1080/13229400.2022.2156379.

Bourdeau, Loïc, ed. 2019. *Horrible Mothers: Representation Across Francophone North America*. Lincoln: University of Nebraska Press.

Buhr, Petra, and Johannes Huinink. 2017. Why Childless Men and Women Give Up on Having Children. *European Journal of Population* 33: 585–606. https://doi.org/10.1007/s10680-017-9429-1.

Clarke, Victoria, Nikki Hayfield, Naomi Moller, and Virginia Braun. 2021. A Critical Review of the Interdisciplinary Literature on Voluntary Childlessness. In *The Truth About (M)Otherhood: Choosing to Be Childfree*, ed. Helen Cummings, Julie Ann Rodgers, and Judith Dunkelberger Wouk, 29–54. Ontario: Demeter Press.

Cummins, Helen, Julie Anne Rodgers, and Judith Dunkelberger Wouk, eds. 2021. *The Truth About (M)Otherhood: Choosing to Be Childfree*. Ontario: Demeter Press.

de Beauvoir, Simone. 1949/2010. *The Second Sex*. Trans. Constance Borde and Sheila Malovany-Chevallier. New York: Alfred A. Knopf.

de Boer, Marjolein Lotte, Cristina Archetti, and Kari Nyheim Solbraekke. 2022. In/Fertile Monsters: The Emancipatory Significance of Representations of Women on Infertility Reality TV. *Journal of Medical Humanities* 43: 11–26. https://doi.org/10.1007/s10912-019-09555-z.

DiQuinzio, Patrice. 1999. *The Impossibility of Motherhood: Feminism, Individualism, and the Problem of Mothering*. New York and London: Routledge.

Donath, Orna. 2017. *Regretting Motherhood: A Study*. Berkeley: North Atlantic Books.

Doyle, Joanne, Julie A. Pooley, and Lauren Breen. 2012. A Phenomenological Exploration of the Childfree Choice in a Sample of Australian Women. *Journal of Health Psychology* 18 (3): 397–407. https://doi.org/10.1177/1359105 312444647.

Edge, Brooke Weihe. 2015. *Barren or Bountiful? Analysis of Cultural Values in Popular Media Representations of Infertility*. PhD diss., University of Colorado.

Engwall, Kristina. 2010. Barnfria män i Sverige. In *Frivillig barnlöshet: Barnfrihet i en nordisk kontext*, ed. Kristina Engwall and Helen Peterson, 331–353. Stockholm: Dialogos and Institutet för Framtidsstudier.

Feasey, Rebecca. 2019. *Infertility and Non-Traditional Family Building: From Assisted Reproduction to Adoption in the Media*. Cham: Palgrave Macmillan.

Fjell, Tove Ingebjørg. 2008. *Å si nei til meningen med livet? En kulturvitenskapelig analyse av barnfrihet*. Trondheim: Tapir Akademisk Forlag.

Gameiro, Sofia, Alexandra W. van den Belt-Dusebout, Eveline Bleiker, Didi Braat, Flora E. van Leeuwen, and Christianne M. Verhaak. 2014. Do Children Make You Happier?: Sustained Child-Wish and Mental Health in Women 11–17 Years After Fertility Treatment. *Human Reproduction* 29 (10): 2238–2246. https://doi.org/10.1093/humrep/deu178.

Gevorgianienė, Violeta, Eglė Šumskienė, and Ciara Bradley. 2022. Still Waters Run Deep: The Invisible Life of Working Mothers with Disabilities in Lithuania. *Qualitative Social Work* 22 (3): 587–605. https://doi.org/10.1177/147332502210919.

Gillespie, Rosemary. 1999. Voluntary Childlessness in the United Kingdom. *Reproductive Health Matters* 7 (13): 43–53. https://doi.org/10.1016/S0968-8080(99)90111-8.

———. 2000. When No Means No: Disbelief, Disregard and Deviance as Discourses of Voluntary Childlessness. *Women's Studies International Forum* 23 (2): 223–234. https://doi.org/10.1016/S0277-5395(00)00076-5.

———. 2003. Childfree and Feminine: Understanding the Gender Identity of Voluntary Childless. *Gender and Society* 17 (1): 122–136. https://doi.org/10.1177/08912432022389.

Goldberg, Abbie E., and Katherine R. Allen, eds. 2020. *LGBTQ-Parent Families: Innovations in Research and Implications for Practice*. 2nd ed. Cham: Springer Nature.

Graham, Melissa, and Stephanie Rich. 2014. Representations of Childless Women in the Australian Print Media. *Feminist Media Studies* 14 (3): 500–518. https://doi.org/10.1080/14680777.2012.737346.

Hays, Sharon. 1996. *The Cultural Contradictions of Motherhood.* New Haven and London: Yale University Press.

Heffernan, Valerie, and Katherine Stone. 2021. #regrettingmotherhood in Germany: Feminism, Motherhood, and Culture. *Signs: Journal of Women in Culture and Society* 46 (2): 337–360. https://doi.org/10.1086/710807.

Henriksson, Helena Wahlström, Anna Williams, and Margaretha Fahlgren, eds. 2023. *Narratives of Motherhood and Mothering in Fiction and Life Writing.* Cham: Palgrave Macmillan.

Herrera, Cristina, and Paula Sanmartín, eds. 2015. *Reading/Speaking/Writing the Mother Text: Essays on Caribbean Women's Writing.* Bradford: Demeter Press.

Houseknecht, Sharon K. 1987. Voluntary Childlessness. In *Handbook of Marriage and the Family*, ed. Suzanne K. Steinmetz and Marvin B. Sussman, 369–395. New York: Plenum Press.

Kačkutė, Eglė. 2023. Orality/Aurality and Voice of the Voiceless Mother in Abla Farhoud's *Happiness Has a Slippery Tail.* In *Narratives of Motherhood and Mothering in Fiction and Life Writing*, ed. Helena Wahlström Henriksson, Anna Williams, and Margaretha Fahlgren, 77–92. Cham: Palgrave Macmillan.

Kelly, Maura. 2009. Women's Voluntary Childlessness: A Radical Rejection of Motherhood. *Women's Studies Quarterly* 37 (3–4): 157–172. https://doi.org/10.1353/wsq.0.0164.

Letherby, Gayle. 1999. Other than Mother and Mothers as Others: The Experience of Motherhood and Non-Motherhood in Relation to 'Infertility' and 'Involuntary Childlessness'. *Women's Studies International Forum* 22 (3): 359–372. https://doi.org/10.1016/S0277-5395(99)00028-X.

———. 2002a. Challenging Dominant Discourses: Identity and Change and the Experience of 'Infertility' and 'Involuntary Childlessness'. *Journal of Gender Studies* 11 (3): 277–288. https://doi.org/10.1080/0958923022000021241.

———. 2002b. Childless and Bereft?: Stereotypes and Realities in Relation to 'Voluntary' and 'Involuntary' Childlessness and Womanhood. *Sociological Inquiry* 72 (1): 7–20. https://doi.org/10.1111/1475-682X.00003.

Letherby, Gayle, and Catherine Williams. 1999. Non-Motherhood: Ambivalent Autobiographies. *Feminist Studies* 25 (3): 719–728. https://doi.org/10.2307/3178673.

Lombard, Maria D., ed. 2022. *Reclaiming Migrant Motherhood: Identity, Belonging, and Displacement in a Global Context.* Lanham: Lexington Books.

Morell, Carolyn. 2000. Saying No: Women's Experiences with Reproductive Refusal. *Feminism and Psychology* 10 (3): 313–322. https://doi.org/10.1177/0959353500100030.

Morison, Tracy, Catriona Macleod, Ingrid Lynch, Magda Mijas, and Seemanthini Tumkur Shivakumar. 2016. Stigma Resistance in Online Childfree

Communities: The Limitations of Choice Rhetoric. *Psychology of Women Quarterly* 40 (2): 184–198. https://doi.org/10.1177/0361684315603.

Notkin, Melanie. 2014. *Otherhood: Modern Women Finding a New Kind of Happiness.* Berkeley: Seal Press.

Park, Kristin. 2002. Stigma Management Among the Voluntarily Childless. *Sociological Perspectives* 45 (1): 21–45. https://doi.org/10.1525/sop.2002. 45.1.21.

Park, Shelley M. 2013. *Mothering Queerly, Queering Motherhood: Resisting Monomaternalism in Adoptive, Lesbian, Blended, and Polygamous Families.* Albany: SUNY Press.

Peterson, Helen, and Kristina Engwall. 2013. Silent Bodies: Childfree Women's Gendered and Embodied Experiences. *European Journal of Women's Studies* 20 (4): 376–389. https://doi.org/10.1177/1350506812471338.

Peterson, Helen, and Tove Ingebjørg Fjell. 2010. Bilden av frivillig barnlöshet i media. In *Frivillig barnlöshet: Barnfrihet i en nordisk kontext*, ed. Kristina Engwall and Helen Peterson, 105–161. Stockholm: Dialogos and Institutet för Framtidsstudier.

Rich, Adrienne. 1976. *Of Woman Born: Motherhood as Experience and Institution.* New York: W. W. Norton.

Rich, Stephanie, Ann Taket, Melissa Graham, and Julia Shelley. 2011. 'Unnatural,' 'Unwomanly,' 'Uncreditable' and 'Undervalued': The Significance of Being a Childless Woman in Australian Society. *Gender Issues* 28 (4): 226–247. https:// doi.org/10.1007/s12147-011-9108-1.

Rodgers, Julie Anne. 2021. Contextualizing the Choice to Be Childfree. In *The Truth About (M)Otherhood: Choosing to Be Childfree*, ed. Helen Cummings, Julie Ann Rodgers, and Judith Dunkelberger Wouk, 11–26. Ontario: Demeter Press.

Rodgers, Julie Anne, and Ciara Gorman. 2023. On ne peut rien contre une fille qui rêve. Teenage Pregnancy as Maternal Empowerment or Maternal Entrapment in *17 Filles. Modern Languages Open* 2023 (1): 1–10. https://doi. org/10.3828/mlo.v0i0.456.

Rotkirch, Anna. 2013. Baby Fever and Longing for Children. In *Fertility Rates and Population Decline: No Time for Children?* ed. Ann Buchanan and Anna Rotkirch, 249–268. Basingstoke: Palgrave Macmillan.

Ruddick, Sara. 1989. *Maternal Thinking: Toward a Politics of Peace.* Boston: Beacon Press.

Rye, Gill, Victoria Browne, Adalgisa Giorgio, Emily Jeremiah, and Abigail Lee Six, eds. 2018. *Motherhood in Literature and Culture: Interdisciplinary Perspectives from Europe.* New York and London: Routledge.

Shaw, Rachel L. 2011. Women's Experiential Journey Toward Voluntary Childlessness: An Interpretative Phenomenological Analysis. *Journal of Community and Applied Social Psychology* 21 (2): 151–163. https://doi. org/10.1002/casp.1072.

Striff, Erin. 2005. "Infertile Me": The Public Performance of Fertility Treatments in Internet Weblogs. *Women & Performance: A Journal of Feminist Theory* 15 (2): 189–206. https://doi.org/10.1080/07407700508571511.

Turnbull, Beth, Melissa L. Graham, and Ann R. Taket. 2016. Social Exclusion of Australian Childless Women in Their Reproductive Years. *Social Inclusion* 4 (1): 102–115. https://doi.org/10.17645/si.v4i1.489.

Vinson, Candice, Debra Mollen, and Nathan G. Smith. 2010. Perceptions of Childfree Women: The Role of Perceivers' and Targets' Ethnicity. *Journal of Community and Applied Social Psychology* 20 (5): 426–432. https://doi.org/10.1002/casp.1049.

Volgsten, Helena, Agneta Skoog Svanberg, and Pia Olsson. 2010. Unresolved Grief in Women and Men in Sweden Three Years After Undergoing Unsuccessful In Vitro Fertilization Treatment. *Acta Obstetricia et Gynecologica* 89: 1290–1297. https://doi.org/10.3109/00016349.2010.512063.

Warrington, Ruby. 2023. *Women Without Kids: The Revolutionary Rise of an Unsung Sisterhood.* London: Orion.

Wirtberg, Ingegerd, et al. 2006. Life 20 Years After Unsuccessful Infertility Treatment. *Human Reproduction* 22 (2): 598–604. https://doi.org/10.1093/humrep/del401.

CHAPTER 2

Reclaiming Non-Motherhood: Abjection, Laughter and Failure in Twenty-First-Century Swedish Narratives of Childlessness

Jenny Björklund

Women who do not have children are often perceived in negative and stereotypical ways. Childfree women are commonly seen as selfish, while involuntarily childless women are viewed as desperate (e.g. see Letherby 2002). In a study of cinematic representations of childlessness, Cristina Archetti (2019) shows how portrayals of childless women are highly pessimistic: "the childless tend to die, either by suicide or killed by others; if

This project has received funding from the European Union's Horizon 2020 research and innovation programme under grant agreement No 952366.

J. Björklund (✉)
Uppsala University, Uppsala, Sweden
e-mail: jenny.bjorklund@gender.uu.se

© The Author(s) 2025
J. Björklund et al. (eds.), *Negotiating Non-Motherhood*,
Palgrave Macmillan Studies in Family and Intimate Life,
https://doi.org/10.1007/978-3-031-66697-1_2

21

they do not die, they acquire a child against all expectations; only men and female (super) heroes can overcome the trauma of infertility; and childlessness by circumstance practically does not exist" (182). Existing scholarship on cultural representations of childlessness has mostly been concerned with media, film and television and highlights how women who do not have children are stereotypically represented as selfish, (too) career-oriented, irresponsible and/or desperate (e.g. see de Boer et al. 2019; Graham and Rich 2014; Peterson and Fjell 2010).

In Sweden in the twenty-first century, childlessness has emerged as a topic in literature across genres. Margaretha Fahlgren (2018) has examined texts where (primarily) women write about their personal struggles to have children, but the theme of non-motherhood also appears in novels, short stories and autofiction. This body of literature on childlessness depicts a variety of ways of being a non-mother: through involuntary childlessness and infertility, through childlessness by choice and through childlessness by circumstance. Each narrative tends to focus on one way of being childless, but similar themes emerge within them, and these themes are not linked to the usual stereotypes of women without children, at least not in the ways discussed in previous scholarship. Instead, the narratives take stories about non-motherhood, which are often invisible and abjected from mainstream society, and tell them in new and defiant ways.

In this chapter, I explore literary representations of women without children in twenty-first-century Swedish literature.[1] I discuss fiction, autofiction and personal essays that deal with childlessness and analyse how these representations reclaim the position of non-motherhood in various ways: by telling stories of failed fertility treatments, by embracing the abjected position of non-motherhood and claiming it as a liveable life, and by using laughter and failure to turn things around and propose alternative ways of living. I bring together theories of abjection (Grosz 1994; Kristeva 1982; Longhurst 2001; McClintock 1995), on the one hand, and theories of laughter and grotesque realism (Bakhtin 1968) and failure (Halberstam 2011), on the other, to analyse stories that are usually expulsed from the public domain in order to uphold the fertility norm. I show how laughter and failure are employed in these narratives to reclaim the position of non-motherhood, to criticise dominant discourses and to imagine different futures.

---

[1] The texts analysed in this chapter have not been translated into English, so all translations of titles and quotes are my own.

REPRESENTING ABJECTION AND FAILURE: INFERTILITY NARRATIVES

In this section, I will discuss three contemporary Swedish stories of infertility, Tove Folkesson's autofictional novel *Hennes ord: Värk I–III* (2019; "Her Words: Ache I–III"), Viktoria Jäderling's short story "Oförklarligt barnlös: uppföljning av en ofullbordad graviditet" (2017; "Unexplained Fertility: Following Up on an Incomplete Pregnancy"), and Sara Lövestam's novel *Ljudet av fötter: Första Monikabok* (2021a; "The Sound of Feet: First Monika Book"). Folkesson's novel depicts Tove who tries to have children through artificial insemination with her female partner Hanna. Jäderling's short story focuses on Hild who goes through in vitro fertilisation (IVF) with a male partner, and Lövestam's novel represents Monika, who is single and does IVF with donated sperm. Rebecca Feasey (2019) has studied US and UK media representations of infertility and non-traditional family building. She shows that mainstream media tends to privilege happy miracle-baby-in-the-end stories, which stands in sharp contrast to the harsh medical reality where infertility treatments fail more than they succeed.[2] Feasey argues that infertility stories have become more visible in the media landscape. Repro-lit—female, first-person, confessional literature on infertility—is a growing genre, and celebrities, such as Michelle Obama and Sarah Jessica Parker, share their infertility stories in the media. While the visibility of infertility stories can have an educational purpose, they typically depict infertility only against the backdrop of a successful outcome: pregnancy and motherhood. Feasey shows that "repro-lit rarely produces stories about living with infertility, without children. Rather, infertility stories are routinely narratives about overcoming reproductive problems in the quest for biological children" (2019, 48). Moreover, the celebrity women "tend only to announce their infertility once they have secured a successful pregnancy outcome, which in itself sends out a rather misleading finale to the infertility narrative" (2019, 129).

Thus, according to Feasey, infertility is rarely represented as an experience in its own right but has to be framed against a successful outcome (see also Archetti 2020). This is not, however, the case in the Swedish fiction on infertility that I discuss here, which could be due, at least partly, to the difference between media and literary representations. While

[2] Feasey states that for women under the age of 35, the chance of getting pregnant from an individual IVF cycle is about 21% (2019, 15).

mainstream media, such as news articles, typically aims for broader audiences and focuses on a few highlights or messages, literature often consists of longer narratives with room for complex plots and detailed depictions of the thoughts and feelings of the characters. As such, literature might be able to add nuance to representations of infertility.[3] The Swedish literary narratives I discuss here document all stages of the female protagonists' struggles to become pregnant in great detail but, in contrast to the media material discussed by Feasey, neither of them ends with children or even a pregnancy.[4]

The narratives depict the minutiae of the fertility treatments in question: gynaecological exams, hormone injections, ovulation tests, insemination, egg retrieval, embryo transfer and the period when the protagonists wait anxiously to see the results of the treatment. In Jäderling's short story, Hild undergoes a seemingly endless number of exams before beginning the treatment: "The investigation with troubleshooting continues. Hild is anesthetized. Carefully punctuated and rinsed clean. They insert cameras, knives, and needles into her. She is injected and inseminated. They look inside her. They measure and calculate" (2017, 296). During the exams Hild is represented with a lack of agency; she is a passive object while things are being done to her by an anonymous medical expertise focused on "troubleshooting", which also indicates that there is something wrong with her body. The malfunctioning body is highlighted in Lövestam's novel too, for instance, in the depiction of the waiting room at the fertility clinic: "To sit here is to be a failure. All of us, who sit here, can see that the others know, we see that, even if we struggle not to make eye contact. Those of us who sit here have not managed to do that which is every biological organism's only task" (2021a, 101).

However, the protagonists are not just represented as passive objects with malfunctioning bodies. They are also depicted as capable and

---

[3] That literature can add nuance to and challenge conventional representations of non-motherhood in other national contexts as well is indicated by Alexandra M. Hill's article (2022) on childlessness in German literature. Hill discusses two literary works that question neoliberal models of femininity and family structures.

[4] Both Tove Folkesson's and Sara Lövestam's books have sequels, and in Folkesson's second book Tove gets pregnant and gives birth to a baby (Folkesson 2021). Read together, Folkesson's two novels thus end in a more conventional way, but if each novel is viewed as a separate work of art, the first novel still breaks with the traditional infertility story plot line. Sara Lövestam's book is part of a trilogy, and Monika does not become pregnant in any of the novels (Lövestam 2021b; Lövestam 2022).

educated, such as when Lövestam's Monika injects hormones: "At a quarter past nine I clean my belly fat with a cotton ball. I take the protective paper off a needle, screw it firmly onto the injection pen and set the dose to 225. I take a breath. Then I use my hand to squeeze a piece of my fat together and perforate it. [...] I keep the needle inside and count to ten before I pull it out" (2021a, 50). Here the female protagonist is represented as active rather than passive, and the quote has an educating tone, since it follows the step-by-step instructions for hormone injection pens used in fertility treatments—even the dose is specified. The details and the educating tone also appear in the description of the egg retrieval: "To punctuate eight follicles in your inner organs feels like it sounds. A dull pain with peaks of something that feels like knife stabs. You can follow everything on a screen, how the thick needle pushes against every follicle until the membrane collapses" (2021a, 119). In this quote, Monika, who is first-person narrator, addresses the reader more directly when describing both the technical aspects and the pain. The descriptions of the fertility treatments in Lövestam's novel can be almost manual-like but the other two narratives do not shy away from in-depth descriptions either. To give the narrators space to describe fertility treatments in detail can be seen as a way of providing the female protagonists with agency to educate the readers about infertility. At the same time, the protagonists are given a voice to tell their stories about abjection and failure.

In Julia Kristeva's (1982) psychoanalytical account, abjection refers to the process in which the subject becomes a social subject by expelling what that society views as impure, such as excrements, vomit, and menstrual blood. However, the subject can never fully expulse these abject elements, and they continue to threaten the subject's sense of self and provoke fear and disgust. As Elizabeth Grosz (1994) points out when discussing Kristeva's concept of abjection, bodily fluids are particularly threatening to the subject's sense of self: "Bodily fluids attest to the permeability of the body, its necessary dependence on an outside, its liability to collapse into this outside [...], to the perilous divisions between the body's inside and its outside" (193). Grosz argues that women's bodies have been constructed in Western cultures as particularly leaky and uncontrollable, and that "women's corporeality is inscribed as a mode of seepage" (1994, 203). Drawing on Kristeva, Grosz and others, Robyn Longhurst (2001) argues that pregnant women's bodies are seen as abject, since they are constructed as seeping, with unstable and unpredictable boundaries and thus as a threat to public spaces.

In Kristeva's, Grosz's and Longhurst's accounts, abjection is in one way or another associated with the mother or motherhood; to put it briefly, for Kristeva, the abject and the instability between self and other are linked to the separation from the mother; for Grosz, women's corporeality and their sexual difference are connected to their reproductive capacities; and for Longhurst, pregnant women's bodies are constructed as abject. In the Swedish fertility narratives, abjection is, rather, associated with failure to become a mother, but as with the theory discussed earlier, the process of abjection relies heavily on bodily fluids, in particular blood. During the period following the embryo transfer, all protagonists continuously scan their bodies for signs of the outcome of the treatment. What is most prominent here is the fear of blood, which would most likely mean that the treatment has failed. Jäderling's Hild and Lövestam's Monika, who both go through IVF, take progesterone, and these vaginal suppositories are a constant source of worry as they melt and seep out of their vaginas: "During the following weeks, Hild inserts a white pill. If she only clears her throat everything ends up like a white wet pulp in her panties. She walks carefully on the streets, focuses on inhaling inside. [Hild and her partner] wake up at night and realise that reality could have changed during sleep. Hild has to go to the bathroom, pull down her panties and check the colour" (Jäderling 2017, 297–298). Hild even checks for blood once when she is outside, hiding between a building and a hedge: "puts a finger all the way in, looks with horror at her moist finger. Smells it, tries to smell forth the red colour" (2017, 300). Like Hild, Monika constantly checks her panties for blood, and throughout the narrative, she reflects on her past periods and different kinds of blood, often with great detail: "Light red streaks that could be interpreted as implantation bleeding, a bleeding you can have even if you are pregnant and that everyone who has gone through in vitro fertilisation therefore hopes for when the first blood appears. More often: flowing, thick, and burgundy red. Thready or petrified, almost brown. Decilitres of disappointment, a reflection I won't share with anyone: how much blood pudding [a traditional Swedish food] it could have made" (Lövestam 2021a, 232–233).

In both Jäderling and Lövestam, the boundaries between inside and outside, self and other, are exposed through detailed descriptions of blood and runny vaginal suppositories. These bodily fluids mark these stories as abjection stories. This is true also in the sense that they are stories that are not usually told in public spaces other than anonymous infertility blogs and online fora. As such, these stories can be seen as abject elements that have to be expulsed from society in order to uphold a certain narrative of fertility, a narrative that also permeates the infertility case studies described by Feasey, with their happy endings. Unlike the media representations in Feasey's study, Jäderling and Lövestam make space for these abject stories to be shared and told. The level of detail, both in relation to the process and the failure, and the educational tone also render these stories accessible to audiences who are less familiar with fertility treatments.

In Folkesson's novel, the need to talk about infertility and miscarriage and to share abject stories is more explicitly stated. When Tove starts to bleed, she cannot get any answers from the midwives about what is happening to her and what to expect. Tove suspects that the midwives know more than they share with her, and Tove cannot understand why every woman has to go through miscarriage on her own when miscarriages are so common. In contrast to the midwives' silence, Tove's miscarriage is described in great detail in the novel. When Tove feels something coming out of her, she pulls down her pants: "I put my whole palm between my legs and get a warm spheric seed capsule in my hand. Big like an iron marble. Heavy. Tight. Veiny" (Folkesson 2019, 254). This is just one of many passages describing blood and lumps coming out of Tove's vagina. Against the backdrop of Tove's questioning of the silence around miscarriage in the fertility and maternity care, the novel's detailed descriptions of Tove's miscarriage can be seen as a way to break the silence and the loneliness around it. The details are not expulsed from society but visible in plain sight in an autofictional novel published by one of Sweden's most prestigious publishers. Miscarriage, in all its bloody, abject detail, is transformed into a theme for art and a story worth telling and sharing. The idea of abjection stories as a theme for art also appears in Lövestam's novel when Monika visits the opera and reflects on how the tragic parts of our real lives are rarely turned into music: "When I tried to become pregnant for eleven years—that would be a long aria" (2021a, 218). This is said jokingly but points to the fact that infertility without a happy ending is rarely seen as a story worth telling and sharing. By telling infertility stories of failure and abjection, Lövestam's, Folkesson's and Jäderling's narratives widen the representational space for infertility (see also Björklund 2023). They also serve an educating purpose; when being published, the blood, pain and sadness of failed infertility treatments and miscarriages are not silenced and hidden in fertility clinics and anonymous online infertility fora. These stories are shared with a general audience, who learn about injections, vaginal suppositories and lumps of blood.

RECLAIMING THE ABJECTED POSITION
OF NON-MOTHERHOOD

In the previous section, abjection was mostly centred around the body and bodily fluids. My discussion of abject stories that need to be expelled from society in order to uphold a particular narrative of fertility points, however, to another way of understanding abjection, which is more in line with Anne McClintock's understanding of abjection. McClintock (1995) sees "the paradox of abjection as a formative aspect of modern industrial imperialism" (72) and argues that there are abject people that imperialism "rejects but cannot do without: slaves, prostitutes, the colonized, domestic workers, the insane, the unemployed, and so on" (72). Abject people inhabit abject zones, which need to be controlled and policed in various ways. While imperialism is, of course, fundamentally different from non-motherhood, McClintock's analysis moves the discussion of abjection to a more societal level; it shows that abjection is not only linked to the body and bodily fluids but could be applied, for instance, to people and places. In this section, I will take my cue from McClintock and discuss non-motherhood as an abject position. I have shown how narratives of failed fertility treatments are abject stories that tend to be silenced. By telling these stories, Lövestam's, Folkesson's and Jäderling's narratives can be said to reclaim the abjected position of non-motherhood, from the perspective of involuntary childlessness. Here I will focus on two books that approach non-motherhood from other perspectives: Malin Lindroth's personal essay *Nuckan* (2018; "The Spinster") and the edited volume of personal essays *Ingens mamma: Tolv kvinnor om barnfrihet* (2013; "Nobody's Mother: Twelve Women on Childfreedom"). Both books reclaim the position of non-motherhood; Lindroth's book does it from the position of childlessness by circumstance, and the edited volume focuses on childfreedom, or voluntary childlessness. While there are undoubtedly differences between the positions of childlessness by circumstance and voluntary childlessness, my readings of *Nuckan* and *Ingens mamma* highlight similarities between these positions. Moreover, some of the themes that appear in the infertility narratives discussed in the previous section feature in Lindroth's and Adolfsson's books as well.

The purpose of Lindroth's book is stated clearly in the foreword: "With this book I want to reclaim the one [of the words associated with shame] that most suits a fifty-two-year-old, childless, involuntarily lonely human being who never felt at home in the narratives of single life that our culture provides. I want to reclaim the word spinster" (2018, 5–6). Lindroth positions the spinster in opposition to our culture's success stories of single women like Carrie Bradshaw in the TV show *Sex and the City*. The spinster did not choose single life; she was just never chosen by anyone. Leading one's life as (involuntarily) single can invoke fear in others. Lindroth describes how acquaintances she meets at dinner parties hurry to tell her that she is not really lonely but rather in possession of precious time for travelling and other self-developing projects. She continues: "Involuntary loneliness was always linked to the others, to the mentally ill, to the addicts and the very old who could be dead for months before their neighbours noticed. Never among us, among Mediterranean dishes and white wine glasses, in the middle of life and affluent neighbourhoods" (2018, 24). Here involuntary loneliness is described as an abject position, as it is linked to "others" and abject people. The spinster becomes a threat through her association with involuntary loneliness, an abject position, and she has to be expelled from middle-class dinner parties and made into a kind of Carrie Bradshaw character with a glamorous single life.

In Lindroth's book, the spinster position is primarily linked to lack of a partner but being a spinster also includes childlessness and involuntary loneliness. Throughout the book, the spinster position is tied to non-motherhood in various ways. The spinster is described as belonging to "the allegedly unfuckable" (2018, 28), which is of course connected to the position of not being able to attract a partner, but being "unfuckable" also, implicitly, implies that there will be no children. There are also more explicit references to how the spinster position is linked to childlessness. Lindroth tells a story of how she engages in a conversation with a mother in a toy store and is assumed to be a mother. She is unable to tell the other woman that she is not a mother, and when she leaves the toy store, she is angry with herself for her inability to reveal her identity as a non-mother.

This passage also contains explicit references to one of Lindroth's friends who is gay and did not want to come out, which suggests that the norm to be a mother is as strong as the heterosexual norm and as difficult to diverge from. Lindroth's life as a spinster is described as a life in hiding: "The feeling of living a semi-lie had accompanied me for several years. I wanted to talk about my life as alone in the same way as the couples talked about theirs, as a lived experience" (2018, 28). The book Lindroth writes is a way to do precisely that; to come out of the closet, break free from norms of coupledom and motherhood, and embrace an abject position. Lindroth points out that her spinster position is not her choice: "Perhaps

I will be a spinster for the rest of my life. That would be a loss. I would lie if I said something else" (2018, 114). In this quote, the idea of a free choice is undermined; spinsterhood is not what she chose but what happened to her. Still, as I have argued, the book establishes a case for this position as a life experience that deserves to be told and not hidden behind norms of coupledom and the nuclear family. Like the infertility narratives discussed in the previous section, Lindroth's book highlights an abjected story about non-motherhood that tends to go unnoticed and presents it as something that concerns everyone.[5]

In the collection of essays *Ingens mamma*, Annina Rabe asks why child-free people are seen as such a threat and tend to invoke aggressions in people. Several of the 12 women in this volume who write about their experiences of being childfree by choice bear witness about how they are constantly being questioned about why they do not have children. Previous scholarship has also acknowledged that women who are childfree by choice are regularly challenged and subjected to other people's efforts to make them comply with the norm to have children (see, for instance, Rodgers 2021). While stories of failed infertility and involuntarily lonely spinsters tend to be abjected from society through silence, childfree women have become increasingly visible (e.g. see Leimbach 2021, 155). However, the way in which childfree women are questioned and feared suggests that they occupy a similarly abjected position. Involuntarily childless women and spinsters can be constructed as having wanted but failed to achieve motherhood, which to some extent upholds motherhood as the norm for women. Childfree women are inscribed with non-motherhood as an active choice, which undermines the presumed link between femininity and motherhood. They need to be challenged in order to uphold normative motherhood, but, like the infertility narratives discussed in the previous section and Lindroth's spinster, the childfree women in *Ingens mamma* embrace the position and use it to tell their stories. This is also explicitly stated in the introduction to the book where editor Josefine Adolfsson acknowledges that it is difficult to find other experiences, especially stories about women who are childfree by choice. She continues: "I decided to put together the book I was looking for myself" (Adolfsson 2013, 8). In

---

[5] That the spinster perspective can concern everyone is confirmed in Lindroth's second book about the spinster, where the spinster takes up writing a love advice column, in the belief that she has something important to contribute with in these matters (Lindroth 2021).

particular, the childfree women in the book use the position to speak back to those who question them and to criticise parents' privileges.

Some writers highlight how non-parents end up working more than parents. Natacha López points out that non-parents are expected to work evenings and weekends to a higher extent than parents. Jane Magnusson argues that the Swedish welfare system, which has facilitated for parents to combine family and professional lives, has led to a situation where parents, despite complaining about stress, take on less of the general workload than non-parents. Parents leave the office early to pick up children from state-funded childcare, and they are absent from work several weeks every winter because the welfare state has provided them with the possibility to stay home to care for a sick child and get reimbursed by the Swedish social insurance agency. The non-parents, on the other hand, end up working more because they need to cover for the parents' absences.

Other contributors discuss how the time of non-parents is valued less than the time of parents. López writes about a childfree woman, Eva, who is expected, both by her boss and her colleagues, to work between Christmas and New Year's because she "doesn't have a family" (Adolfsson 2013, 44). In this passage, Eva herself is given space to question her colleagues: "I do have a family! I have a mother and a father and I'm very close to both of them. I have a brother and a new-born nephew and an older nephew and a sister-in-law. But just because I don't have children... What is family? Do only the ones I have given birth to count?" (Adolfsson 2013, 44–45; ellipsis in original). This quote highlights how Swedish norms around family—such as child-centeredness, the nuclear family norm and pronatalism—have contributed to a narrow definition of what family entails. But it also gives room for the childfree people to speak back to the parents by providing their own definitions of family. While López highlights how childfree people are less free to make decisions around vacation, Anna Sol Lindqvist discusses a different dimension of time. She shows how childfree people have to adjust their schedules around families' schedules: "As childfree among parents I have become used to that social life is often governed by how the parents have defined the needs of the children, while the needs of the adults who are not part of the family can always be negotiated. Suddenly I have, too, become included in a schedule where dinner is eaten at five o'clock sharp and where children are put to bed between quarter past seven and eight" (Adolfsson 2013, 87). Both López and Lindqvist point to how the time of parents and children are prioritised over the time of childfree people.

Together the essays in *Ingens mamma* highlight the privileges of parents and how these often impact childfree people in negative ways. Helen Peterson and Tove Ingebjørg Fjell (2010) have studied Swedish and Norwegian media representations of childfreedom, and they note that the media debate between parents and non-parents is less polarised in Sweden and Norway than in other European countries and the United States. Childfree people in Swedish and Norwegian media are represented as relatively friendly people who like children, and critique of parents' privileges and child-centeredness in society is virtually non-existent. Peterson and Fjell suggest that such critiques are too controversial to be given space in the media, and parenthood thus appears to be unassailable (2010, 140–146). Unlike the media representations discussed by Peterson and Fjell, the essays in *Ingens mamma* are explicitly critical of how non-parents need to adjust their lives to parents and families, both in the workplace and in their personal lives. Instead of adjusting to the unassailable parenthood norm, the writers embrace the abjected position that being a childfree woman entails and use it as a platform for critique of this norm and how it negatively impacts the lives of non-parents.

LAUGHTER, FAILURE AND NEW WAYS OF SEEING THE WORLD

While non-motherhood is linked to abjection and failure in the Swedish narratives discussed in this chapter, many of the stories also contain laughter, often in the context of the body. In this section, I use Mikhail Bakhtin's (1968) theories of grotesque realism to discuss how the material bodily principle is used in some of the previously discussed Swedish narratives of non-motherhood to laugh at something usually not associated with humour, namely infertility. I also draw on Bakhtin's discussion of degradation and renewal and Jack Halberstam's (2011) theories of failure to explore what new possibilities degradation and failure can offer in narratives of non-motherhood.

In Bakhtin's discussion of Rabelais's work, the material bodily principle—images of the body, eating, drinking, sexual intercourse, defecation and urination—plays a key role. Bakhtin refers to Rabelais's use of such images as grotesque realism, an aesthetics grounded in the medieval carnival, and defines the material bodily principle as deeply positive, as it includes degradation and renewal at the same time: "To degrade is to bury, to sow, and to kill simultaneously, in order to bring forth something more and better. To degrade also means to concern oneself with the lower stratum of the body, the life of the belly and the reproductive organs; it therefore relates to acts of defecation and copulation, conception, pregnancy, and birth. Degradation digs a bodily grave for a new birth; it has not only a destructive, negative aspect, but also a regenerating one" (1968, 21). Another component of grotesque realism is the carnivalesque laughter—a universal laughter that includes everyone and everything. In the context of the medieval carnival, the whole world is perceived as ridiculous and humorous and the carnivalesque laughter thus challenges power, official truths and the current world order.

In the infertility narratives discussed above, the level of bodily detail and the protagonists' reflections on them sometimes become humorous. The description of Jäderling's Hild hiding in the bushes to check if she has started bleeding and Monika's reflections, in Lövestam's novel, on how much blood pudding she could have made with all her menstrual blood are not only abject stories but can evoke laughter. Read with Bakhtin's theories on grotesque realism, the humorous images of bodily fluids open up another dimension of these narratives. According to Bakhtin, the grotesque body is not complete and closed; it transgresses itself and is open to and blends with the outside world. The grotesque body's unfinished and open character is particularly visible in the act of eating, often in images of the banquet: "the confines between the body and the world are overstepped by the body; it triumphs over the world, over its enemy, celebrates its victory, grows at the world's expense. […] [The banquet] is the triumph of life over death. In this respect it is equivalent to conception and birth. The victorious body receives the defeated world and is renewed" (1968, 282–283). While menstrual blood is connected to failure to become pregnant in Lövestam's novel, Monika's reflections on making blood pudding out of it also link it to food. Her menstrual blood represents the material bodily principle which both destroys and creates, and the creative dimension is particularly visible in the image of the blood pudding, something nutritious and life-preserving.[6]

---

[6] In contemporary French literature, menstrual blood is sometimes represented as purifying and sacred rather than as impure and abject. Maria Kathryn Tomlinson (2021) argues that these representations can be seen as a corporeal protest against societal discourses that define women's bodies as abject (63, 93). Infertility and childlessness are, however, not the focus of Tomlinson's study, which deals with literary representations of the female fertility cycle. In contrast, in Lövestam's novel the creative dimension of the menstrual blood is linked to failure to become pregnant.

Food also appears in connection with fertility treatments in Jäderling's short story. When Hild and her partner drive home after the embryo transfer, "they buy a large cinnamon roll and take a picture of it while laughing. They think that the roll swells and that it is surrounded by a glorified light" (Jäderling 2017, 297). For Bakhtin, the official Medieval culture and its truth are primarily linked to the church and Christianity, which had a "tone of icy petrified seriousness" (1968, 73). The carnivalesque laughter challenged the official culture and truth by degrading it to the material bodily level, and the mockery "was deeply immersed in the triumphant theme of bodily regeneration and renewal" (1968, 75). The laughter in the quote from Jäderling is a carnivalesque laughter; even if it is not explicitly linked to religion, the idea of pregnancy as a glorified state can be seen as an official truth that is ridiculed and laughed at by being linked to food and eating, the material bodily principle. Lövestam's novel more explicitly references the Bible in connection with fertility and food. Throughout the novel, Monika's follicles, which start to grow as a result of the hormone injections, are compared to grape clusters. This simile appears, for instance, when Monika draws her family tree on a piece of paper, thinking: "*Stina slept with a strange man and gave birth to a son Micke. Micke took a wife who reminded him of Stina. She gave birth to a daughter Monika. Monika became the mother of twenty grapes*" (Lövestam 2021a, 80; italics in original). This passage alludes to the Biblical genealogies, which highlight kinship and heritage. By representing Monika's inability to conceive in a context where it breaks with a long genealogy this quote emphasises barrenness. At the same time, by including food and ovaries in the Biblical genealogy and thus invoking laughter and the material bodily principle, this passage degrades and challenges truths about the importance of these genealogies and paradoxically also links Monika's barrenness to renewal.

For Bakhtin, the carnivalesque laughter mocks and defeats power, "all that oppresses and restricts" (1968, 92). An element of mocking power is particularly visible in Lövestam's novel. For instance, when Monika visits the fertility clinic, the doctor makes some insensitive comments about Monika's age, and while Monika does not object explicitly, the reader has access to her inner monologue in which she constantly speaks back to the doctor and belittle him by comparing him to a mole (the animal). The mole dwells in the earth, and the comparison thus degrades the doctor to the material bodily level. Even if Monika's resistance is quiet, she is a first-person narrator and controls the narrative; she can invoke the carnivalesque laughter and degrade the authoritarian doctor.[7]

In the infertility narratives, laughter thus works to turn things around and challenge what we take for granted. Degradation and laughter are used to mock power and to resist official truths of pregnancy as a glorified state and conventional kinship bonds like the ones in the Bible. In line with the material bodily as a creative principle, degradation and laughter also, perhaps paradoxically, change barrenness into renewal and regeneration. For Bakhtin, degradation and regeneration are intertwined in grotesque realism: "Carnival (and we repeat that we use this word in its broadest sense) did liberate human consciousness and permit a new outlook, but at the same time it implied no nihilism; it had a positive character because it disclosed the abundant material principle, change and becoming, the irresistible triumph of the new immortal people" (1968, 274). The idea that degradation and negativity can carry with them a seed to renewal appears also in Jack Halberstam's book *The Queer Art of Failure* (2011). Key to Halberstam's theory is how failure can be a way of resisting the norms of what it means to succeed in a society that is governed by a neoliberal ideology that prioritises individualism over collectivity. Similar to Bakhtin, Halberstam argues that the questioning of taken-for-granted truths can open up new ways of living in the world, but Halberstam ties those new ways of living closer to collectivity.

As we have seen, the Swedish narratives of non-motherhood are in various ways stories of failure. While the infertility narratives depict failing fertility treatments, *Nuckan* and *Ingens mamma* highlight failure to live up to norms of femininity and motherhood. In many of these stories, however, degradation and failure make possible new ways of living in the world. In the infertility narratives, grotesque realism and failure are intertwined, linked to bodily fluids and degradation, but this process leads to something new. At the end of Jäderling's short story, Hild has miscarried, and even if the last paragraphs emphasise emptiness and lack of meaning, Hild is also filled by happiness when realising that she is at the bottom. Degradation leads to something positive, and even if it is unclear in Hild's case what this happiness entails, it is obviously not associated with having children.

---

[7] In another twenty-first-century Swedish novel about a woman who struggles to have children, Martina Haag's *Glada hälsningar från Missångerträsk: En vintersaga* (2011; Happy Greetings from Missångerträsk: A Winter's Tale), laughter is used to challenge "official truths" about what a good life entails for women: husband and children (Björklund 2023).

In Lövestam's novel, new possibilities are connected to a relationship to a child who is not Monika's: her neighbour, 14-year-old Texas, who needs a stable adult in his life since his own mother has addiction problems. The novel depicts not only how Monika tries to become pregnant but fails but also how she receives a family by becoming a kind of mother figure in Texas's life: she feeds him, talks to him about his life, and even saves him from being sexually abused by an older man. The development of their relationship parallels Monika's fertility treatment, such as when Monika's embryos grow in petri dishes at the hospital during a weekend she spends growing closer to Texas. At another occasion, during an intimate conversation with Texas, she feels a movement in her cervix, which makes her think about the fertility treatment. But while the fertility treatment fails, her relationship with Texas thrives, and the references to growing embryos and cervix movements can be seen as a way to emphasise how caring for a child is linked to Texas rather than the embryo. This is even confirmed by Texas, who after learning about Monika's struggle to become pregnant reveals that he does not want her to have a child. At first, Monika gets upset, but then realises why:

"You don't want me to have children because you want to keep me to yourself, right?"
I see the answer in Texas's shrug.
"At least you're normal," he says.
Rarely has a declaration of love felt so real. (Lövestam 2021a, 244)

By emphasising the relationship between Monika and Texas, Lövestam's novel challenges biogenetic motherhood as the only way to care for children and opens up new ways of leading one's life.

While Folkesson's novel includes grotesque elements in the representation of Tove's miscarriage, it does not invoke the carnivalesque laughter. Still, failure and the connection to the material bodily principle reveal the possibilities of new ways of living, as collectivity is presented as an alternative to the nuclear family. Tove, her partner Hanna, Tove's grandmother and Tove's uncle care for each other like family members, and when they all sit together in grandmother's kitchen, Tove refers to them as a family: "Grandmother looks so happy because we will stick together when she dies. A strange little family consisting of two + uncle + dog" (Folkesson 2019, 99). Even if grandmother is not included in this family, since she will soon die, she is part of the community in the present. This is also a cross-species family, since the dog is included.

Some of the essays in *Ingens mamma* offer similar examples of alternatives to biogenetic bonds and the nuclear family. These essays do not evoke grotesque realism, but in light of Halberstam's theories, their representations of failure to live up to norms of fertility and femininity also suggest other ways of leading one's life. Similar to Lövestam, both Josefine Adolfsson and Faranak Rahimi highlight the possibility to care for children beyond biogenetic bonds. Adolfsson points to the paradox that lies in society's prioritisation of artificial reproduction over taking care of existing children in need, and Rahimi writes about her experiences of caring for the children in her low-income neighbourhood. Other essays in the volume argue for the need to upgrade other close relationships than parent-child relations. Anna Sol Lindqvist dreams of a large family that is only partly based on biogenetic connections; a group of friends who live together and who would not differentiate between their biogenetic children and the other children in the group. Natacha López highlights how childfree people spend quite a lot of time caring for others, such as ageing parents, lonely friends, their partners and even children who need more adults in their lives, and she states: "Maybe it's time to upgrade the significance of other relationships than the one between parents and small children?" (Adolfsson 2013, 49–50). In these essays, failure to adjust to motherhood norms frees human consciousness to reflect on other ways of organising close relationships.

CONCLUSION

The Swedish narratives of non-motherhood discussed in this chapter encompass a wide variety of genres and represent a range of women who do not have children for numerous reasons. And yet, similar tropes and themes emerge within these texts, including the reasons for being childless. Together, the texts recount stories that are usually invisible—stories of blood, loneliness and less-privileged positions—and they do so with an educating and defiant tone. In the narratives, non-motherhood is linked to abjection; in the infertility narratives, abjection is expressed through bodily fluids, in particular blood, and in Lindroth's *Nuckan* and the edited volume *Ingens mamma*, non-motherhood becomes an abjected position. Non-motherhood is also associated with failure; the infertility narratives are stories about failed fertility treatments, and the other two books represent failure to comply with norms. Abjection and failure are embraced and reclaimed in these narratives and used to showcase non-motherhood as a liveable life and to criticise the motherhood norm and the rarely discussed parents' privileges. Abjection and failure are also combined with laughter in some of these stories, a laughter that is carnivalesque and thereby linked to degradation and renewal. Subsequently, laughter mocks power and offers new ways of being, making possible a world where close relationships are not necessarily organised around biogenetic bonds and the nuclear family. Even if the carnivalesque laughter does not appear in all the narratives discussed in this chapter, they are all characterised by a defiant attitude; they challenge motherhood and family norms and provide alternative ways of leading one's life. They suggest that happiness is unrelated to having children, they promote collectivity and/or caring for children beyond biogenetic bonds and they valorise other forms of relationality, including connections between friends.

Acknowledgements I am very grateful to those who have given valuable feedback on earlier versions of this text: Ulrika Dahl as well as my co-editors and the contributors to this volume, especially those who served as assigned readers at a workshop, Valerie Heffernan and Laura Lazzari.

REFERENCES

Adolfsson, Josefine, ed. 2013. *Ingens mamma: Tolv kvinnor om barnfrihet.* Stockholm: Atlas.
Archetti, Cristina. 2019. No Life Without Family: Film Representations of Involuntary Childlessness, Silence and Exclusion. *International Journal of Media & Cultural Politics* 15 (2): 175–196. https://doi.org/10.1386/macp.15.2.175_1.
———. 2020. *Childlessness in the Age of Communication: Deconstructing Silence.* London and New York: Routledge.
Bakhtin, Mikhail. 1968. *Rabelais and His World.* Trans. Helen Iswolsky. Cambridge, MA, and London: The MIT Press.
Björklund, Jenny. 2023. Struggling to Become a Mother: Literary Representations of Involuntary Childlessness. In *Narratives of Motherhood and Mothering in Fiction and Life Writing,* ed. Helena Wahlström Henriksson, Anna Williams, and Margaretha Fahlgren, 55–75. Cham: Palgrave Macmillan.
de Boer, Marjolein Lotte, Cristina Archetti, and Kari Nyheim Solbrække. 2019. In/Fertile Monsters: The Emancipatory Significance of Representations of Women on Infertility Reality TV. *Journal of Medical Humanities.* https://doi.org/10.1007/s10912-019-09555-z.

Fahlgren, Margaretha. 2018. Babyfeber: När längtan tar över livet. In *Mamma hursomhelst: Berättelser om moderskap*, ed. Margaretha Fahlgren and Anna Williams, 183–194. Möklinta: Gidlunds.

Feasey, Rebecca. 2019. *Infertility and Non-Traditional Family Building: From Assisted Reproduction to Adoption in the Media*. Cham: Palgrave Macmillan.

Folkesson, Tove. 2019. *Hennes ord: Värk I–III*. Stockholm: Bonnier.

———. 2021. *Den stora kyrkan*. Stockholm: Bonnier.

Graham, Melissa, and Stephanie Rich. 2014. Representations of Childless Women in the Australian Print Media. *Feminist Media Studies* 14 (3): 500–518. https://doi.org/10.1080/14680777.2012.737346.

Grosz, Elizabeth. 1994. *Volatile Bodies: Toward a Corporeal Feminism*. Bloomington and Indianapolis: Indiana University Press.

Haag, Martina. 2011. *Glada hälsningar från Missångerträsk: En vintersaga*. Stockholm: Piratförlaget.

Halberstam, Judith "Jack". 2011. *The Queer Art of Failure*. Durham and London: Duke University Press.

Hill, Alexandra M. 2022. Family Without Futurity, Kinship Without Biology: Childlessness in Contemporary German Literature by Women. *Feminist Media Studies* 22 (4): 816–830. https://doi.org/10.1080/14680777.2020.1743735.

Jäderling, Viktoria. 2017. Oförklarligt barnlös: Uppföljning av en ofullbordad graviditet. In *Åh Lunargatan*, 279–316. Stockholm: Bonnier.

Kristeva, Julia. 1982. *Powers of Horror: An Essay on Abjection*. Trans. Leon S. Roudiez. New York: Columbia University Press.

Leimbach, Joselyn. 2021. Queering Cristina Yang: Childfree Women, Disrupting Heteronormativity, and Success in Failed Femininity. In *The Truth About (M)otherhood: Choosing to Be Childfree*, ed. Helene A. Cummins, Julie Anne Rodgers, and Judith Dunkelberger Wouk, 155–177. Bradford: Demeter Press.

Letherby, Gayle. 2002. Childless and Bereft?: Stereotypes and Realities in Relation to 'Voluntary' and 'Involuntary' Childlessness and Womanhood. *Sociological Inquiry* 72 (1): 7–20. https://doi.org/10.1111/1475-682X.00003.

Lindroth, Malin. 2018. *Nuckan*. Stockholm: Norstedt.

———. 2021. *Nuckans hjärtespalt*. Stockholm: Norstedt.

Longhurst, Robyn. 2001. *Bodies: Exploring Fluid Boundaries*. New York and London: Routledge.

Lövestam, Sara. 2021a. *Ljudet av fötter: Första Monikabok*. Stockholm: Piratförlaget.

———. 2021b. *Bära och brista: Andra Monikabok*. Stockholm: Piratförlaget.

———. 2022. *Nu levande: Tredje Monikabok*. Stockholm: Piratförlaget.

McClintock, Anne. 1995. *Imperial Leather: Race, Gender and Sexuality in the Colonial Contest*. New York and London: Routledge.

Peterson, Helen, and Tove Ingebjørg Fjell. 2010. Bilden av frivillig barnlöshet i media. In *Frivillig barnlöshet: Barnfrihet i en nordisk kontext*, ed. Kristina

Engwall and Helen Peterson, 105–146. Stockholm: Dialogos Förlag and Institutet för Framtidsstudier.

Rodgers, Julie Anne. 2021. Introduction: Contextualizing the Choice to Be Childfree. In *The Truth About (M)otherhood: Choosing to Be Childfree*, ed. Helene A. Cummins, Julie Anne Rodgers, and Judith Dunkelberger Wouk, 11–26. Bradford: Demeter Press.

Tomlinson, Maria Kathryn. 2021. *From Menstruation to the Menopause: The Female Fertility Cycle in Contemporary Women's Writing in French.* Liverpool: Liverpool University Press.

CHAPTER 3

Non-Motherhood and the Narrative of the Self in Nuria Labari's *The Best Mother of the World*

Dovilė Kuzminskaitė

INTRODUCTION

The Best Mother of the World (2019) is an autobiographical novel by Spanish writer and journalist Nuria Labari. The main focal point of the book is the life journey of a self-actualized middle-class Catalan woman in her thirties. After going through IVF treatment several times and giving birth to two girls with a small age gap between them, Labari's protagonist

This project has received funding from the European Union's Horizon 2020 research and innovation programme under grant agreement No 952366

D. Kuzminskaitė (✉)
Vilnius University, Vilnius, Lithuania
e-mail: dovile.kuzminskaite@flf.vu.lt

© The Author(s) 2025   41
J. Björklund et al. (eds.), *Negotiating Non-Motherhood*,
Palgrave Macmillan Studies in Family and Intimate Life,
https://doi.org/10.1007/978-3-031-66697-1_3

tries to reconstruct her identity through the lens of a new maternal experience. The main character is a modern big-city woman, who claims to never have had a 'maternal instinct', yet one day she was suddenly struck with an overwhelming desire to have children. Lauren Jade Martin (2017) argues that biology also plays a greatly important part, since each body dictates an individual timeline that cannot be ignored. Hence, becoming or not becoming a mother is not only a moral/ethical choice. Instead, it is rather a complex decision or circumstance related to various factors, such as the body of the individual and the ones surrounding them (the partner or the surrogate, when necessary), the time (both individual and shared), the place, the political, economic, and cultural context. Therefore, what is believed to be an individual decision might in fact be the result sum of circumstances.

After facing fertility issues and thereby requiring an 'artificial' way of conceiving, she feels a deep fracture both in her own consciousness and her relationships. The novel then becomes an exercise in auto-analysis. Labari's character goes through her key experiences, related to femininity, focusing on her identity in relation to public discourse. Trying to articulate her new self, the woman rediscovers her relationship with her partner, her mother, her work, her children, her career, and, of course, herself. Yet the book ends with a twist, which is rarely seen in cultural representations of fertility struggles and renders Labari's work unique and worthy of discussion: the main character decides to abort her third, unexpected, pregnancy. Moreover, she does not have a 'socially justified' reason to do that: she simply does not want a third child.

When approaching reproduction-related topics and, subsequently, the discourse surrounding them, three factors should be taken into consideration: time, space, and politics, all of which go hand in hand with individual decisions (Stuvøy 2018, 34). Labari's novel was published in 2019 in Spain, where feminist modes of thinking are well articulated and visible even on the superficial cultural level. As María Luisa Balaguer (2019) explains, the Francoist regime framed women as passive objects with a predestined life purpose: to reproduce and to take care of others. When the dictatorship came to its end, Spanish feminist discourse re-emerged based on individual voices that aimed to de-codify patriarchal system and redefine women as active subjects (29). In recent decades, Spanish feminists have been keen to eliminate persisting forms of discrimination and violence (Heffernan and Stone 2021, 126) and to revisit women's roles in society, concentrating on very specific issues. Nowadays, feminism in Spain has gained a micro-focal perspective, with each voice in the feminist chorus focusing on a specific problem: migration, work conditions, reproductive choices and rights, sexual identity, public image of women, and equality in child-care, among many others.[1] During the II Republic and the Francoist regime, feminists had to tackle basic foundational issues, such as representing women as citizens and human beings equal to men. Nowadays, Spanish feminism has the possibility of focusing on more specific needs and demands, which means that feminism in Spain can be considered to have been successfully embedded in culture and society and feminist modes of thinking well-established. Yet it shouldn't be forgotten that social context is impactful too: feminist values will be shared more widely among middle-class, educated, urban women than in closed suburban communities. The revival of women's fiction, together with vivid feminist expressions in social media (e.g. Instagram accounts of Moderna del pueblo, Marta Piedra, and Lola Vendetta, amongst others), annual manifestations of 8M, numerous artists from pop culture (such as the singer Rosalía), all of which respond to the feminist discourse, provided the ideal context for Labari's book to emerge.

Since ART and abortion constitute an important component of Labari's book, before diving into the analysis of the novel, I will briefly touch upon the situation of fertility-related matters in Spain. According to the data provided by Eurostat, Spain's fertility rates are low and decreasing (from 1.32 in 2012 to 1.19 in 2020) (Eurostat n.d.). As Heffernan and Stone explain, low natality rates lead to glorification of pregnancy and motherhood and the emergence of pro-natalist discourse (124): since society wants or needs to propagate itself, it becomes keen to push individuals into making the 'right' decision and leaves very little to no place for alternative life practices or experiences. Pro-natalist

---

[1] It is worth mentioning that, as well as responding to feminist ideas, Labari's book also pertains to a specific modern literary tendency of journalists producing literary or auto-fictional texts on 'trendy' topics, which seems to be an international process (a similar example could be Caitlin Moran's bestseller *How to Be a Woman*). This type of writing, while not necessarily considered as prestigious by the literary elite, is nonetheless important in that it provides easy-to-connect discourse and content which are accessible to broader audiences. Labari's novel was published with a slightly non-mainstream, yet still reader-friendly, publishing house (Literatura random house) and contributes to the type of lively discussion on womanhood and motherhood that is characteristic of contemporary maternal, autofictional texts.

discourse also causes polarization in society: the representations of the ones who want/or have children and the ones who do not become fixed and framed. The narratives about not wanting children, abortion, or infertility become lateral, marginal ones. Labari's novel, then, seems to be intent on broadening the spectrum of images and narratives that surround motherhood.

Due to socioeconomical circumstances and increased emancipation, Spanish women start planning families later, which may also lead to reproductive challenges. As stated by Ido Alon and Jaime Pinilla (2021), "since 2008, the volume of Assisted Reproductive Technologies (ART) in Spain has increased by nearly 50%, reaching 149,337 In-Vitro Fertilization (IVF) and 34,100 Intrauterine Insemination (IUI) cycles in 2018. Spain is the largest European ART provider and fourth globally" (1). It is also worth mentioning that, while there is social security cover for these procedures, only 10% or 20% of the centres are public and there is also a list of criteria for eligibility, where age, other children or civil status can be significant factors (Romero Caro 2022). Decreasing natality rates and increasing demand for ART might constitute factors that influence Labari's particular representation of motherhood: on one hand, she reflects on the process of becoming a mother through ART and discusses this in contrast to the 'natural' way of getting pregnant, thereby introducing alternative ways of becoming a parent into the discourse. On the other hand, the author concludes her text with an abortion, thus providing an indirect response to pro-natalist narratives.

After having been strictly banned by the Francoist regime which imposed strict catholic values on society, abortion emerges in Spanish legal discourse from 1978. However, it took several years of debate and research until the more liberal abortion laws were established in 2010, when women gained the right to abort until 14 weeks of gestation without medical reason (Márquez Murrieta 2010). In 2022, the Spanish government announced the follow-up of the abortion law and plans to allow teenagers to abort without parental consent. According to the official statistics of the Spanish Health Ministry, annually about 10 of 1000 women have an abortion, the predominant age group is 20–29 years (around 15% of total abortions), and around 85% of women choose private centres over the public hospitals (Sanidad 2022). Different issues related to abortion, such as pro-natalist concern in health sector or lack of accessibility to legal abortion for the more socially vulnerable groups seem to be widely discussed both in legislative institutions and via various types of media. However, it seems that individual narratives of abortion, especially atypical ones when pregnancy is not a threat to a woman or the woman is not characterized by any level of social vulnerability, are not pronounced loudly enough. This might be the reason why Labari chooses to conclude her own narrative about motherhood precisely with this topic.

The aim of this chapter is to show how Labari's protagonist seeks to find her individual self while negotiating the various pressures imposed by society. As previously noted, contemporary Spanish society still incites its members to procreate, disregarding the fact that circumstances now are very different: more women become mothers later in life and use ART, while others choose abortion and childlessness. Therefore, the concept of motherhood is undergoing a shift, becoming more complex, less unilateral. Correspondingly, fragmented and individualized narratives about motherhood, as is the case for Labari's character, are emerging, yet they still have to find a valid place within official discourse. In the following analysis of the novel with its rather ironic title, *The Best Mother of the World*, I will centre on three aspects, aiming to underline the protagonist's way of negotiating infertility and motherhood: economics and ethics of non-motherhood; infertility and femininity; and abortion and the narrative of choice. Since Labari's book is written from an openly socio-critical perspective, I will use the concepts of power and biopolitics, established by Michel Foucault in his lectures, published in *Society Must Be Defended* (2003) together with Nancy Chodorow's concept of individuation, introduced in "Family Structure and Feminine Personality" (1995).[2] Both Foucault and Chodorow think about individual existences as the ones that are tightly interwoven in social tissue: Labari's female is also trying to understand her place in the society and keep her head above the stream of unifying narratives about motherhood. Foucault's approach will help to underline the clash between individual and official powers, while Chodorow's reflection on individuation will shed light on the protagonist's struggle to maintain her subjectivity while being cornered by the master discourse.

---

[2] Chodorow's (1995) central argument is that women define themselves more in relation to other people than men do (44). While this argument might seem opposed to the modern feminist aim to represent women as independent creatures, Labari's book allows us to engage with Chodorow's perspective, as the protagonist reflects on her experiences precisely based on her social binds.

ECONOMICS AND ETHICS OF NON-MOTHERHOOD

Assisted reproduction in Labari's novel is presented using three main leit-motivs: first, the emphasis on the artificiality of the process in contrast to the narratives of pregnancy as an almost mystical experience; second, the economic aspect in relation to the ethics; and third, the power struggle. The perspective from which Labari's character approaches ART in *The Best Mother in the World* is a peculiar one, since it is depicted from the critical socio-political lens, rather than an intimate one. Curiously enough, Labari's narrator is distinctively open about her body, emotions, and choices, yet the reader never gets to know the reason why she must choose ART. Discursive ambivalence is one of the most important descriptors of the protagonist: she combines rational, almost 'sterile' reasoning with cha-otic, emotional outbursts; her critical, woke, feminist ideas are at times replaced by poetic reflection. While, on one hand, these narrative clashes create a certain scepticism towards the integrity of the protagonist, from my perspective they also generate a sense of authenticity: Labari's charac-ter seems to be a real and genuine person who shifts and changes, rather than an inflexible representation of certain ideals or ideologies.

The dichotomy of 'natural' vs 'unnatural' reproduction is depicted in the novel through the generational quarrel considering women's choice to use IVF. One of the peak conflicts in the book is the one between Labari's character and her mother, and which evolves around the spontaneity of getting pregnant. The mother argues that infertility and even the con-scious desire to have children is a modern problem, while the 'traditional' way to have children is by accident: "I will seem very old to you, but these things only happen to your generation now. I never wanted to have chil-dren. Not like your generation does now, I want to say. I ended up preg-nant without knowing it, without going for it or thinking about it" (Labari 2019, 14). To begin with, the mother's statement highlights the problem-atic of choice: in her times, having children was not something to reflect on, rather, it was something that happened to a woman. Hence, the 'natu-rality' of having children is not only related to the physical side of the process, the way to conceive them, but also to the lack of deliberate deci-sion: the woman falls pregnant as one becomes ill, without having an active say in it. This statement forms part of a traditionalist discourse, based on a collective frame of thinking instead of the individual narrative: the mother does not listen actively to her daughter, she reacts with prees-tablished polarized phrasing, implying that there is a right way to do things

the modern, 'problematic' way. Here, we observe the ten-
_ctween two generations of women and two interiorized ways of
narrating themselves: the mother is 'trained' to assume her role without
reflection while the daughter is a part of a modern, self-analytical generation. This conflict reminds us of Chodorow's scholarship which argues
that, in Western middle-class families, the mother-daughter conflict is normally a conflict between "regression, passivity, dependence" and "pro-
gression, activity, independence" (65). However, it must be noted that the
independence and individuality of Labari's protagonist are complex: her
having to make a conscious decision about how and when to have children
is forced on her by her body and the process itself is a regulated one.
Therefore, the process of individuation becomes a real struggle.

Labari's narrative about ART almost immediately starts with numbers:
"control of ovarian stimulation: 500 euros. Extraction of oocytes: 1200
euros. Lab: 1500 euros. Transfer of embryos: 300 euros" (2019, 23), the
woman enumerates in the chapter "I Can't Have Children". She also
comments bluntly on all the additional costs and indicates prices for her
prescription in a chart (see Fig. 3.1).

These passages of the text are written in a sterile, emotionless prose,
which allies with the bureaucratic aspect of the process itself: while 'natural' parents celebrate the surprise of the pregnancy, the woman of the
novel is dealing with receipts, payments, and forms. The woman quotes
the document that her husband is asked to sign, which indicates that his
"reproductive material can be used 'twelve months after his death to
fecundate Ms. _____'" (Labari 2019, 35). The use of documents and
medical records demystifies the process of becoming parents, almost

– Puregon 900 ui.	359,00€
– Puregon 600 ui.	274,74€
– Cetotride. 7 viales de 0,25 mg	248,70€
– Ovitrelle, 250 mg (1 dosis)	50,63€
– Blastoestimulina, 10 óvulos	6,95€
– Zitromax 1 g, 1 sobre	3,93€
– Azitromicina Ratio 500MG, 3 c.	5,90€
– Proggefic, 60 cápsulas. 250 mg	38,90€
Total:	988,75€

Fig. 3.1   Fragment of the page 24 of *The Best Mother of the World*

dehumanizes those going through it, and even renders the experience vulgar: as the protagonist comments, "there is nothing dirtier than paying to be a mother, yet I put the bill into my wallet as softly as a whoremonger slips bills on some naked chest" (24). Labari's character deliberately desentimentalizes everything related to the IVF, and, later on, abortion,[3] because that is how the subject is presented in the clinic: the woman assimilates and mimics the official discourse. Since she is the object of the procedure, the woman seems to be positioned on the lower scale of the hierarchy and becomes absorbed by the power that is performed over her.

The economic aspect of IVF implies an ethical dilemma which Labari's character discusses with similar acuity: "The market is incredibly flexible when it comes to buying women's bodies based on hours, months or even parts. By contrast, it becomes more conservative, when it comes to the negotiating parts of the unisex body. The blood or the kidneys cannot be sold, only donated. Yet the maternal milk is sold. The uteruses are being rented" (2019, 79). Here Labari reveals the regulatory aspect of biopolitics: the power over an individual body is not an individual matter after all, it is delegated (or not) to the individual by the higher system. The consumerist aspect of IVF is explained in Ingvill Stuvøy's (2018) study on surrogacy: she argues that, unlike 'natural' parents, the ones that choose or must choose alternatives for having children normally face the role of the client, rather than the one of the 'true parent' (36). Foucault argues that regulatory systems tend to replace ritualization with regulation (247): from my point of view, the sections of the novel where Labari's protagonist harshly discusses the lack of humanism in the process depict just that. 'Artificial' reproduction has little to no mystery and intimacy, it is something that is being allowed, apprised, and performed on an individual by others, hence the question about the limits of individuality arises.

Yet Labari's character is sceptical not only about the system surrounding ART but also about herself as a subject who is actively choosing the procedure:

---

[3] Yet the prose surrounding the husband and the children is more subtle and at times rather edulcorated. When narrating her experience of becoming a first-time mother the woman says: "D1 is six months old, and Husband holds her in his arms in a corner of our room. Both are flesh, both naked, both mine. We were hunters, we were collectors, and we are the only thing that we needed to not to be cold. This is how it was when D1 came. Love shot up and drowned it all, as simple as that" (56).

"I want to have a child", I thought. I even repeated it to the Husband's ear. Then he caressed my hair or neck before we fell asleep.

Want+have+child=Error.

From the point of view of 'having' I should be ok with adoption. For example, when you want to have a dog, everyone knows that it is better to adopt. There is no difference if it's a puppy or if it's an elder dog, everybody knows that adopted dogs are more noble. And it's exactly the opposite with children. […]

I didn't want to adopt. Yet I knew that it is bad to pay for the baby with my own genetics. Much worse than to buy a dalmatian from a breeder. Without a doubt, adoption for me was the only morally acceptable thing. But I wanted a baby of a certain breed.[4] (2019, 44)

In this segment of the text, the protagonist observes herself from a critical distance and recognizes that she is also part of a power-based system. Later in the text the woman concludes: "DNR is 99.9 per cent the same in every human being. The differences between us (despite sex and race) are genetic and very irrelevant. Yet thanks to the ideology of narcissism and singularity, to pay for being mother (or father) without trying to adopt a child who already exists and needs a mother is a desire whose ethics are never questioned" (Labari 2019, 45). Here Labari addresses the question that frequently accompanies discourse surrounding assisted reproduction: why not choose adoption? The comparison to animal breeding may seem cynical, yet it could be seen as a narrative strategy that Labari implements: irony implies distance, which helps to form a more individual way of thinking. At the same time, this reflection could be read as a criticism of pro-natalist politics: the decision to go through IVF instead of adoption is not criticized quite so harshly because of the biopolitical desire to increase the body of society.

Foucault argues that every society tries to take control over the reproductive decisions of its members and specifically guide them in a direction that is beneficial for the system, often disregarding the individuals (241). As previously stated, Labari introduces the regulatory aspect of IVF while mentioning its cost, but there is also an interesting passage in the novel where she reveals the more subtle manifestations of pro-natalist politics:

---

[4] Labari is not the only one who establishes the parallel between being childless and owning a pet: it is frequently seen in social media and other cultural representations. For example, a childless character in the novel by Mexican writer Guadalupe Nettel, called *La hija única* (2020), talks about owning a dog as a 'light' version of having children.

Despite the doctor, in fertility clinics there are three types of women that have a say about the future of all women: actors, princesses and spouses of football players. They are always present in the waiting rooms. [...] Women that are always of some brand, women that erase images of women not born from the market. All of us: the infertile ones, the old ones and the lesbians are hypnotically going through the pages of sentimental magazines, the ones about fashion or the ones about beauty. Those are supposedly the magazines that we, women, read. Regarding the experiences of their protagonists, the thesis is always the same: to have a child is the ultimate external confirmation that you deserve to be alive. [...] Private fertility clinics are full of sentimental magazines, because they are the best marketing strategy for the business. (2019, 35–36)

In this image, the clinics are not depicted as sterile 'sanctuaries' where struggling people go to get help to fulfil their lifelong dreams: rather, they are portrayed as carefully strategized mechanisms, that treat their clients in a certain way to obtain certain results (stimulate the desire to have children to benefit economically). By depicting this aspect, Labari shows that the discourse surrounding women and reproduction is never innocent, it is carefully designed to trigger their subconsciousness and make the individuation harder. From this arises one of the most important questions related to identity discourse: are the 'individual' choices always individual? Further on in the text the woman adds: "Looking at it from the distance, I don't know how I managed to go through it all. I'm not talking about the pinching, the hormones and the analytics, the waiting and the having to begin again, the mild clinical stumbles. I refer strictly to the sentimental magazines of the waiting room" (2019, 38). The perfect women in the magazines point to the 'defectiveness' of the ones that are waiting for the procedure and make them feel their supposed lack of fulfilment more keenly. Labari makes an interesting shift when it comes to the discourse surrounding infertility: it is commonly depicted as physical and emotional pain, yet Labari's character also suffers intellectually, as she analyses the socio-political aspects of her journey and understands how women are being objectified and manipulated, how their individual power is diminished through encounters with the official discourse and power.

The depiction of the waiting room is common both in visual and textual representations of people who use ART. Guadalupe Nettel in *La hija única* also mentions a waiting room in the infertility clinic, located in a tall building that overlooks the slums: Almost a Foucauldian panopticon.

While sitting there, the woman's gaze also falls on women's magazines and brochures. The waiting rooms of fertility clinics seem to be used in fiction to underline the uncomfortable and, moreover, the public aspect of artificial reproduction: while the 'natural' conception happens behind closed doors and inside, the 'artificial' one exposes individuals and makes their experience a shared one. Again, to reference Foucault, the individual decision becomes a public one where external influences shape and, indeed, manipulate personal choices.

The use of IVF in Labari's novel is morally uncomfortable not only because the ones who are going through it are objectified, but also because of the internal hierarchies within the group: "when life is submitted to scientific efficacy, science puts a price on it, and procreation becomes another form of power" (2019, 137). Labari pushes Foucault's ideas about system vs individual choice slightly further. Instead of focusing on a stable dichotomy between the state that regulates and the individuals that are being regulated, she shows that within the regulated segment there are internal systems. Being able to decide 'what kind' of child one wants and to pay copious amounts of money and dedicate time and effort to the strenuous process automatically makes that person more powerful than the one that cannot do so. *The Best Mother of the World*, therefore, diverges from the linear cause-effect representations of fertility struggles, avoids emblematic characters, and reveals the complexity of the power struggle.

INFERTILITY AND FEMININITY

Labari's reflections on infertility begin with puberty, which is quite unique when it comes to infertility discourse in general as the latter is normally focused on the 'here and now', the struggle and effort to have children and not so much on early experiences of reproductive challenges. Both in film and literature, people who are struggling to conceive are represented as stuck in the present moment of childlessness: there is no past and there seems to be no future unless their desire is fulfilled. Since Labari's aim is to represent the construction of the self as woman and the changes in her identity, she broadens the scope of information given to the readers. In analysing her encounters with infertility, the protagonist starts with her adolescent years, when a lack of menstruation was a differentiating factor and a form of social protest. She comments: "I remember myself baren from the early years. Since childhood my panties announced that, always so white. The spotless message: if you are not bleeding, you do not give birth. I think I felt like a guy in that sense. A lucky guy, as they say. Or, more precisely, a fortunate woman. I liked the non-bleeding very much. I felt as if I were 'the chosen one', when at fourteen, fifteen, sixteen and seventeen I didn't have to cover my menstrual haemorrhages. I felt sorry for my friends" (Labari 2019, 21).

This fragment of the text allows us to see how women are constantly in negotiation with the narrative around them and how the frame of thinking changes over time: in adolescence, a girl is supposedly lucky if she does not have to 'suffer' menstruation, but when the 'right' time to have children comes, she is portrayed as lacking something. Labari's protagonist describes herself as an individual displaced from the official discourse of womanhood and explains: "I wanted to be read by men and renounced to pronounce the word 'uterus' for anything in this world. After all, I was almost a guy" (2019, 21). It seems that detaching from femininity is women's way to individuation. Instead of aligning herself with others of her kind which, Chodorow argues, women are expected to do as more socially dependant individuals, she tries to ally with the group that has more power, hence, men. For her, being baren is related to intellectual work: she must be like a guy (unable to become pregnant) to be able to break through 'feminine' writing and be taken seriously. In this case, Labari indirectly dialogues with Simone de Beauvoir in *The Second Sex* (1949), who also stated that women must renounce having children if they want to be successful: only in Labari's protagonist's case, the choice is made for her, she is just a consciousness that processes it, but has little or no power over her body.

The formulation of an individual self (which Chodorow depicts as "individuation" or "sense of self" and Diana Tietjens Meyers (2001) calls "self-narrative") is an underlying leitmotiv in Labari's texts. Here, the previously mentioned tendency towards ambivalence also prevails. Whilst the decision to use ART is a conscious one, the urge to consider having children appears to be an innate condition, a state related to being a woman: "I was a mother long before giving birth to H1" (Labari 2019, 20). The protagonist says: "I imagined a fertile woman humid like a green mountain. But I was wrong. It was not my imagination. It is an image constructed in stone and time, made even bigger with our economic culture, like the belly of a Palaeolithic Venus" (20). On a superficial level, Labari's position on motherhood might seem shallow (motherhood=instinct), yet there is more complexity to it: she reveals that all women are exposed to narratives of exuberant fertile goddesses, which is supposed to form the core of womanhood. Labari's protagonist implies that motherhood is not only the fact of having a child, but rather an idea attached to womanhood that every woman must make her peace with. For women struggling with fertility, this part of one's self-construction is a particularly difficult one: "All the women that I know have a hole [...]. To be born with a hole. This is what being a woman means. And this is what not being a mother is" (24). Hence, the inability to have 'natural' pregnancies is not simply the loss of a baby, but rather a loss of identity: "Woman, you are infertile. Woman, you are not bleeding. Woman, you are not a woman. Woman, you are nothing. Woman, go disappear" (22). For Labari's protagonist, being unable to have children also means a shift in language: "When I knew that I was unable to have children, my words went blank, equal to my panties: useless" (25). It seems that, for the protagonist, being detached from motherhood is an indicator of overall emptiness, yet barrenness is not only (or not at all) a defect of the body. The woman states: "The fact that I am unable to have children *naturally* is one of the reasons why I decided to write about maternity. I think that my impossibility to get pregnant legitimizes me in this matter. Because you must be very female to be barren" (20). Here Labari's character references the image of a hole or a void: if all women are born with a void (which is Labari's key metaphor for motherhood), the barren ones are the most female of them all, because their void is never filled in a 'proper' way, and so they cannot escape it.

Labari also tries to debunk the myth that being able to have children is a continuum and fertility is something given for life: "In the end, all of us will be barren. It does not matter if the woman has given birth to four, five or twelve children, we are all condemned to the same end. Do not be fooled, to have a child also means to dry. One day, a child will look into his mother's eyes and will announce to her that she will never be fertile again" (21). In this fragment, we can see that infertility for Labari is not an 'issue' or a medical state, that one must go through and then, hopefully, come to the other end of and forget about. (In)fertility in a broader, metaphorical sense, is a definition of a woman that she is predestined to struggle with her entire life, the axis around which the feminine identity twirls: it seems to be, in fact, the core element to the process of individuation of every woman.

ABORTION AND NARRATIVES OF CHOICE

As observed in the previous section of this article, *The Best Mother of the World* overtly challenges the cultural myth of motherhood as the ultimate fulfilment of womanhood. In her text, Labari endeavours to deconstruct the representation of pregnancy and abortion as completely opposing experiences: one related to birth, and the other, to death, as is the case for pro-natalist discourse which claims that abortion is akin to murder. In Labari's narrative, the choice to take part in the process of having children is as strong (and valid) as the choice to not to do so. In an atypical fashion, the abortion forms a parallel narrative to the one that centres on the desire to have children: the woman chooses abortion just as she chose IVF ("I chose the goodbye" she states (Labari 2019, 197)) and must go through the protocol and formal procedures to achieve the goal. Once again, the woman is presented with documents and questionnaires, her behaviour is regulated, but the aim this time is the opposite. Similar to the discussion of IVF, there are two main leitmotivs: money ("The intervention costs 354 euros with local anaesthesia and 454 with deep sedation, a type of general anaesthesia that does not require to intubate the patient" (208)) and power, embodied by figure of the doctor. In the chapter entitled "Interruption",[5] Labari presents the dialogue with the doctor who will perform the abortion:

- – Did you use any contraception?
- – No.
- – Is anyone forcing you to make this decision?
- – No.
- – Would your significant other support you if you decided to continue with this pregnancy?
- – Yes.
- – Do you have children?
- – Yes.
- – Ages?
- – Five and two and a half.
- – Civil status?
- – Married.

---

[5] The name of the chapter itself is significant: the woman interrupts the pregnancy, but also her own perpetuation as a new mother, she stops reinitiating herself into motherhood.

- Previous abortions?
- None.
- Would you have resources to maintain this child?
- Yes.
- Have you been sleeping well since falling pregnant?
- Yes.
- How would you imagine this baby?
- I lost various embryos implanted in vitro. It is clinically premature to talk about a baby of six weeks of gestation, doctor. There is no baby. (206–207)

In the dialogue, one can sense explicitly the power struggle at play: to acquire the right to go through the procedure, the woman is forced to engage in a conversation that she does not feel comfortable with, as is evident from her short answers. The conversation is controlled by the medic who selects very specific questions and seems to be leading the woman towards rethinking the abortion, as if it was the logical thing to do or in line with a certain norm. Foucault argues that biopolitics imply that society is seen as a mass with unified needs and desires, not as individuals (2003, 245), which means that official institutions will tend to have one type of discourse which will be applied to all. The dialogue presented by Labari depicts just that: the universal questionnaire shows how medical language is not interested in the individual situation, it is designed as a 'one-size-fits-all' model. The doctor never reacts to woman's answers, only ticks a box until the woman interrupts the procedure by inverting the roles: she is the one reminding the doctor about the 'proper' way of talking about the embryo, since she has already appropriated the discourse of the doctors with whom she interacted during the IVF.

Labari depicts the hypocrisy of language in medical institutions in relation to reproduction: while during IVF, the embryos are mere particles that are bought and their failure is treated more as a discharge than an actual loss of a human being, the pre-abortion embryo is considered to be a baby and abortion implies a concrete loss. This part of the novel also contrasts vividly with the beginning of the chapter "The Failure and the Chewing Gum", where the woman explains how during IVF, the doctors were reluctant to answer her questions and avoided guaranteeing any success, quite the opposite in fact:

The doctors don't guarantee anything by definition. My doctor has black hair and wears it in a braid in such a manner that there is not a single loose hair by the roots. Her hair is as tense as an arrow before shooting. Her words are arrows. "It depends on the age of the woman and the causes that lead to the procedure. Generally, there is 45–50 percent of pregnancy possibility per cycle, although there are exceptions. The average rate of pregnancies after three cycles is approximately 75 per cent. And the percent of abortion in every cycle is 15 per cent. If the transferred embryos are not frozen ones, the average percentage of pregnancy for every trying is 25 per cent, and the one for de-vitrificated embryos is 35 per cent." I count my possibilities to save the 30000 euros that would cost me to access the 80 per cent possibility to become a mother. (Labari 2019, 34)

In the abortion interview, the six-week foetus is already a baby and the doctor uses a language that implies its future (asking about the maintenance, for example). By contrast, when discussing IVF with the person who clearly desires to have a baby, the doctor merely gives statistics and emphasizes the possible loss, showing a refusal to connect with the patient and adopt her point of view. Both in representation of abortion and that of IVF, the discourses of the doctors and the patient are parallel, they do not share the same language and expression, since the patient is interested in her individual needs and desires and the doctors are acting according to the norm. The embryo in IVF seems to be narrated as a possible failure, while the pre-abortion foetus is treated as an undeniable success (or a blessing in a traditional wording) that the woman refuses to accept. Again, Labari indirectly points to the guilt that women seem to be predestined to experience: the discourse surrounding abortion is formulated in a way that pushes a woman towards the 'right' path (from a pro-natalist perspective). Therefore, the medical system, which we normally tend to understand as objective and just, is shown as manipulative, a system that tries to dominate the individual.

In the short segment of the book concerning the abortion and its parallel narrative about IVF, Labari emphasizes the discursive difference surrounding different aspects of non-motherhood. Also, she continues with her representation of motherhood as a dynamic condition, when depicting a woman's right to decide when to stop 'renewing' herself as a mother. In this manner, Labari also challenges the stereotype that people who struggle with infertility want children almost obsessively: no matter how nor

how many[6]. Furthermore, Labari proclaims a woman's right not to experience abortion in a dramatic way: "after the intervention we do not know
what to do. We are not too affected; we are not that kind of people"
(2019, 210). With this statement, the protagonist once again dissolves
typical representations: abortion is not depicted as something that breaks
a woman's life and consciousness and inevitably implies loss and tragedy.
Perhaps Labari's woman assumes her abortion so calmly because she is
already content with her life or, perhaps, because she has already interiorized that, no matter what, the maternal void is always within her.

CONCLUSION

Labari's novel responds to the topic of infertility and childlessness in a very
specific way. Instead of reproducing the common polarization between
childless people and the ones who have children, people who struggle to
conceive and those who have never encountered such issues, she opts for
a multidirectional approach. The complex protagonist of *The Best Mother
of the World* embodies the struggle to conceive, the difficult process of
negotiation with new motherhood and the active decision to limit the
number of children in the family all at once, showing that life might be
more complicated than a 'pure' experience of having children/deciding
not to have them/struggling to have them. *The Best Mother of the World*
explores how childlessness grows into motherhood and then back into
non-motherhood, and shows how these shifts impact the identity of a
woman. Together, the focus on (in)fertility as a pragmatic issue grows into
a reflection on barrenness as a core quality of womanhood, which, in turn,
becomes an existential concept.

Labari approaches motherhood and non-motherhood as concepts that
are bound together. Depicting non-motherhood as a composite phenomenon, the author is acutely aware of the different factors that affect wom-
en's experiences when facing reproduction-related decisions. In the novel,
Labari shows the economical side of ART, depicts societal pressure and
generational conflicts, and spots the incongruities of medical discourse:
all of which frame women's experiences of non-motherhood. Combined
together, these aspects show that being or not being a mother is not always
(or only) an individual choice that women make by themselves and for

---

[6]Although one may also argue that here Labari falls into a rather cliche representation of
family: big city, middle class, two children with a 'reasonable' age difference between them.

themselves, nor it is made 'on the spot': both being and not being a mother require negotiation with one's surroundings and oneself. Hence, *The Best Mother of the World* allows the reader to see that motherhood is not a singular, homogeneous theme; it is a constant anxiety and inherently complex.

REFERENCES

Alon, Ido, and Jaime Pinilla. 2021. Assisted Reproduction in Spain, Outcome and Socioeconomic Determinants of Access. *International Journal for Equity in Health* 20 (156): 2–12. https://doi.org/10.1186/s12939-021-01438-x.

Balaguer, María Luisa. 2019. El movimiento feminista en España. Influencias de los modelos americanos y europeos. *IgualdadES* 1: 19–42. https://doi.org/10.18042/cepc/IgdES.1.01.

Chodorow, Nancy. 1995. Family Structure and Feminine Personality. In *Feminism and Philosophy: Essential Readings in Theory, Reinterpretation, and Application*, ed. Nancy Tuana and Rosemarie Tong, 43–66. New York: Routledge.

Eurostat. n.d. Fertility Indicators. (website). Accessed 27 May 2022. https://tinyurl.com/39jzffxj

Foucault, Michel. 2003. *Society Must Be Defended*. Trans. David Macey. New York: Picador.

Heffernan, Valerie, and Katherine Stone. 2021. International Responses to Regretting Motherhood. In *Women's Lived Experiences of the Gender Gap*, ed. Angela Fitzgerald, 121–133. Singapore: Springer.

Labari, Nuria. 2019. *La mejor madre del mundo*. Barcelona: Literatura Random House.

Martin, Lauren Jade. 2017. Pushing for the Perfect Time: Social and Biological Fertility. *Women's Studies International Forum* 62: 91–98. https://doi.org/10.1016/j.wsif.2017.04.004.

Ministerio de Sanidad. 2022 Interrupción voluntaria del embarazo. (Website). Accessed 27 May 2022. https://www.sanidad.gob.es/profesionales/saludPublica/prevPromocion/embarazo/tablas_figuras.htm.

Nettel, Guadalupe. 2020. *La hija única*. Barcelona: Anagrama.

Márquez Murritea, Alicia. 2010. *España y sus leyes sobre interrupción voluntaria del embarazo: contexto y actores*. Mexico City: GIRE.

Romero Caro, Inés. 2022. Radiografía de la reproducción asistida en España: los límites de acceso en la sanidad pública y la situación por comunidad. *Ondacero*, January 24. Accessed 26 November 2023. https://www.ondacero.es/noticias/sociedad/radiografia-reproduccion-asistida-espana-limites-acceso-sanidad-publica-situacion-comunidad_2022012461eea5999890160001c4a1a3.html.

Stuvøy, Ingvill. 2018. Troublesome Reproduction: Surrogacy Under Scrutiny. *Reproductive Medicine and Society* 7: 33–43. https://doi.org/10.1016/j. rbms.2018.10.015.

Tietjens Meyers, Diana. 2001. The Rush to Motherhood: Pronatalist Discourse and Women's Autonomy. *Signs* 26 (3): 735–773. https://doi.org/10.1086/495627.

CHAPTER 4

Meanings, Experiences, and Perspectives on Non-Motherhood in a Spanish Context

Anna Morero Beltrán and Elisabet Almeda Samaranch

INTRODUCTION

This chapter analyses "non-mothers" or, in other words, women who have actively chosen not to become mothers. The trend towards non-motherhood is part of broader structural changes in Spain, a country which, like several other Western societies, is undergoing significant transformation in the field of reproduction. Such transformations also affect the meanings of motherhood, the representations of family, and gender

This project has received funding from the European Union's Horizon 2020 research and innovation programme under grant agreement No 952366.

A. Morero Beltrán • E. A. Samaranch (✉)
Universitat de Barcelona, Barcelona, Spain
e-mail: anna.morero@ub.edu; elisabet.almeda@ub.edu

61
J. Björklund et al. (eds.), *Negotiating Non-Motherhood*,
Palgrave Macmillan Studies in Family and Intimate Life,
https://doi.org/10.1007/978-3-031-66697-1_4

relations (Bogino Larrambebere 2020). This particular study aims to explore the various reasons why women choose non-motherhood. To this end, we conducted a series of interviews with a group of women fitting this profile and asked them to explain why they opted to remain childless. Our survey included questions specifically designed to explore and examine the arguments provided by our interviewees, identify those aspects of their life experiences that led them to reject motherhood, and understand what the realities of being a non-mother are for them. Our chapter is also careful to contextualize this study within contemporary Spanish culture and society.

Our contribution is relevant and innovative for a number of reasons. Firstly, official data reveals that, since the 1990s, the total fertility rate (TFR) in Spain has been below 1.5 children per woman. More precisely, the number of women who remain childless in Spain rose from 11 per cent for women born in 1945 to 20 per cent for those born in 1965, and it is estimated to reach 25 per cent for women born in 1975 (Esteve et al. 2016). This means that one out of every four women in this latter generation will not become a mother, making it the Spanish generation with the fewest number of children in the last 130 years (Esteve et al. 2016).

Secondly, according to existing research, the reasons that influence the decision not to have children are primarily related to financial difficulties, work-family (im)balance, and the almost non-existence of public policies designed to attenuate these adverse circumstances, followed by the lack of a partner or, in the case of having one, not considering him to be suitable for fatherhood (Cabré Pla 2003; Esteve and Treviño 2019). However, it should be noted that, in socio-demographic reports, the response "I don't want to be a mother" was found across all age groups, and it rose from 11 per cent for women 25 or younger to 33 per cent for women aged 45–49, a period when motherhood is more often determined by personal choice than by the possible adverse circumstances associated with maternity (Esteve and Treviño 2019).

However, Spanish scholarship on the subject has paid little attention to these non-mothers and the reasons why they freely decide to remain childless. Scholarship on non-motherhood has frequently been engulfed by studies on the wider networks of family relationships. In academic literature, as in cultural experience, childless people have been socially silenced in some way or another (Piella Vila 2013, 1). This chapter, therefore, marks an important contribution to a still scarce but growing theoretical framework on non-motherhood by choice in Spain. Initial research on this issue was slow to emerge, focused almost exclusively on heterosexual women, and based almost exclusively on one "childlessness" framework, namely: women who were unable to have children for various reasons. More specifically, this body of literature focused mainly on the postponement of motherhood due, above all, to a very precarious labour market for women and an even more precarious employment horizon once they became mothers (González and Jurado-Guerrero 2006; Seiz 2013; Baizán 2006; Devolder and Merino-Tejada 2007).

Thirdly, early work on non-motherhood tended to focus on the lack of public policies in place to properly support families (Comas d'Argemir et al. 2016; Meil 2006; Bianculli and Jordana 2013). Often, public policies designed to support families were wrongly perceived as maternity support policies because women have been traditionally positioned as the main caregivers and, as a consequence, they were considered to be the main benefactors of this type of non-transformative public policy.

Later research underwent a shift towards a "childless-by-choice" or "childfree" framework, which emphasizes the fact that, for some women, not being a mother is an active choice rather than an act of renouncement. This concept of free choice in relation to non-motherhood can also be explained as a consequence of the entrenchment of feminist discourses that have contributed to a reformulation of non-motherhood as desirable and acceptable (Piella Vila 2013; Bogino Larrambebere 2016; Ávila 2005).

To briefly recapitulate, therefore, this chapter will add to the more recent body of theory on non-motherhood as a valid life-choice, a body of work that regards women who freely choose not to be mothers as political subjects and gives a unique voice to their personal desires beyond all the difficulties associated with labour markets, public policies, the absence or not of a partner, and so forth. In what follows, we shall present a feminist framework which complements the accounts of seven female interviewees who freely chose not to become mothers.

CHOOSING TO BE A "NON-MOTHER" IN THE SPANISH CONTEXT

Spain provides an interesting case-study for research concerning the growing trend towards non-motherhood, given the intense socio-demographic and family changes that have taken place over the course of the last five decades. During this time, the country has evolved from a pronatalist state, with high birth rates and authoritarian family-oriented public policies, into one of the European countries in which the birth rate has declined most significantly and which has experienced a notable increase in the number of women who voluntarily decide to remain childless (Alberdi 1995).

In fact, until well into the 1980s, traditional family structures and high birth rates still characterized the lives of most Spanish families and women, who continued reproducing traditional gender stereotypes and roles. The mothers and grandmothers of women born in the 1960s had lived through 40 years of Franco's dictatorship, with its patriarchal culture that treated women as a "full-time housekeeper" (Valiente 2003). However, the women born in the late 1960s and the 1970s became the first generation in the democratic period to subvert the heteronormative models of traditional nuclear families (Cabré Pla 2003; Meil 2006), although this occurred in a context in which society still conceived of and organized the family and the household around a traditional view which saw the rigid division of gender roles as essential. For decades, the country had not had any meaningful family-friendly public policies (Bianculli and Jordana 2013, 505), that is, there had been a stark absence of family policies truly supporting women and allowing them to develop their families at their will, or making financial contributions and providing services that permitted them to find a balance between paid employment, on one hand, and home-life and childcare, on the other. In fact, the weak Spanish welfare regime, broadly speaking, has been—and continues to be—quite insensitive to the real needs of women who look after their families.

Furthermore, the legitimacy crisis of the welfare state and a precarious labour market have shaken traditional welfare structures to their foundations, leading to the emergence, not only of new social risks, but also of new ways of understanding the family, the couple, motherhood and non-motherhood. Therefore, slowly but surely, many women born in the 1980s and 1990s began to actively live their lives outside the values of the traditional family. Accordingly, this generation of women has embraced a range of different individual and family trajectories and experiences which may not include having children. It is precisely this generational group of women that our interviewees belong to. On the one hand, they strive for autonomy and individuality, while, on the other hand, their freedom comes up against—and is restricted by—a patriarchal society in Spain where male-chauvinistic values continue to prevail. Unsurprisingly then, women are continually forced to justify their decisions regarding non-motherhood.

Moreover, these women who increasingly opt for non-motherhood by choice still have to negotiate the dilemma of having to confront some of the same traditional cultural values on conception and family life that characterized earlier generations of women in Spain. They also face the reality of having to carve out their own trajectories against a lack of pre-existing models, even though they are certain that they are better off fulfilling their desires and expectations with respect to not having children. Although they may not have clear reference points, their situation provides them with a broader range of life options, which, despite everything, also comes at a cost in terms of prejudice and discrimination, as it is demonstrated by this study.

METHODOLOGY

In order to analyse the experiences of our interviewees, we adopted a qualitative methodology, as it favours a more in-depth examination of the participants' subjective realities, meanings, lived experiences, perceptions, attitudes, and cultural codes (Ruiz Olabuénaga 2012). Seven in-depth interviews lasting between an hour and an hour and a half were conducted either in person or online. The interviews took place in their homes or in a café, according to their choice. They were semi-structured interviews, designed to encourage our informants to reflect upon their own perceptions and speak frankly about their childfree lives and what had led them to make that choice. All the interviews were recorded with the participant's consent. The sample was selected until discourse saturation was reached.

The sampling followed the snowball method, a non-probability sampling method where new informants are recruited by other informants to form part of the sample. More specifically, to set up the sample, the authors distributed messages through WhatsApp, specifically targeting feminist and women's groups, ensuring wide dissemination of the message. Later, informants were asked to share the message with other women who might qualify. This methodology has benefits and limitations. While the snowball sampling method has the ability to recruit hard to reach populations and the implementation process is short and simple (Ruiz Olabuénaga 2012), the primary limitation of this methodology is that the sample is not randomly selected, thus snowball sampling can lead to a homogenous sample.

Our interviews included cisgender, lesbian, bisexual, and heterosexual women born between 1976 and 1990 in the province of Barcelona, Spain. All of them identified as feminists, and they had a partner, a paid job, and higher education; they held fourth-level postgraduate qualifications such as PhDs, with the exception of one of the interviewees, who had done specialist training. As for their occupations, four of them were employees, and the rest were self-employed. Their professions were diverse: a visual artist, an illustrator, a dog trainer, a consultant, a journalist, and two women worked for public administration. At the time of the interviews, all of the women lived in the city of Barcelona, with the exception of one participant, who lived in a nearby town. However, the most important characteristic shared by all of them was that they believed they had the biological capacity to have children, but they had chosen not to do so.

In this respect, it can be stated that our interviewees were committed to their decision not to have children and, in the words of Ireland (1993), they could be defined as "transformative women," that is, women who have actively chosen non-motherhood. They did not want to have to accommodate the worries and responsibilities that accompany motherhood and understood that the time and the flexibility that characterized their daily lives were the result of their own choice, which, in turn, opened up several possibilities for personal autonomy, creative work, political activism, professional development, leisure time, and care of their environment. The interviewees also fit into two other categories of women who do not want to become mothers: early articulators and postponers. On the one hand, some of them would identify as early articulators, that is, women who knew from an early age that they would never want to be mothers. Postponers, on the other hand, are women who have not yet decided whether they want to become mothers. Postponers, at the same time, can be divided into two further subgroups: those who always imagined that they would be mothers but postponed doing so due to certain life circumstances such as lack of a stable relationship or lack of stable income; and those who have always been undecided about motherhood (Houseknecht 1979). Eventually, while our participants' personal accounts provide information about the ambivalence surrounding the desire to experience or not experience motherhood, they also reveal the pressures, prejudices, and value judgements that can challenge and complicate the counterhegemonic model represented by non-motherhood.

Results and Discussion

Arriving at the Non-Motherhood Decision and the (Almost) Constant Need to Justify It

A woman who voluntarily decides to remain childless is defined as a person who currently has no children, has no expectations of having children in the future, has the intention and has made the choice not to have children (Dykstra and Hagestad 2007). For most of our interviewees, the decision not to become a mother was not innate; rather, they usually reached this position over the course of their adult lives. Initially, some of the participants had considered the idea of becoming mothers, having envisioned themselves as mothers when they were young in the form of symbolic play, or at other times in their lives, such as when becoming involved in an emotional relationship as adults: "I did consider becoming a mother at some point. It was the result of a relationship that I had six or seven years ago, but in the end, I decided not to. Generally speaking, I've always been on the side of 'no' but, sometimes, depending on my partner, because I was in love, I wanted to make her happy, and so on, I did consider the possibility of becoming a mother, but I always ended up deciding not to" (Interview 4, 34 years old, who lives in a lesbian relationship). Another interviewee once entertained the notion of motherhood during her preadolescent years. However, after observing the experiences of her friends and reflecting on her own experiences while sharing her life with a woman who had children from a previous relationship, she opted to structure her relationship without assuming any responsibility or role in her partner's children's lives: "When I was very young, I always used to say that I wanted to have many children—12, in fact! My mother still recalls that vividly. However, as I grew older and witnessed the reality of parenting, seeing friends who had children and then seemed to disappear from their own lives, my perspective shifted. So, when I found myself in a relationship, I initially agreed from a distance to the idea of motherhood. But now, being with a partner who has children, the question arises: do I want to be involved in this? And the answer, for me, has been no. I'm willing to spend time with you and your children, I can make that effort. However, it remains just that—an effort. And for me, effort alone doesn't equate to genuine desire" (Interview 2, 30 years old, who lives in a lesbian relationship).

However, when we asked those interviewees who had initially considered becoming mothers why they had entertained the idea, they generally identified social inertia as the main cause, that is, a vision of motherhood as a fixed fate requiring little decision. This is closely related to the fact that the identity of women as such has always been defined with reference to the family, that is, with reference to the fact of having children and not to the absence of these: "like suddenly you find someone you feel good with and you feel this urge to start a family, but it's just that the idea came to me, and as I grew older I became more convinced that it's an idea that probably came to me because… because of the patterns instilled in you: you have to study, you have to work, find a partner, and have children" (Interview 7, 35 years old, who lives in a heterosexual relationship).

Another interviewee noted that, during the time when she contemplated biologically becoming a mother, the lack of public debate on non-motherhood as a real option made it difficult for her to make this decision and, at times, delayed it: "I had considered being a mother […] out of social inertia. Maybe there's more debate around motherhood now, but when I was 30, 30-something, this debate was not part of my world. You were simply a heterosexual woman with a partner and you were expected to have not one, but two children" (Interview 1, 44 years old, who lives in a heterosexual relationship).

Most of our participants stated that if the current debate about motherhood had existed at that time, they would have made the decision in a more confident manner, understanding that motherhood is one of several biological possibilities, not an instinct or the fate of all women. Nonetheless, all of our interviewees were confident about their decisions, even when they were not innate or motivated by circumstance, but the result of a genuine desire not to become mothers: "For me, not becoming a mother was not something circumstantial, like I'm in an unstable situation or I am… The reasons really changed over time; when I was 14, I didn't see things the same way I do now at the age of 36" (Interview 6, 36 years old, who lives in a heterosexual relationship). This other participant questions the maternal instinct that supposedly prompts women to desire motherhood: "I remember when I was 14 years old, I didn't want to be a mother. I didn't understand why I had to be a mother just because I was a woman; I never understood that. I've never had that maternal feeling they talk about. I don't know what it is, I've never felt it" (Interview 5, 35 years old, who lives in a heterosexual relationship).

It is important to understand the rupture that this signifies, given that, in the Western imaginary, motherhood is still considered the most relevant identity trait of femininity (Badinter 2011). Moreover, the fact that motherhood involves a biological component has served to ensure that it is presumed natural and proper to women, and is therefore considered to be their destiny above all others. For this reason, the representations that make up the social imaginary of motherhood have the ability to reduce the full spectrum of desires of all women to a single desire: that of having children. They also create a homogeneous identity for all women around motherhood (Tubert 1996).

Because of the perceived irregularity of their choice, many of the women we interviewed had had to deal with social pressure and confront a construction according to which their decision not to have children made them non-mothers, egotists, women who prioritize their work or personal projects over family. However, when non-motherhood is a personal choice, these women are forced to face an additional type of interrogation which is the result of their positioning themselves as counterhegemonic models. In the case of most of our interviewees, such questioning came from their close circles, although they also encountered it in circles where they did not have any reliable emotional ties, as was the case with this interviewee: "maybe it's me, but I often find myself needing to justify […] the 'no's' and how to explain it, it has to be explained beyond just 'I don't feel like it' or 'I don't want to,' […] Sometimes you have to find an excuse… and when you're younger, they tell you that you're too young: 'I'm not going to validate this, because you're very young, and you're going to change your mind' […] you always have to validate this 'no,' I mean, that you don't want to be a mother, the 'no' never just stops there" (Interview 6, 36 years old, who lives in a heterosexual relationship). This other interviewee, on the other hand, faced pressure from her closest family circle, her parents, who persistently inquire about her plans regarding motherhood, even to this day: "There was a period when I lived with them [their parents] when there was always this message: let's see when you make us grandparents, let's see when you make us grandparents… and when, when, when. There came a point where it was like, 'I won't make you grandparents, and if I ever do it's because I've decided to do so'" (Interview 7, 35 years old, who lives in a heterosexual relationship).

In relation to this, we must point out that many of our interviewees stated that, in their circles of friendship, both mothers and non-mothers speak about the social pressure they had to endure regardless of whether they were mothers or not. The idealization of motherhood is something that both mothers and non-mothers have to negotiate. All of our participants maintain that these spaces for debate are restorative and offer the mutual recognition that is needed but cannot be found in public policies or general public opinion.

The Main Reasons for Not Becoming a Mother

As noted above, our interviewees made the decision not to become mothers consciously, without any connection to infertility, chance or other circumstances beyond their control. In general, these women had many diverse reasons for it, reasons that changed over the course of their life cycle. Accordingly, some studies have identified the different reasons that women have for not wanting to become mothers, including, for example, a lack of maternal instinct or interest in motherhood, or a fear of motherhood, specifically childbirth (Peterson and Engwall 2013). Most studies on women who have chosen not to have children predict that the percentage of women who are non-mothers by choice will continue to grow due to other reasons, such as economic, cultural and social changes, and, more recently, reasons related to the climate change crisis (De Rose and Testa 2015; Abma and Martinez 2006; Agrillo and Nelini 2008; Mulder 2003). Besides this, their main motivations include arguments connected to the discourse of freedom too. As observed by Helen Peterson (2015), we find two types of discourse in the construction of voluntary non-motherhood. The first one has to do with the different positive experiences associated with certain elements of the freedom that childless women enjoy in their everyday lives. This discourse sees freedom as part of a wider deeply rooted identity involving other life choices besides that of rejecting motherhood. The second kind of discourse is founded on the danger that children pose for women's autonomy and freedom, with motherhood consuming time and mothers trapped in child-rearing activities.

All the participants in this study regarded motherhood as a sacrifice and a renouncement, meaning that they ceased to be the protagonists of their own lives. As noted by Paloma Fernández-Rasines and Mercedes Bogino Larrambebere (2019), many women see motherhood as an intensive practice, and they are not ready to take on the cultural mandate that extols the experience of motherhood as a social merit. On the contrary, they consider motherhood as a threat to their individuality. One of the main reasons given by our interviewees to explain their childless status had to do with the need to safeguard a central value of their identity: their autonomy, that is, the possibility of making decisions about their own lives and defining personal projects (Lagarde 1999). They viewed autonomy and motherhood as incompatible largely due to the meaning that the women in our study conferred upon maternity, considering it an activity that prevents them from making decisions in alignment with their own wishes, since mothers must subordinate their aspirations and desires to the needs of the child. Thus, according to all of our interviewees, the development of personal projects ceases to be a priority in the lives of women who opt to become mothers, who are forced to focus their time and energy on child care and the welfare of their children. Consequently, the interviewees expressed a need to establish the conditions that will allow them to make choices about their own life projects and have time to pursue their own professional aspirations and consolidate their careers: "At this point, my professional career takes priority over motherhood... I still don't know what I want to be when I'm older, but I'd like to have my own project and see it through, and I know that it's very complicated to pursue my professional dream and raise a child. If I have children, I want to be a present mother; I don't want to be everywhere and nowhere at the same time" (Interview 2, 30 years old, who lives in a lesbian relationship). Another interviewee justifies her choice based on the incompatibility of pursuing a professional life with motherhood. Additionally, she introduces generational difference as a variable that makes a distinction: "Professional women represent a significant change. We now have opportunities that didn't exist before [...] We do many things, and being mothers doesn't fit in. We approach things very differently from women of previous generations because we have more options; we can say what we want and what we don't" (Interview 5, 35 years old, who lives in a heterosexual relationship). This idea, which all our interviewees share, is partly due to the way in which different social discourses have created a sort of an ultimatum for women which dictates not only that they must become mothers but also that they should execute their motherhood in a certain way. In line with this, motherhood has been perceived as a homogeneous experience for all women and as their sole destiny, the only fate that they all have in common. This also implies that there is a lack of positive and/or diverse models of "other" mothers, and this was another observation shared by many of our interviewees: "The models of motherhood that I have around me haven't helped in terms of deciding to become a mother [...] There are very few mothers who enjoy it in my circle. Or, they seem to really enjoy it, but it doesn't seem real to me. Generally speaking, I don't have any mothers around me who make me feel jealous" (Interview 1, 44 years old, who lives in a heterosexual relationship).

As mentioned earlier, despite the fact that since the 1970s, in Spain, the family has been mutating towards a greater plurality of relational and parental arrangements, accompanied by changes in legislation, values, representations, and practices, the word "family" remains inextricably linked to the heterosexual bi-parental model. In addition to this, the traditional nuclear family is still considered to be the best environment to raise children and remains the gold standard against which all other family types are measured (Golombok 2015). This implies a model of motherhood that was not desired by the participants, who also rejected the intensive two-parent model: "Many more women would be mothers if [having a family] was not so individualistic: you and your couple. For many women, that's too much, as it is for me as well. Although if it were organized some other way, it would be different" (Interview 4, 34 years old, who lives in a lesbian relationship).

In other words, the organization of the traditional family does not make sense for certain segments of society today. Thus, there is a need for a wider approach to maternity, which should be seen from a more communitarian, interdependent perspective. There is an urgent need for real alternatives to the prevailing bi-parental model, alternatives in which child care and rearing become collectivized.

This lack of alternative to the traditional family, in turn, raises questions about public policies and how women are abandoned, even today, as mothers. As we mentioned earlier, the lack of policies to support families is an obvious reality in the framework of what is actually a family-oriented welfare regime, like the Spanish one, a regime with permanent dependence on the family, its intergenerational solidarity and its gender structure as providers of work and care services, and as aggregators of inadequate income support measures (Saraceno 1995; Vergés Bosch et al. 2019).

On the other hand, it should be noted that the transformation of the family during the twentieth century—not only in Spain, but also in other Western countries—has reinforced a kind of gender syncretism for women, that is, caring for others in the traditional fashion while striving, at the same time, to achieve their individual development and be part of the modern world through success and competition. The result is that women are trapped in an inequitable relationship between care and individual development. The patriarchal culture that builds such gender syncretism fosters in women a satisfaction of the duty to care, which has come to be viewed as a

cal duty of women and, therefore, experienced as if it were
\t the same time, women also feel the social and economic
e in educational, labour, and political processes to survive
society of advanced capitalism (Lagarde 2013). This form
of being a mother is no longer a desirable goal for the women in our sample;
so, if they cannot be mothers in a different way, they are not interested in it.

Finally, reasons related to climate change have more recently been indicated by a variety of studies as a new explanation for non-motherhood
(Schneider-Mayerson and Ling 2020; Rieder 2016; Arnocky et al. 2012;
Marks et al. 2021). We asked our interviewees whether climate change was
a factor influencing their decision not to become mothers. However, and
contrary to the hypothesis of the referenced authors, this argument did
not play a role in any of our cases. They often relativized this issue by arguing that climate change is just one issue among the many difficulties the
world is going through, such as pandemics or wars, and which now constitute part of our daily lives: "The end of the world is not a reason why I
wouldn't become a mother if I wanted to; it wouldn't be a compelling
reason; in the end, the world has gone through so many things... and this
[climate change] is just one more thing" (Interview 5, 35 years old, who
lives in a heterosexual relationship).

It should be clarified that the hypothesis about the influence of climate
change in our interviewees' decision to remain childless was based on the
growing literature on the subject, the discourse of social movements, and
cultural initiatives such as the Birth Strike movement, a voluntary organization of women and men who have decided not to have children in
response to climate change. However, all our interviewees agreed that
they based their decision not to have children exclusively on reasons
directly related to their own well-being and personal development but did
not equate their decision with a means of contributing to the combat
against climate change, nor was the latter an issue of sufficient importance
to change their reproductive decision (see also Bodin and Björklund
2022). In fact, as it has been revealed, the reasons given by these women
are, in many cases, the same as those why other women decide to become
mothers, for example: their own well-being, happiness and personal fulfilment. This might suggest that it is pointless to establish any sharp contrast
between the motives of childfree women and those of women who choose
to be mothers, as it is often done.

Internalizing Stereotypes and Prejudices About Non-Mothers

It is still widely assumed that women's wish to be mothers is a direct and natural result of their biological capacity to procreate and, subsequently, a series of ingrained notions are often tied to the fact of being a mother (Donath 2015), such as the idea that there is a maternal instinct that automatically prepares women to take care of their offspring. In addition, motherhood is still considered to be a primary role for women, and women who do not mother, biologically or socially, are often stereotyped as selfish, desperate, or living barren lives, and are subject to the ideologies of the dominant discourse on motherhood (Letherby 2002). The existing scholarship on the subject has addressed an extensive list of these myths, and many of them continue to be seen as valid today, as was established by our study. The responses of all our participants echoed some of the most deeply rooted social conceptions of motherhood that legitimize these stereotypes as natural, such as the fact that motherhood is a unique and unsurpassable experience: "My mother told me that I would miss out on the best that life as a woman has to offer, which is to create life" (Interview 6, 36 years old, who lives in a heterosexual relationship). Another participant referenced the idea that being a mother involves a kind of unconditional love that one can only feel for a child: "a love that you can only feel for a son or daughter" (Interview 1, 44 years old, who lives in a heterosexual relationship).

In their responses, our interviewees also mentioned some of the most widely held social prejudices about women who decide to remain childless. Motherhood is still considered to be a fundamental function for women, and childfree women continue to be viewed today as "imperfect" women who have failed to achieve their most valuable accomplishment in this world, namely: being a mother (Donath et al. 2022). Moreover, motherhood is seen as an altruistic act of generosity and, therefore, the choice of non-motherhood is linked to egotism. The responses of the women we interviewed show the extent to which they have internalized these prejudices and they apply those same labels to themselves in their explanations.: "Culturally, the fact of being a mother is very closely tied to altruism and generosity, and so I, myself, made myself understand that not being a mother was selfish, but I don't know if it is or it is not, but that's what I've read my whole life about the culture that we have" (Interview 4, 34 years old, who lives in a lesbian relationship). This reveals that dominant ideologies strongly affect the personal experiences of those women who remain childless by choice (see also Letherby 2002).

Other studies (Peterson 2015; Gillespie 2000; Donath et al. 2022) note that voluntary non-mothers are often stereotyped as selfish, egomaniacal, self-centred, immature, and self-indulgent. These stereotypes were referred to by one of the participants: "My family, especially my parents, has been quite challenging. From a very young age, they told me that I'd change my mind; over the years they've seen that I haven't changed it, and, in any case, when they talked about the topic itself and we talked about the reasons, they said that I was selfish, that not wanting to be a mother is selfish, because you're only thinking about yourself" (Interview 5, 35 years old, who lives in a heterosexual relationship).

Additionally, the absence of children can be perceived as signalling a lack of happiness and personal realization. Thus, in a way, we can see how female identity is closely related to women's ability and willingness to become mothers. In this ideological context, the myth that equates motherhood with happiness stands as a mirror in which not all women are reflected, leading some of them to choose not to be mothers. This is another idea which is traditionally associated with non-mothers: "I remember the first time I said that I didn't want to have children when I was 13; it was at a family dinner with my cousin's partner, and I was struck that their response was: what do you mean that you don't want to be a mother? If you're not a mother, you're going to be bitter your whole life" (Interview 6, 36 years old, who lives in a heterosexual relationship).

It is important to acknowledge the extent to which these ideas associating non-motherhood with a void and something vital that is missing from a woman's life continue to persist even today (Gillespie 2000). Also, this shows that, although more and more women openly articulate that they do not want to be mothers, today there is still no correlation in Spanish society between the increasing number and presence of these women and the way non-motherhood is socially perceived.

Conclusion

To conclude, this study provides useful insight into the discourses surrounding non-motherhood as a personal choice, from the perspective of women who have personally lived through the experience. More specifically, it helps to develop and extend the analysis of the phenomenon of non-motherhood by choice in Spain, a subject that has received very little academic attention to date, both theoretically and in the form of more quantitative research using demographic texts or public policies. Our study, therefore, was designed to provide an introduction to the subject and a base from which further debate could evolve.

There are a number of key findings that can be extracted from this study. Firstly, while the women we interviewed provided a variety of reasons for their voluntary non-motherhood, one particular comment stands out, namely: their refusal to believe that "being mothers will make us happy as a matter of course." Behind this statement lies the true transgression committed by these women, since it reflects a clear rupture with the supposedly inevitable nature and desire of women: motherhood as a central component of the normative construct of womanhood. Additionally, while the existing literature suggests that the environmental crisis is now an important factor in reproductive decisions due to the social anxiety that it generates, curiously enough, none of our interviewees expressed this concern as part of their decision not to have children.

Finally, although non-motherhood was a freely elected choice for the group of women interviewed for this study, almost all of them indicated that they had also internalized some of the preconceived ideas related to the construct of the "selfish" or "embittered" childless woman; this, in turn, serves to prove that injurious stereotypes and myths about non-mothers and their personal decisions remain pervasive within a predominantly patriarchal culture that continues to impose itself socially on motherhood. In spite of this, however, the actual individual life paths of many women who do not want to have children constitute a growing reality, one that is slowly gaining acceptance, and non-motherhood is becoming a life project, which is truly eroding traditional female roles and related expectations. In short, women who choose not to become mothers reveal a profound transformation of the institution of the family and our understanding of it, as well as of our vision of emotional and gender relationships. For this reason, women who decide not to become mothers must be appreciated in their full complexity.

Within this study, the voices of a cohort of women sharing significant commonalities are depicted. However, this analysis does not encompass the experiences of women with highly diverse socio-demographic traits and political stances beyond feminism. Indeed, an exploration of the motivations behind alternative profiles of women opting out of motherhood may reveal additional reasons beyond those presented here, as well as varied experiences. In spite of this, while the findings of this study cannot be used to make generalizations nor should they, they can nonetheless usefully inform the overall debate and highlight the need for further research into non-mothers by choice particularly in the Spanish context.

Ethics Approval Informed consent was sought from the participants, and all interviewees were anonymized and non-traceable.

REFERENCES

Abma, Joyce C., and Gladys M. Martinez. 2006. Childlessness Among Older Women in the United States: Trends and Profiles. *Journal of Marriage and Family* 68: 1045–1056.

Agrillo, Christian, and Cristian Nelini. 2008. Childfree by Choice: A Review. *Journal of Cultural Geography* 25: 347–363.

Alberdi, Inés. 1995. Informe sobre la situación de la familia en España. *Revista Española de Investigaciones Sociológicas* 70: 171–176. https://doi.org/10.2307/40183811.

Arnocky, Steven, Darcy Dupuis, and Mirella Stroink. 2012. Environmental Concern and Fertility Intentions Among Canadian University Students. *Population and Environment* 34 (2): 279–292. https://doi.org/10.1007/s11111-011-0164-y.

Ávila, Yanina. 2005. Mujeres frente a los espejos de la maternidad: las que eligen no ser madres. *Desacatos. Revista de Antropología Social* 17: 107–126.

Badinter, Elizabeth. 2011. *La mujer y la madre*. Madrid: La esfera de los libros.

Baizán, Pau. 2006. El efecto del empleo, el paro y los contratos temporales en la baja fecundidad española de los años 1990. *Revista Española de Investigaciones Sociológicas* 115 (6): 223–253.

Bianculli, Andrea, and Jacint Jordana. 2013. The Unattainable Politics of Child Benefits Policy in Spain. *Journal of European Social Policy* 23 (5): 504–520. https://doi.org/10.1177/09589287134991.

Bodin, Maja, and Jenny Björklund. 2022. 'Can I Take Responsibility for Bringing a Person to This World Who Will Be Part of the Apocalypse!?': Ideological Dilemmas and Ethical Concerns When Bringing the Climate Crisis Into Reproductive Decision-Making. *Social Science and Medicine* 302: 1–8. https://doi.org/10.1016/j.socscimed.2022.114985.

Bogino Larrambebere, Mercedes. 2016. No-maternidades: entre la distancia y la reciprocidad en las relaciones de parentesco. *Quaderns-e de l'Institut Català d'Antropologia* 21 (2): 60–76.

———. 2020. Maternidades en tensión. Entre la maternidad hegemónica, otras maternidades y no-maternidades. *Investigaciones Feministas* 11 (1): 9–20. https://doi.org/10.5209/infe.64007.

Cabré Pla, Anna. 2003. Facts and Factors on Low Fertility in Southern Europe: The Case of Spain. *Journal of Population and Social Security* 1: 309–321.

Comas d'Argemir, Dolors, Diana Marre, and Beatriz San Román. 2016. La regulación política de la família. Ideología, desigualdad y género en el Plan Integral de Apoyo a la Familia. *Política y Sociedad* 53 (3): 853–877. https://doi.org/10.5209/rev_POSO.2016.v53.n3.48880.

De Rose, Alessandra, and María Rita Testa. 2015. Climate Change and Reproductive Intentions in Europe. In *Italy in a European Context*, ed. Donatella Strangio and Giuseppe Sancetta, 194–212. London: Palgrave Macmillan.

Devolder, Daniel, and Marta Merino-Tejada. 2007. Evolución reciente de la infecundidad y la fecundidad total: España en el contexto europeo. In *La constitución familiar en España*, ed. Anna Cabré, 139–198. Bilbao: Fundación BBVA.

Donath, Orna. 2015. Choosing Motherhood? Agency and Regret Within Reproduction and Mothering Retrospective Accounts. *Women's Studies International Forum* 53: 200–209. https://doi.org/10.1016/j.wsif.2014.10.023.

Donath, Orna, Nitza Berkovitch, and Dorit Segal-Engelchin. 2022. "I Kind of Want to Want": Women Who Are Undecided About Becoming Mothers. *Frontiers in Psychology* 13: 1–15. https://doi.org/10.3389/fpsyg.2022.848384.

Dykstra, Pearl A., and Gunhild O. Hagestad. 2007. Roads Less Taken: Developing a Nuanced View of Older Adults Without Children. *Journal of Family Issues* 28 (10): 1275–1310. https://doi.org/10.1177/0192513X07303822.

Esteve, Albert, and Rocio Treviño. 2019. Els grans perquès de la (in)fecunditat a Espanya. *Perspectives Demogràfiques* 15: 1–4.

Esteve, Albert, Daniel Devolder, and Andreu Domingo. 2016. La infecunditat a Espanya: tic-tac, tic-tac, tic-tac!!! *Perspectives Demogràfiques* 1: 1–4.

Fernández-Rasines, Paloma, and Mercedes Bogino Larrambebere. 2019. Paradojas de género: Mujeres que declinan la maternidad y padres que reclaman la crianza. *Revista de Antropología Iberoamericana* 14 (3): 491–514. https://doi.org/10.11156/aibr.140307.

Gillespie, Rosemary. 2000. When No Means No: Disbelief, Disregard and Deviance as Discourses of Voluntary Childlessness. *Women's Studies International Forum* 23 (2): 223–234. https://doi.org/10.1016/s0277-5395(00)00076-5.

Golombok, Susan. 2015. *Modern Families: Parents and Children in New Family Forms*. Cambridge: Cambridge University Press.

González, María-José, and Teresa Jurado-Guerrero. 2006. "Remaining Childless in Affluent Economies: A Comparison of France, West Germany, Italy and Spain, 1994-2001 / Rester sans Enfant Dans Des Sociétés d'abondances: Une Comparaison de La France, l'Allemagne de l'Ouest et l'Espagne, 19994-2001." *European Journal of Population / Revue Européenne de Démographie* 22 (4): 317–52. http://www.jstor.org/stable/20164350.

Houseknecht, Sharon. 1979. Timing of the Decision to Remain Voluntarily Childless: Evidence for Continuous Socialization. *Psychology of Women Quarterly* 4 (1): 81–96. https://doi.org/10.1111/j.1471-6402.1979.tb00700.x.

Ireland, Mardy S. 1993. *Reconceiving Women: Separating Motherhood from Female Identity.* New York: Guilford Press.

Lagarde, Marcela. 1999. *Claves feministas para el poderío y la autonomía de las mujeres.* España: Instituto Andaluz de la Mujer.

———. 2013. Mujeres cuidadoras entre la obligación y la satisfacción. In *Cuidar cuesta: Costes y beneficiones del cuidado.* Bilbao: Emakunde.

Letherby, Gayle. 2002. Childless and Bereft? Stereotypes and Realities in Relation to 'Voluntary' and 'Involuntary' Childlessness and Womanhood. *Sociological Inquiry* 72 (1): 7–20. https://doi.org/10.1111/1475-682x.00003.

Marks, Elizabeth, Caroline Hickman, Panu Pihkala, Susan Clayton, Eric R. Lewandowski, Elouise E. Mayall, Britt Wray, Catriona Mellor, and Lise van Susteren. 2021. Young People's Voices on Climate Anxiety, Government Betrayal and Moral Injury: A Global Phenomenon. *Lancet Planetary Health* 5: 863–873. https://doi.org/10.2139/ssrn.3918955.

Meil, Gerardo. 2006. Welfare Policies, Work and Family Lives in Modern Spain. In *Reconciling Family and Work: New Challenges for Social Policies in Europe*, ed. Giovanna Rossi, 7–58. Milano: Franco Angeli.

Mulder, Clara H. 2003. The Effects of Singlehood and Cohabitation on the Transition to Parenthood in the Netherlands. *Journal of Family Issues* 24 (3): 291–313. https://doi.org/10.1177/0192513X02250885.

Peterson, Helen. 2015. Fifty Shades of Freedom. Voluntary Childlessness as Women's Ultimate Liberation. *Women's Studies International Forum* 53: 182–191. https://doi.org/10.1016/j.wsif.2014.10.017.

Peterson, Helen, and Kristina Engwall. 2013. Silent Bodies: Childfree Women's Gendered and Embodied Experiences. *European Journal of Women's Studies* 20: 376–389. https://doi.org/10.1177/1350506812471338.

Piella Vila, Anna. 2013. Infecundidad y parentesco (hijos sin hijos): una perspectiva histórica y transcultural. *Ankulegi* 16: 29–42.

Rieder, Travis. 2016. *Toward a Small Family Ethic: How Overpopulation and Climate Change Are Affecting the Morality of Procreation.* Switzerland: Springer.

Ruiz Olabuénaga, Jose Ignacio. 2012. *Metodología de la investigación cualitativa.* Bilbao: Universidad de Deusto.

Saraceno, Chiara. 1995. Familismo ambivalente y clientelismo categórico en el Estado del bienestar italiano. In *El Estado de bienestar en la Europa del Sur*, ed. Sebastiàn Sarasa and Luis Moreno. Madrid: CSIC.

Schneider-Mayerson, Matthew, and Leong Kit Ling. 2020. Eco-reproductive Concerns in the Age of Climate Change. *Climatic Change* 163: 1007–1023. https://doi.org/10.1007/s10584-020-02923-y.

Seiz, Marta. 2013. Voluntary Childlessness in Southern Europe: The Case of Spain. *Population Review* 52 (1). https://doi.org/10.1353/prv.2013.0006.

Tubert, Silvia. 1996. *Figuras de la madre*. Madrid: Cátedra.

Valiente, Carmen. 2003. Central State Childcare Policies in Postauthoritarian Spain: Implications for Gender and Care Work Arrangements. *Gender and Society* 17 (2): 315–334.

Vergés Bosch, Núria, Anna Morero Beltrán, Joaquina Erviti Erice, and Elisabet Almeda Samaranch. 2019. Violence Against Women in Female-Headed Households: Generating Data on Prevalence, Consequences and Support. *Women's Studies International Forum* 72: 95–102. https://doi.org/10.1016/j.wsif.2018.12.007.

CHAPTER 5

Alternative Happy Endings? A Qualitative Study of Non-Mothers in Lithuania

Lina Šumskaitė

INTRODUCTION

Women's decisions whether and when to have children are often influenced by circumstances and internalised cultural beliefs (Meyers 2001). The vast majority of studies in this area address voluntary (Houseknecht 1982; Kelly 2009; Cummins et al. 2021) and involuntary childlessness, mostly focussed on couples'/women's experiences facing infertility (Gouni et al. 2022; Peterson et al. 2011). Authors claim that reasons for remaining childless or choosing not to have children should be analysed at

This project has received funding from the European Union's Horizon 2020 research and innovation programme under grant agreement No 952366.

L. Šumskaitė (✉)
Vilnius University, Vilnius, Lithuania
e-mail: lina.sumskaite@fsf.vu.lt

J. Björklund et al. (eds.), *Negotiating Non-Motherhood*,
Palgrave Macmillan Studies in Family and Intimate Life,
https://doi.org/10.1007/978-3-031-66697-1_5

81

both macro and micro levels. The impact of structural changes on societal and cultural attitudes are analysed as macro-level causes of rising childlessness rates in Europe (Kreyenfeld and Konietzka 2017). From a micro-level perspective, Gayle Letherby (1999, 2002) and Jeanne Safer (1996), in their autobiographical reflections of their paths from infertility to their conscious decision not to have children, show the overlap of circumstances and autonomous agency. Comparing their own experiences with other women's, they reach the conclusion that decisions about children are complex and continuous throughout the entire period of the reproductive age.

Demographic studies in Lithuania show that the presence of childless women in fertility rates has, until now, been fairly low, less than 10 per cent (Stankūnienė et al. 2013; Stankūnienė and Baublytė 2009; Stankūnienė et al. 2003) and it is only in recent years that a marked rise in the proportion of childless women can be detected (Tretjakova et al. 2020). In light of these statistics, women's experiences of non-motherhood have not received much scholarly or scientific attention in Lithuania, although this is beginning to change. For example, the first notable small-scale qualitative research on the voluntary decision not to have children was completed in 2012 by a Master's student of Sociology (Leonavičiūtė 2012). Another qualitative study on two generations of women's experiences of living without children was carried out in 2017–2018.[1] The research on 44 reproductive age and older women reveals that women's decisions if and when to have children are very much dependent on circumstances such as finding a suitable partner and feeling secure financially (Tretjakova et al. 2020). It is clear that women in Lithuania, as in other Eastern European countries, experience the pressure of pronatalist society (Gedvilaitė et al. 2020). The dominant discourse of motherhood serves to intensify childless women's feelings of exclusion (ibid.), even if they take care of children in their close surroundings (Šumskaitė and Gevilaitė-Kordušienė 2021).

The aforementioned qualitative study dating from 2017–2018 explores women's experiences of non-motherhood as captured at a specific moment in time through the forum of the interview process. While the original group was much larger in size, this particular chapter concentrates on the narratives of a specific sub-set of 12 women. This is because the overall

---

[1] Interviews were gathered in the framework of the project "Childlessness in Lithuania: Socio-Cultural Changes and Individual Experiences in Modern Society," No. S-MOD-17-3, financed by the Research Council of Lithuania.

study was carried out by a number of colleagues, with each individual being responsible for their own sub-group. One of the most salient points that emerges when analysing the narratives of the 12 reproductive-age women (the focus group for this chapter) is that they considered having a child at least several times in their life and faced questions about their non-motherhood and their own personal trajectory throughout their whole reproductive lives, possibly longer. In this chapter, I will discuss the experiences of women who are non-mothers, showing (a) how women relate their non-motherhood experiences to the widespread notion in society that children should bring meaning to life; (b) how women live in familial relationships and how they describe *family;* and (c) what it means to women to be independent and to seek self-realisation. The findings show that almost all of the women in their teenage years had a vision of future marital life with children, while later on only a few still believed that raising children was most important in bringing meaning to their lives. Extended familial relationships were stressed by most of the women, and only a few highlighted the relationship with partners as the most important thing in their lives. Employment status was the primary facet for maintaining high self-esteem, as it provided feelings of independence and financial security.

The term 'non-motherhood' is used in this chapter as it is more accurate than 'childlessness' and 'childfreeness.' Only a few women from the sample could be described using the terms 'childless' or 'childfree.' Those who experienced failures in getting pregnant and possibly were involved in fertility treatments expressed deep feelings around their lack of children, so the term 'childless' was applicable for them. Only one woman told a story of making a conscious decision not to have children; her narrative corresponds with the term 'childfree.' Still, others shared complex pictures of experiences of their own decisions and the circumstances they faced. Those women who were postponing having children hadn't felt a lack of children yet, so the term 'childlessness' was not suitable to describe their position or feelings. And for those who were at the end of their reproductive age but remain without children because of circumstances, the term 'childfreeness' is not applicable either. Hence, the term 'non-motherhood' is used as an umbrella term that covers a wide range of experiences of not having children. This chapter contributes to the volume presenting empirical evidence about various experiences of non-motherhood during women's reproductive life.

METHOD

The sociological analysis is based on 12 semi-structured qualitative interviews, conducted in 2017 with 29- to 47-year-old single and coupled women who did not have children for various reasons. Most of women lived in the capital or another big city. Interviews were conducted with women with post-secondary education, even though the study did not purposely focus exclusively on highly educated women. Nevertheless, research shows that not having children is more widespread among women with tertiary education and living in big cities (Gedvilaitė- Kordušienė et al. 2019). Nine women had a partner, four of them were married, only three women were single. Most of the women engaged in heterosexual relationships with only one woman living in a same sex partnership. Seven women were living with a partner, four were living alone, and one was living with parents. Nine women were employed, two were studying and one was unemployed during the interview.

Interviewees were found using the snowball method. Some women I knew from my own leisure activities, one woman belongs to my work environment, one woman is a relative living in another city, and others were recommended by colleagues and friends. In relation to women I knew personally, the status of the relationship prior to the interview was not one of close friendship, nor did it evolve in this direction post-interview. I met 5 women from the group of 12 for the first time during the interview process. The majority of interviews were conducted in public places, mostly in cafés, with one in a library, one at the home of the interviewee, and several at their places of work. The interviews lasted between 45 minutes and 2 hours each, with the average duration being 1 hour, 13 minutes.

All of the women described themselves as non-mothers, even the one whose husband had children living with an ex-wife. She did not label herself as stepmother, even though she looked after children occasionally. The questions directed to the women were broad, covering the women's romantic relationships, professional lives, relationships in their parents' family, most important events in their lives and circumstances around how the question of children appeared. The interview material was coded and analysed using the Maxqda programme (version 18) using content analysis method.

IDEA OF CHILDREN AS THE MEANING OF LIFE

Non-motherhood as a valid identity and a lived experience has only recently begun to be acknowledged. This can be seen both in women's postponing of reproduction (Lebano and Jamieson 2020) and, more directly, in overt declarations of the decision not to have children (Kelly 2009; Cummins et al. 2021). In this study, pronatalist norms and the idea of motherhood as central to feminine identity were present in the women's narratives, and the women negotiated these norms in different ways. Some of the women explicitly stated that family and children were most important to them and would give their lives meaning. Dagnė (45) refers to having an "empty life" without family and children: "If I could have a family and children, that would be most important. [...] As there is not, there is nothing important (laughing), I don't know, I live for today." Inga (35) and Eglė (29), facing fertility issues, decided to adopt a child, as they could not imagine a family without children. And Neringa (35)[2] prioritised children and family over professional achievements: "I see meaning in life in the family, not at work, career or something else [...]. You bring up a new person, to whom you give your own values, I think that is life's biggest secret and meaning."

However, most women were less upfront about children as the meaning of life. Younger interviewees talked about how they wanted to postpone having children until they were married and had followed other plans and goals. Grytė (29) considered having children a life stage, when your friends began having children and you need to have something to take care of, and Goda (31) stated that children brought positive changes in life—"life becomes a bit different when you have children." Still Goda and some other women around the age of 30 expressed conflicting feelings about their reproductive plans. Goda felt younger than her biological age and had postponed her plans to have children until after marriage and building a home with her partner:

In my heart I feel very good because I feel like I'm 24 years old [...] I realise [...] that 31 is already a limit, when you're supposed to have had children, because you should at around 27 or so according to doctors [...] older age is a risk of not having children at all, and you can have a lot of problems [...]

---

[2] During interview Neringa was single, but she had a plan to fulfil her wish to have a child as a solo mother using a sperm donor, if she doesn't meet the right partner in the next few years.

my Evaldas³ wishes we already had children, but again there is no home, no family, I mean marriage, and we come back to the beginning, where we started. (Goda 31)

These women positioned having children within a temporality, according to which some things, such as marriage, should happen first. This illustrates the impact of what Jack Halberstam (2005) refers to as "a middle-class logic of reproductive temporality" (4). According to Halberstam, normative temporality is structured around reproduction, and a normative life is supposed to follow a certain course: "birth, marriage, reproduction, and death" (2). Goda's wish to marry and build a house for a family before trying to have children can be positioned within the logic of reproductive temporality. She places these markers of life experience in a particular order—marriage before reproduction—and she does not question the need to fulfil all these elements of what she considered to be a mature adult life. At the same time, Grytė and Goda also placed reproduction in the vague future, and Goda considered herself younger even if she was aware of the medical recommendations for the ideal biological age to have children. In these cases, the women's sense of time seems to be more in line with Halberstam's concept of queer time, which breaks with normative temporality. Crossing youth/adult boundaries and postponing reproduction does not follow the linear thinking of reproductive temporality.

Monika (31), though the same biological age as Goda, treated the time for children as passing by. However, she stressed several other reasons for not having children. The main ones were that her partner doesn't want children, society's negative attitudes towards same-sex relationships, and some financial and emotional barriers. Monika expressed feeling trapped in negative circumstances and stated that the decision to not have children was made for her.

M.: It seems to me that it has already been silently decided [...] that I will not have my own biological child anyway, I don't know.
I.: Who has decided?
M. Well, it seems so to me. Well, because I'm so old ... [...] I'm not 25 anymore, well, my partner doesn't want to, the financial possibilities don't allow it now, and in a year, I don't think it will have changed much, maybe

³The name of the partner has been changed.

in three years [...] If I bring a child to the world I have [...] to be financially and emotionally stable. So far I am neither of those. (Monika 31)

In her youth, before stepping into a same-sex relationship, Monika imagined having a husband and children. She states that she "loves children," and when she considers the question of having her own, she thinks raising a child alone would be an easier solution than in a same-sex partnership in an unaccepting society. Monika's statement illustrates the impact of the negative societal attitudes towards same-sex families in Lithuania, as she anticipates breaking with the linear thinking of normative temporality to cause less resistance than building an alternative same-sex family. Even if normative temporality is a heteronormative construction and can be placed within a heteronormative framework (Halberstam 2005, 10), explicit homosexuality is thus considered to deviate even more from heteronormativity than raising a child outside of marriage. However, at the moment Monika only considers this possibility on a theoretical level and chooses to be content with being with a *loving partner*.

Prioritising a partner or a partner's needs over having children is a recurring trope in the women's narratives. Norvilė (36) declares conflicting feelings about the idea of children as the meaning of life, as she prioritises her relationship with her husband over children. As Norvilė and her husband faced unwanted non-parenthood, her attempts to find out the biological reasons for not getting pregnant raised conflicts between the partners. Her husband has been convinced he is infertile since childhood, though he refused to go to a doctor for a confirmed diagnosis. He also had negative attitudes towards adoption. Norvilė's attempts to talk about having children openly ended in her husband's ultimatum, with a threat of breaking up. Therefore, Norvilė accepted living without children, as she appreciated her relationship with her partner. She revealed that both partners experience some sadness about not having children; still they cope by rationalising their situation. The major argument for accepting non-parenthood was based on deeper fears: Norvilė's husband has a sister suffering from epilepsy and with a minor intellectual disorder, and Norvilė witnessed her grandmother, who lost her sons: "My husband and I sometimes think very philosophically. Giving birth and having a child is not necessarily happiness, it's ok if everything is fine and healthy. [...] Maybe you should be happy that it [reproduction] isn't given, because maybe that protects you from more difficult experiences."

Jorė (29) told a different story. She did not imagine having children until she was a student and fell in love with a man with whom she went to university. Only then did she feel a desperate desire to have a child with him: "I thought that it doesn't matter, if he will be with me or not, at least let me have his baby (laughing)."

When Jorė (29) thought about children with her husband she also reflected that the wish to have a child did not appear at the beginning of their relationship. Only after living together and feeling safe did she try to get pregnant. Some reproductive health issues were disclosed, and at the time of the interview, Jorė was not sure about the right time to have a child. She also had doubts as to whether she needed to have children at all. On the one hand, she wanted to feel free to run her business (she teaches yoga and opened her studio recently). Sometimes she also felt tired looking after her husband's children from a previous marriage and her neighbours' children. On the other hand, she regularly felt an *instinctive wish* to have a child during her menstrual cycle, which she ties to hormones. After sharing that feeling with her husband, she got his assurance that he would help with the childcare in order to let her continue her occupation after giving birth. Since her husband was more experienced from having children from a previous marriage, she listened to his encouragements and planned to try getting pregnant in the near future. According to Diana Tietjens Meyers (2001), it's very difficult for women to make autonomous decisions about reproduction. A woman has to put constant efforts towards becoming conscious about her own inner feelings of making the decision whether or not to have children and separating them from the outside pressure from close surrounding and internalised cultural beliefs from society.

For most women in the sample, it was important to be married before having children, which suggests that they positioned reproduction not only within the temporality mentioned above but also within a heteronormative framework. Those who remained single, Toma (39), Dagnė (45), and Virga (47), reflected on not having considered the option of raising a child alone. Virga (47) and Dagnė (45) experienced encouragement to become solo mothers. Virga heard such views from female acquaintances when she bought a flat. Having a stable job and her own place to live was considered a good situation for raising a child. Dagnė (45) got an offer to have a baby with a former romantic partner, who was married but offered her financial support for raising a child. Dagnė refused this offer and remained strict in her attitudes that a child should be raised in a normative configuration of a family. She tried to get pregnant with her current

ner, but she refused to consider adoption if they remained
,...t: "A child is not an object that you can purchase when you cannot give him a family. I never considered it."

Toma (39) and Virga (47) hadn't had any long-lasting romantic relationships. Though they were open to that, they were not actively looking
for a partner. Toma did not mind being a stepmother to her future partner's children. Both women did not reveal a deep desire to have children;
a big portion of their interviews focused on how they experienced their life
as single women and how they were treated by others.

One of the interviewees, Rugilė (44), explicitly contradicted the idea of
children as the meaning of life. She admitted that in her teenage years, she
was influenced by society and had an image of a traditional family with
children for herself as well. Still, she always followed her inner voice and
realised she did not want children in any of her romantic relationships,
even though she faced this expectation from some of her ex-partners and
their parents: "Thank God that I had something, I don't know what to
call it, maybe confidence in myself. [...] When you're really aware, what
you want. [...] It is not that I don't like children. I like children. I think
you can make children only then, when really an inner wish comes to have
them. [It] really never came to me. [...] I thought that this wish for children might come sometime later, and I would want that, but now I certainly don't" (Rugilė 44). Rugilė declared that the feeling of happiness
does not relate to having a child or relationship with a partner. According
to her, inner satisfaction with life should come first, and then it spreads
into other areas of life: "I look at families, and I see that children do not
make you happy. Or your husband doesn't make you happy [...] Often
[parents] don't have anything in common, but a child came along and it
becomes so sad. [...] If you're content inside, then you're content there
and there, and there [...]. Not the other way [around]."

In short, the women in the study discussed how children fit into their
lives (or not) in different ways. Several women stated that children mean a
lot to them and that they had plans to raise a child in the near future.
Almost all interviewed women had a vision of their future in a family with
children when they were young, which suggests that the idea of children
as the meaning of life for women holds strong. For most of the women,
children were inseparable from partnership and a particular image of family, which indicates that they placed reproduction within a logic of reproductive temporality and a heteronormative framework. Some of the
interviewed women had doubts about the idea that children brought

meaning to life, and one of them, Rugilė, openly confronted the idea. She instead stated that inner satisfaction with life is not related to having a child or partner. Other women, like those who faced external barriers to having children—such as remaining single in their forties or encountering their partners' refusals to try some alternative ways to have children (repro- ductive technologies or adoption)—had just begun to be comfortable with the idea of non-motherhood as an alternative path to a happy life.

WHAT DOES FAMILY MEAN?

Sociology of the family has focused on the nuclear model since the begin- ning of the twentieth century (Burgess 1926). The Industrial Revolution and urbanisation led to structural changes in the extended family, and the nuclear family became a new ideal in Western societies and sociological research. At the end of the twentieth and the beginning of the twenty-first centuries, a diversity of family forms and relationships were acknowledged (Stacey 1998), and that raised questions about the meaning of the family (Levin and Trost 1992). Sociological research on the family in Lithuania started much later, only at the end of the twentieth century, and predomi- nantly focused on the nuclear family institution (Česnuitytė 2015). Subsequently, it has taken Lithuanian society longer to accept new forms of family, such as looking more favourably on children born out of wed- lock, accepting migrant families and acknowledging men's and women's decisions not to have children.

However, even if the concept of family has become more diversified in Lithuania in recent years, the norm to have children still holds strong. The non-mothers in the study negotiated this norm in various ways during the interviews, even if few of them questioned it explicitly. Only Rugilė (44) criticised the overvaluing of family and children in Lithuania in compari- son with Western countries. She states that in Lithuania, she observed more families where partners have a distant relationship, connected only through their child. Even if most of the women in the study were not criti- cal of the importance of family, they talked about family in a much broader sense than the nuclear family.

There was no direct question about the meaning of family in the inter- views, but the women often stressed that family is the most important area in their life. However, for many of the women, 'family' did not refer to the nuclear family, and their more expansive ways of talking about their fami- lies widen the definition of family and as such can be seen as a resistance to the nuclear family norm. Those women who had a partner usually saw their partner as the most important person in their life and underscored that a family does not have to include children. As previously mentioned, Norvilė (36) prioritised the relationship with her husband over children: "I always thought that the most important relationship is with my husband, that family is a man and woman and children are a result. So I never […] desperately wanted children. […] We heard among our friends that when we had children we would become a real family. […] It doesn't match with my point of view."

Eglė (29) and Inga (35) also stressed their husbands as the most important persons in their lives, giving them emotional support, which was crucial for them during the process of infertility treatment. Eglė emphasised, "It is very important to support each other. If one breaks down, the other has to lend a hand—help them up." A longitudinal study on couples' relationships after five years of unsuccessful infertility treatment shows that relationships among partners might get stronger (Peterson et al. 2011). However, Norvilė (36) faced undiagnosed fertility issues as a source of conflict with her husband when she raised the question of children. As mentioned in the previous section he refused to go to fertility specialists and was against adoption[4] and assisted reproductive technologies. When Norvilė offered one of these options, she faced an ultimatum for separation and finding another partner to have children. Still, according to social exchange theory (Rank and LeCroy 1983) Norvilė gets more from the relationship with her partner in comparison with the costs of conflicts about having children. Mark R. Rank and Craig W. LeCroy (1983) emphasise that looking for rewards and costs of the communication explains why some relationships become more valuable than others. Norvilė describes her husband as "the biggest present in my life. […] Even as a sign of God, because my husband is very good to me. He accepts all of me, with all my disabilities, I mean, being in a depressed mood, being unemployed, in short, everything … (tears appear)."

Other interviewees stressed the importance of familial bonds beyond the nuclear family. Some highlighted family members such as their own parents and siblings, and some women distinguished extended family relationships with relatives such as aunts, uncles, and cousins. For Virga (47), it remained important to have a stable relationship in her extended family.

---

[4] His argument against adoption is that the majority of kids in children's homes have health issues. As he studied pedagogy, he used to visit children's homes.

None of her aunts and uncles had been divorced. However, recently her younger brother faced divorce, and since then Virga's sense of what makes a family has changed: "we knew all along: parents, grandparents, brothers, sisters, uncles, aunts... everyone, you knew who was who."

When Jorė (29) recently got married, she moved to the countryside near her parents and some other relatives. She treated relationships in the extended family as a community: "The community in the village, it is my family also (laughs). Since I also live near my parents, when someone comes to see my parents, [...] they come to my place [...] If there is any work [...] potato digging or something, then everyone is together."

When Virga (47) moved from her hometown for studies, she lived with her aunt. It was treated as a privilege to live with relatives instead of in the dormitory. Since then, she prioritises keeping close relationships with siblings and cousins. Inga (35) also treated her aunt's and cousins' home as her own, as she used to spend a lot of time there after the death of her mother, when she was 18 years old: "during holiday I always came back to [my aunt's] from the dormitory, so I always had a home."

The exchange of social support was seen as one of the characteristics of a family relationship. It could be given in extended families and did not have to be limited to the nuclear family. Virga (47) and Jorė (29) grew up in large families. Jorė has three sisters; Virga, four siblings. Both women witnessed practical support in the extended family. Virga saw how the siblings of her father helped to build their house: "They come for the weekend and the floor is plastered [...] or they cover the roof."

However, some of the interviewees had problems with the exchange of social support in their extended families. Toma (39) missed practical and emotional support from her parents and brother. She thought that family should be the most important source of support in life: "It should be like a harbour." However, Toma faced unfulfilled requests; therefore, she stopped asking her brother and father for favours, as the emotional costs outweighed the benefits: "Unfortunately, family is [...] as God gives [...]. For example, if I ask you to do something, and you agree and later you do it your own way [...] It's better not to ask [...] It's too hard on your nerves."

Inga (35) disclosed the emotional costs of financially supporting her brother's family. She reflected on not feeling close to her brother and supporting him only because she felt bad for his children. Her husband also provided practical support for his mother and sister's family as they both live without partners. This situation sparked Inga's thoughts about emigration. She wanted to escape "living the lives of others": "Yes, partly to run away, because we both are the kinds of people that we would take off our last pair of pants so that others would be fine (laughing), but sometimes it's very tiring as you take on others' problems as your own and you're worrying and stressing."

Having children was also seen by some interviewees as a way to strengthen other familial bonds. Grytė (29) and Goda (31) thought that having children might refresh communication with their own parents. Grytė noticed that her parents spend more time with her older sister, as she has small children, and Goda witnessed her parents provide childcare support for her older sister as well. Grytė wished to work less and to spend more time with her parents, and having children could be a rational excuse to make a break from the intensive schedule of her professional life.

What stands out in the women's narratives is that 'family' does not necessarily refer to the nuclear family. Their more expansive definition of family can be seen as resistance to the nuclear family norm, which is still strong in Lithuania. The women describe the family as a source of emotional and practical support, and this could be given by various people around them: partners, parents, siblings, and extended family members. Greater emotional support was mainly expected and received from romantic partners. In the extended family it was more often expected to keep in touch (to meet more often) and to exchange practical support. Still, some interviewed women faced conflicts in their extended familial relationships when practical or emotional support was needed. Unfortunately, these conflicts remained unresolved, and for some of them, it caused a greater distance or burnout in the relationship with their own or their partner's siblings and parents.

FINANCIAL SECURITY, INDEPENDENCE, AND SELF-REALISATION

Family sociologist Martha McMahon (1995) emphasises that self-realisation in adult life is very important in Western society. However, the connection between motherhood and self-realisation is not clear. From her empirical research with full-time working mothers, she draws the conclusion that becoming a mother changed women's identities. However, British sociologist Catherine Hakim (2003) points out that women should not be treated as a homogenous group. While analysing fertility decisions according to preferences, women are usually grouped as home-oriented, work-oriented and adaptive, the latter organising their employment according to family policy and social circumstances (Hakim 2003). Family-friendly policies mainly focus on the third group of women, aiming to enhance fertility rates; however, some women's fertility decisions are less influenced by cultural norms or social policy (Maher 2005). Therefore, Maher suggests that perceiving motherhood as an activity rather than an identity minimises the social pressure mothers experience.

The theme of self-realisation was revealed in women's interviews while talking about their professional occupation, free-time activities and important events in their lives. Women were also asked how content they felt with their current life. A professional career was seen as key to self-realisation by most women. In some interviews the questions about education and work raised a long conversation about the importance of being employed as well as likes and dislikes in their previous or current occupation. For instance, for Inga (35), Norvilė (36), and Goda (31) being employed was an important aspect of independence. Inga stressed that she began to work when she was eighteen years old. Therefore, depending on her current husband's financial support while she studied in order to change her occupation made her feel uncomfortable. Her expectations to gain some profit soon reduced the discomfort. Goda (31) also stressed financial independence from her partner and sought to ensure some security for the future: "because today you have a husband, tomorrow he may not be there [...] you don't know. If your health fails or something else happens, you have to be able to do something."

Norvilė (36) stated that her professional life is more important to her well-being than having children. She experienced unemployment periods several times during recent years, and that lowered her self-esteem a lot. She stressed that not having children did not make her feel so low in comparison with not having a job: "I really don't feel good, but it's not related to the question of children [...] It is related to work, to employment, to earnings, in that sense, to income ... [...] I feel very insecure." Norvilė even doubted her ability to raise a child since she could not keep a job for a long period of time. On the one hand, she found reasonable explanations for not finding a suitable job in a smaller city, where she moved after marriage, in comparison with more successful periods of employment in the capital, where she lived before marriage. On the other hand, she remembered having good experiences of looking after children of friends and came to the idea of trying a nanny job, as being with children made her happy.

Working towards a PhD degree seemed to bring a sense of self-realisation as well. After spending many years in a job Dagnė (45) disliked, she decided to enter a PhD programme. At the time of the interview she was occupied with writing a dissertation and was living from savings. She described her satisfaction with her current situation: "although it's not very logical when you're sitting without work (laughs), but anyway ... It's a subjective approach (laughs)."

Other women saw children who were not their own as a road to self-realisation. Virga (47) reflected on realising her emotional needs with nephews and nieces. Since youth she had sewn clothes for Barbie dolls as a hobby. As she had too little time to work with her younger sister's dolls in the past, she now pursued her hobby of sewing for her niece's dolls.

For some women, however, a successful career was not enough for self-realisation. While talking about her occupation, Neringa (35) described feeling content in her current job.[5] As her salary was above the professional average, she found freedom in making choices in daily life. Still, recently Neringa realised that the gained freedom did not make her happy anymore. Therefore, she was considering having a child: "all those advantages do not bring a sense of joy that you have everything—you are not happy with those things, because you do not share them with anyone."

Jobs and careers were also viewed by some women as things to achieve *before* having children. Being financially secure was also important for Monika (31) and Jorė (29). Jorė highlighted job security and related that to the decision to have a child: "If you don't have a permanent job, some normal job, when you get a stable salary every month, [...] what will you do with that child. ... It is nonsense, you cannot make a normal daily routine for a child." And Monika stressed the ability to provide for children financially, as she witnessed financial insecurity while living with a single mother in her teenage years. Still, having a child was perceived by Monika as a huge obligation that restricted independence, and she did not feel ready for that: "This obligation is every day [laughing], every week, every month for many years, and your life quality changes regarding trips, finances, where you put them, etc."

Some women had other things they wanted to achieve before having children. For Grytė (29) and Toma (39), travelling was connected to independence and self-realisation. Grytė took long trips with her partner, and

---

[5] She invented her position by writing a well-financed project under the supervision of foreign leaders.

it was important for them to take a dream trip before having children. She agreed with her partner's statement that "when you have done everything in your life, you can plan for children, not because surroundings push you, but you want it yourself." Only then can a person enjoy parenting. Still, she was concerned about consequences to her fertility because of the postponement and set a timeframe of a couple of years. Toma (39) considered travelling as more important in her life than renovating a flat, which she bought eight years ago. Although some friends do not understand her choice, she keeps going on trips at least once a year: "it bothers people, how can you not manage [to do it] for so many years [...] everyone has different priorities. Some have said, for example, I wouldn't go anywhere until I tidied up my environment [...]. I choose to leave my place of residence for as long as I can and while my health allows me to go somewhere. I don't know what will happen next."

For most of the women in the study, self-realisation was closely linked to profession and occupation. The strong emphasis the woman put on being employed could be understood in the Lithuanian context. Scholars note that history and social norms of employment practices in the society form women's attitudes towards employment regardless of their motherhood status (Bernardi and Keim 2017). Therefore, Eastern European countries show higher rates of female employment in comparison with Western and Southern European countries, where a tradition of a male breadwinner and a partly working or stay-at-home mother were more widespread. Lithuanian women inherited a dual earner family model from the Soviet period and have one of the highest employment rates among women in Europe (Eurostat 2022). For the woman, having a job meant emotional and financial security, as well as independence from partners. It also provided the freedom to travel, even though this had a cost in other spheres in life. At the same time, employment was also viewed by some as a requirement before having children. The decision to have a child for some women who had partners was closely bound with employment status and stable financial resources, as it brought not only financial but also emotional security, allowing for future plans.

CONCLUSION AND DISCUSSION

Non-motherhood is often studied from the perspective of causes and consequences (Kreyenfeld and Konietzka 2017; Peterson et al. 2011), and as a temporal stage in women's lives until they pass their reproductive age.

Cultural norms of motherhood as central to feminine identity have just recently begun to be questioned (Lebano and Jamieson 2020). Lithuania's pronatalist society can in part be traced to 1990, when, post-independence, the Catholic Church regained political power, influencing public discourse and family policy (Šumskaitė and Rapolienė 2019). Today, younger generations agree with more liberal statements that people should decide on motherhood by themselves; still, there is a belief that children bring meaning in life, more so for women than for men (Gedvilaitė-Kordušienė et al. 2019).

Most interviewed women had not questioned the reproductive temporality and heteronormative life path, which suggest that adult life should follow a normative life cycle—become an adult, create a family (by marrying a partner of the opposite sex), and have children (Halberstam 2005). Those women, who faced unwanted non-motherhood, kept trying for children. Others felt pressure to think about reproduction as central in their lives and created plans for how to fulfil it. Only those few women who were in their forties and were single for a long period of their adult life felt more comfortable with their non-motherhood status, as they perceived solo-motherhood in a negative way. They stated that reproduction should happen only in married heterosexual relationships. Only one interviewee openly confronted reproduction and living in partnership as the foundations of a woman's life. She found an alternative inner satisfaction in her life.

Even though reproduction remained central in the women's lives, for most of them family meant more than nuclear family. Despite heteronormative values in society, women valued extended family networks, which were the sources of emotional and practical support. Some women thought of relationships with relatives as living in a community. To keep up with relationships in extended familial networks was important not only for single women but also for those living in partnerships. Therefore, the interviews suggested that despite pronatalist norms, family may have broader and more inclusive meanings.

Profession, occupation, and employment status were important for women's self-esteem, feelings of independence and financial security. One of the explanations for parenthood becoming less attractive is perceiving parenthood as a duty and focusing on individual self-realisation goals and couple relationships (Schneider 2010). To have a breadwinning partner was not enough to feel secure financially or to plan for children, and for single women, income from work was the main means of securing independent living and fulfilling desires such as travelling. Lithuanian families' dependency on the labour market can also be explained by a lack of state financial support for bringing up children, as the main focus of family policy remains on paid parental leave, which depends on a woman's previous employment. Benefits levels remain low and other family support measures are less developed (Steinbach and Maslauskaitė 2022). That could explain the crucial importance of employment to women's feelings of current and future financial and emotional security. For some of them, only stable employment and financial security allowed them to consider reproduction.

The qualitative interviews demonstrated that reproduction was seen as central in women's lives. Only a few women felt comfortable with not having children. Others negotiated with themselves about the timeframe for trying for biological children and other alternatives like adoption, becoming a stepmother or being a single mother by choice. Finally, even those women who were at the end of their reproductive age and did not have any plans to try for children in the near future hadn't talked about a final decision to live without children. This indicates that pressure for motherhood remains strong, and experiences of non-motherhood do not yet hold sufficient weight to demonstrate an alternative path for a happy life.

Acknowledgements I'm very grateful to the editors of this volume, Jenny Björklund, Julie Anne Rodgers, and Dovilė Kuzminskaitė, for feedback and suggestions for improvement on the earlier versions of this text. Results incorporated in this chapter received funding from the European Union's Horizon 2020 research and innovation programme under grant agreement No 952366.

Ethics Approval Informed consent was sought from the participants, and all interviewees were anonymised and non-traceable.

References

Bernardi, Laura, and Sylvia Keim. 2017. Childless at Age 30: A Qualitative Study of the Life Course Plans of Working Women in East and West Germany. In *Childlessness in Europe: Contexts, Causes, and Consequences,* ed. Michaela Kreyenfeld and Dirk Konietzka, Demographic Research Monographs, 253–268. Springer Open.
Burgess, Ernest W. 1926. The Family as a Unity of Interacting Personalities. *The Family* 7 (1): 3–9. https://doi.org/10.1177/104438942600700101.

Česnuitytė, Vida. 2015. *Lietuvos šeima: sampratos ir praktikos [Family in Lithuania: conceptions and practices]*. PhD diss., Vilniaus universitetas: 25–53.
Cummins, Helene A., Julie Anne Rodgers, and Judith Dunkelberger Wouk. 2021. *The Truth about M(O) Therhood: Choosing to be Childfree*. Demeter Press.
Eurostat. 2022. Employment Rate by Sex. https://ec.europa.eu/eurostat/databrowser/view/tesem010/default/table?lang=en. Accessed 17 Nov 2022.
Gedvilaitė-Kordušienė, Margarita, Vaida Tretjakova, and Rūta Ubarevičienė. 2019. Bevaikystė Lietuvoje: tendencijos, normos ir regioninė diferenciacija. *Socialinė teorija, empirija, politika ir praktika* 18: 96–111. https://doi.org/10.15388/STEPP.2019.6.
Gedvilaitė-Kordušienė, Margarita, Vaida Tretjakova, and Łukasz Krzyżowski. 2020. Women's Feelings About Childlessness in Two Pro-Natalist Countries. *Polish Sociological Review* 210: 229–244. https://doi.org/10.26412/psr210.06.
Gouni, Olga, Gabija Jarašiūnaitė-Fedosejeva, Burcu Kömürcü Akik, Annaleena Holopainen, and Jean Calleja-Agius. 2022. Childlessness: Concept Analysis. *International Journal of Environmental Research and Public Health* 19 (3): 1464. https://doi.org/10.3390/ijerph19031464.
Hakim, Catherine. 2003. Competing Family Models, Competing Social Policies. *Family Matters* 64: 52–61.
Halberstam, Judith "Jack". 2005. *In a Queer Time and Place: Transgender Bodies, Subcultural Lives*. New York and London: New York University Press.
Houseknecht, Sharon K. 1982. Voluntary Childlessness: Toward a Theoretical Integration. *Journal of Family Issues* 3 (4): 459–471. https://doi.org/10.1177/019251382003004003.
Kelly, Maura. 2009. Women's voluntary childlessness: a radical rejection of motherhood?. *Women's Studies Quarterly, 37* (3/4): 157–172.
Kreyenfeld, Michaela, and Dirk Konietzka. 2017. *Childlessness in East and West Germany: Long-Term Trends and Social Disparities*. Springer International Publishing.
Lebano, Adele and Lynn Jamieson. 2020. Childbearing in Italy and Spain: postponement narratives. *Population and Development Review, 46* (1), pp. 121–144.
Leonavičiūtė, Živilė, and Zenonas Norkus. 2012. *Savanoriška bevaikystė: Lietuvos moterų patirtys ir viešoji nuomonė: magistro tezės*. Vilnius: Vilniaus Universitetas.
Letherby, Gayle. 1999. Other Than Mother and Mothers as Others: The Experience of Motherhood and Non-Motherhood in Relation to 'Infertility' and 'Involuntary Childlessness'. *Women's Studies International Forum* 22 (3): 359–372. https://doi.org/10.1016/S0277-5395(99)00028-X.
———. 2002. Challenging Dominant Discourses: Identity and Change and the Experience of 'Infertility' and 'Involuntary Childlessness'. *Journal of Gender Studies* 11 (3): 277–288. https://doi.org/10.1080/0958923022000021241.
Levin, Irene, and Jan Trost. 1992. Understanding the Concept of Family. *Family Relations*: 348–351.

Maher, JaneMaree. 2005. A mother by trade: Australian Women Reflecting Mothering as Activity, Not Identity. *Australian Feminist Studies* 20 (46): 17–29. https://doi.org/10.1080/0816464042000334500.

Mcmahon, Martha. 1995. *Engendering Motherhood: Identity and Self-Transformation in Women's Lives.* Guilford Press.

Meyers, Diana Tietjens. 2001. The Rush to Motherhood: Pronatalist Discourse and Women's Autonomy. *Signs: Journal of Women in Culture and Society* 26 (3): 735–773.

Peterson, Brennan D., Matthew Pirritano, Jessica M. Block, and Lone Schmidt. 2011. Marital Benefit and Coping Strategies in Men and Women Undergoing Unsuccessful Fertility Treatments Over a 5-Year Period. *Fertility and Sterility* 95 (5): 1759–1763. https://doi.org/10.1016/j.fertnstert.2011.01.125.

Rank, Mark R., and Craig W. LeCroy. 1983. Toward a Multiple Perspective in Family Theory and Practice: The Case of Social Exchange Theory, Symbolic Interactionism, and Conflict Theory. *Family Relations*: 441–448. https://doi.org/10.2307/584622.

Safer, Jeanne. 1996. *Beyond Motherhood: Choosing a Life Without Children.* Pocket Books.

Schneider, Norbert F. 2010. Family and Parenthood in Contemporary Europe: Sociological Considerations and Their Political Implications. *Family Science* 1 (3–4): 135–143. https://doi.org/10.1080/19424620.2010.570009.

Stacey, Judith. 1998. *Brave New Families*, 17–18. Berkeley and Los Angeles, CA: University of California Press.

Stankūnienė, Vlada, and Marė Baublytė. 2009. Gimstamumo ir prokreacinės elgsenos kaita. In *Lietuvos šeima: tarp tradicijos ir naujos realybės*, ed. Vlada Stankūnienė and Aušra Maslauskaitė, 99–166. Vilnius: Socialinių tyrimų institutas.

Stankūnienė, Vladislava, Aiva Jonkarytė, and Alfonsas Algimantas Mitrikas. 2003. Šeimos transformacija Lietuvoje: požymiai ir veiksniai. *Filosofija. Sociologija* 2: 51–58.

Stankūnienė, Vlada, Aušra Maslauskaitė, and Marė Baublytė. 2013. *Ar Lietuvos šeimos bus gausesnės?* Lietuvos socialinių tyrimų centras.

Steinbach, Anja, and Aušra Maslauskaitė. 2022. Childcare in Lithuania and Belarus: How Gendered Is Parenting in Eastern European Countries? *Journal of Family Studies* 28 (3): 1181–1197. https://doi.org/10.1080/1322940 0.2020.1806903.

Šumskaitė, Lina, and Margarita Gedvilaitė-Kordušienė. 2021. Childless Women's Relationships with Children of Others: Narratives from Two Generations in

Lithuania. In *Close Relations. Family, Kinship and Beyond*, ed. Helena
Wahlström Henriksson and Klara Goedecke, 171–192. Singapore: Springer.
Šumskaitė, Lina, and Gražina Rapolienė. 2019. Motinystės diskurso paraštėse:
bevaikystė 1991–1996 m. Lietuvos moterims skirtuose žurnaluose. *Informacijos
mokslai* 86: 133–156. https://doi.org/10.15388/Im.2019.86.30.
Tretjakova, Vaida, Margarita Gedvilaitė-Kordušienė, and Gražina Rapolienė. 2020.
Women's Pathways to Childlessness in Lithuania. *Social Sciences Bulletin*: 7–21.

CHAPTER 6

The Incomplete Mother as Non-mother: A Study of Secondary Infertility in Helen Davies' *More Love to Give*

Julie Rodgers

While it is true that the first two decades of the twenty-first century have borne witness to a marked increase in academic publications on the subject of the non-mother (e.g. Cain 2002; Joubert 2010; Notkin 2014; Daum 2015; Edwards 2015; Heti 2018; Blackstone 2019; Cummins et al. 2021), there remains a problematic tendency in maternal scholarship to bifurcate and standardise the lived experience of non-motherhood as an either/or phenomenon, positioning it as unequivocally voluntary (childfree through choice) or involuntary (childless due to circumstance or infertility) but

This project has received funding from the European Union's Horizon 2020 research and innovation programme under grant agreement No 952366.

J. Rodgers (✉)
Maynooth University, Maynooth, Ireland
e-mail: julie.rodgers@mu.ie

© The Author(s) 2025
J. Björklund et al. (eds.), *Negotiating Non-Motherhood*,
Palgrave Macmillan Studies in Family and Intimate Life,
https://doi.org/10.1007/978-3-031-66697-1_6

103

rarely allowing for anything more fluid or nuanced. Within these two categories, there are further layers of homogenisation with voluntary frequently positioned as a wholly static choice and involuntary (especially in the case of infertility) almost exclusively aligned with having no children whatsoever. This chapter aims to challenge this tendency towards rigid and circumscribed definitions of non-motherhood by focusing on the obscured figure of the woman suffering from secondary infertility. Despite already having a child, secondary infertility leads to acute feelings of incompleteness and deficiency and gives rise to a paradoxical experience of motherhood which, in terms of the overriding sense of lack and loss, can more readily be aligned with that of involuntary non-motherhood resulting from primary infertility.

In medical discourse, secondary infertility is defined as the inability to conceive or carry a pregnancy to term following the birth of one or more children (Simons 1995, 2). And yet, as noted by Trisha Raque-Bodgen and Mary Ann Hoffman (2015), in spite of their "unique experiences and their greater prevalence than women with primary infertility, women with secondary infertility are relatively absent from psychosocial and medical-based infertility research" (485). Pragya Agarwal (2021) supports this observation, noting that secondary infertility is poorly tracked and, more often than not, subsumed by primary infertility (161). Subsequently, the condition remains inadequately discussed and frequently misunderstood which, in turn, erroneously implies that it matters less and reduces it to "a side note [...] a luxury, an indulgence" (236). The pain and anguish of those with secondary infertility is overshadowed by the experiences of those with primary infertility in what could be termed a hierarchy of reproductive suffering which situates the absolute involuntary non-mother at the top and privileges her account over that of other women negotiating somewhat more nebulous but no less significant forms of unchosen non-motherhood.

The primary focus of this chapter will be British writer Helen Davies' little-known autobiographical account of secondary infertility entitled *More Love to Give* and published in 2017. In spite of some stylistic literary weaknesses, *More Love to Give* is nonetheless worthy of scholarly attention for its detailed scrutiny of the experience of secondary infertility from a first-person perspective. As well as the dearth of formal research on the causes and consequences of secondary infertility previously noted, there are also very few narrative accounts (fictional and non-fictional) dedicated to the experience, with *More Love to Give* existing as a lone text of sorts among a much larger body of literature devoted to the narration of primary infertility. In this respect, both the subject of this chapter and the primary source selected for analysis are unconventional in their treatment of non-motherhood. By approaching non-motherhood as multi-faceted and sometimes contradictory in nature, this chapter therefore offers a valuable contribution to our understanding of the experience and helps to expand the term outwards to become more inclusive of a diverse range of lived realities on the part of non-mothers.

Through a close reading of *More Love to Give*, this chapter will interrogate the various ways in which secondary infertility causes the author-narrator to feel like a non-mother, thereby deconstructing the hypothesis proffered by Lynn White and Julia McQuillan (2006) that women who already have a child suffer less when struggling to conceive than those who do not. In the first instance, I will examine the overwhelming sense of loss and lack that underpins secondary infertility, feelings which are, of course, concomitant with primary infertility, but which are further complicated by the fact that the author-narrator in *More Love to Give* already has a child and, therefore, feels unentitled to these emotions. Secondly, I will consider the invisibility and voicelessness of the sufferer of secondary infertility within discourses of non-motherhood which often seek to stymie the articulation of such stories, given that the woman concerned is not considered to be an 'authentic' non-mother. Such silencing and pervasive oversight, I will argue, compound the suffering of the author-narrator through the creation of an additional layer of 'nothingness' and 'non-existence' that stems from the presumed invalidity of secondary infertility as a recognisable form of non-motherhood. Finally, I will discuss the concept of the imperfect family as being interrelated with the experience of non-motherhood. What I mean here is that the single-child family continues to be viewed by society as incomplete and it is expected that when a woman has one child, she will inevitably go on to produce more. When the latter is desired but does not materialise, the mother is left with the feeling that she has failed and that her maternal status is defective. This, in turn, leads to feelings of non-motherhood in that there is always something missing or unachieved within the family as far as the mother figure is concerned.

THE SENSE OF LOSS AND LACK IN SECONDARY INFERTILITY

Writing about representations of infertility in the media, Rebecca Feasey (2019) draws our attention to the fluctuating nature of the condition and states that there is not always a clear demarcation between infertility and fertility and, moreover, infertility and maternity, because women often have the possibility or at least the hope of moving from one position to another (8). In a similar vein and with specific reference to secondary infertility, the boundaries between mother and non-mother can shift and women who already have a child/children but cannot conceive another can find themselves caught up in a physical and psychological crisis which corrupts their maternal identity. As the reader navigates Davies' autobiographical account of her own personal struggles with secondary infertility, what becomes clear is that the author-narrator's sense of self is increasingly defined by feelings of loss and lack in relation to motherhood, irrespective of the fact that she already has a young son. Unfortunately, as Harriet Fishman Simons (1995) informs us, these feelings of loss and lack in secondary infertility tend to go unrecognised by society and, consequently, unsupported (39).

There are several ways in which loss and lack overpower the author-narrator's maternal identity to the extent that she identifies more with being outside of rather than within motherhood. In fact, as previously mentioned, the loss experienced due to secondary infertility mirrors, in many respects, that of women suffering from primary infertility. Perhaps the key difference is that the identity of the latter as non-mother is acknowledged by society and afforded empathy, whereas women struggling to conceive a second time are largely overlooked and, moreover, judged for wanting more children when, allegedly, they should be satisfied with their lot. However, as highlighted by Arthur Greil et al. (2010), both women suffering from primary infertility and those with secondary infertility are entangled in a painful negotiation of their identity against societal and cultural norms that presuppose that women should be able to conceive easily and naturally which, in turn, produces feelings of loss and inadequacy when this fails to occur (141). Furthermore, in their comparative scientific study of mental health during primary and secondary infertility, Yoldemir et al. (2020) report similar depression scores in both cohorts suggesting, therefore, that the sense of loss and lack emanating from this particular type of reproductive crisis is felt just as keenly even when the woman trying to conceive is already a mother (1133). Whether their infertility is primary or secondary, the emotional, physical, logistical and financial journey is similarly overwhelming and both groups of women are subject to the dehumanising rhetoric of sterility, reductive definitions of femininity and the pronatalist gaze of society. In both instances, for the women concerned, the loss of the child that they cannot conceive is experienced as traumatic and their maternal identity becomes synonymous with lack and an acute sense of non-motherhood.

Another similarity that links both primary and secondary infertility and feeds into the overriding sense of a dislocated identity relates to the complex choreography of appointments, treatments and timings in which the women find themselves caught up when seeking medical assistance. For the author-narrator of *More Love to Give*, there is no doubt that her feelings of loss and lack as a result of her secondary infertility are amplified by the state of paralysis into which she is unexpectedly thrust when undergoing IVF. Davies describes the relentless tracking and checking of ovulation as akin to being "on a non-stop merry-go-round, on and on, round and round" (13). Time becomes the enemy for as each month passes, there is increased panic at the thought that it is running out and that soon it will be too late for her (in terms of her age) to conceive a second child. The rigorous requirements of the various medical interventions, the constant appointments and injections, trap the author-narrator in a seemingly never-ending present and consume her very existence. Davies reveals, "It impacted every single thought or action, every single day. From the food I ate, what I drank, my ability to concentrate [...]. It affected when we went on holiday and what sort of holiday. It impacted what time I had to leave meetings to get acupuncture and so it went on and on. There was hardly a minute I didn't think about it or had to consider it" (72).

This temporal stagnation becomes particularly acute following the transfer of embryos in the IVF process which the author-narrator describes as a time of utter fixation on the moment and the taunting possibility that you might be pregnant but, equally, you may not. Davies writes, "It's like walking round with a brick wall in front of your face that you can't see through [...]. It's ever present from the moment you rouse in the morning [...] to the moment you fall asleep at night" (89). In addition to this, but no less consequential, the narrator is confronted with what she perceives as constant markers of her inability to conceive—other pregnant women, bump pictures, strollers, in short, a baby-saturated society of which she feels she is now on the outside (28). This, in turn, intensifies the feeling of being frozen in time and unable to propel her life forward and expand her family in the way that she had hoped. Of the trauma that such seemingly innocuous daily occurrences give rise to, she writes, "rubbing salt into an open wound is a good metaphor to describe what it's like, going around your normal day when everything around you seems to remind you of your pain at not being able to get pregnant" (17).

The space of the clinic where the author-narrator undergoes treatment for secondary infertility is also worth commenting on. The language and images used to describe it—the continuous waiting, the lack of interaction between the various couples who, despite sharing similar forms of suffering, do not acknowledge one another, and the strained atmosphere of a longed-for transition to somewhere else—are evocative of Marc Augé's (1992) concept of *a non-lieu* ('a non-place'). The *non-lieu*, Augé informs us, is characterised by the ephemeral, the provisional and the liminal—it is a space that lacks identitary and historical fixity and which can appear fragmented, disconnected and/or incomplete. Examples of *non-lieux* cited by Augé include hotels, squats, refugee camps, airports, train stations and hospitals. In the early chapters of *More Love to Give*, numerous scenes very pertinently unfold in the waiting room of the clinic. The overriding sense of the author-narrator being (unwillingly) caught between two phases of her life, motherhood and non-motherhood, is amplified by her frequent appearances in the *non-lieu* of the clinic. There is no doubt that this dependence on having to repeatedly return to a non-space for various treatments heightens her feelings of lack and nothingness at her inability to conceive and further underscores her positionality as a non-mother.

An additional point to make, and which is interconnected with the representation of the clinic and its waiting room as non-places, is the way in which they come to be associated with lack of agency and loss of control on the part of the author-narrator. Davies is conscious of her vulnerability in this particular space, where she feels coerced into adhering to the instructions of the medical team, side-lined in relation to the decisions that are being made about her and the treatment that she is undergoing for her secondary infertility, and, moreover, powerless with regard to the potential outcome (167). She writes, "What struck me [...] was the feeling of total, utter helplessness. The horrid reality that no amount of money, effort or positivity could help me. I had nothing more to give, there was simply nothing more I could have done and still, I couldn't conceive. That feeling of helplessness was horrendous and scary [...]. I wasn't in control of my destiny and despite every fibre in me doing everything it possibly could, I still could not control the outcome" (176).

While acknowledging the similarities between the experience of primary and secondary infertility serves to bolster the assertion that the woman struggling to conceive a second or subsequent child struggles in her negotiation of non-motherhood just as much as the woman who has not managed to conceive any children, it is crucial, of course, to consider the new dimensions that are introduced by the specific condition of secondary infertility. It is possible to argue, for example, that the lack of control felt by the author-narrator is all the more difficult to navigate given her previous experience of being able to reproduce and carry a child to term in accordance with her own internalised family plans. Secondary infertility, however, has interrupted this process and abruptly propelled the author-narrator out of motherhood and into non-motherhood. In her personal account of her own arduous journey through motherhood, Agarwal elaborates on this particular aspect of secondary infertility. She writes, "When one has conceived so easily the first time [...] it is hard to reconcile this with the idea of being infertile. The notion of your body not being what it used to be, when not much else seems to have changed overall, can come as a shock" (161). Agarwal returns to this idea of a very specific type of agentic loss that is brought about by secondary infertility a few pages later, stating, "I couldn't get my head around being barren. Suddenly, inexplicably, my body had decided it would not co-operate. I had been used to keeping tight control of my life and its course for the most part" (167). These observations are reinforced by Simons who states that the shock of secondary infertility is "even greater if you have proven your fertility and must later redefine your self-image to include the possibility and then the reality of infertility" (13). Unsurprisingly, the emotions that arise from this unforeseen lack of control and loss of agency for the author-narrator are both chaotic and virulent and range from panic and paranoia to failure, devastation and inadequacy. The impact of such turbulent emotionality is fiercely corrosive—the overwhelming sense of lack and loss that emerges from her secondary infertility gnaws away at her identity as a mother, causing the author-narrator to feel more like a non-mother, or, at the very least, an incomplete mother.

Ironically, one of the most recurrent manifestations of loss and lack that is emblematic of secondary infertility relates to the child that she already has. Fixated as she is on having a second child, the author-narrator begins to associate her young toddler with that which is lacking in her life (another baby) rather than that which she has already become (a mother). When speaking of her son, the overall tenor veers towards the negative and, more specifically, bereavement. The child who exists becomes conflated with the child whom she has failed to conceive and, as a result, the existing child's achievements are experienced more as a form of grief. As her son reaches developmental milestones, the author-narrator describes her anguish at him "becoming independent and not really needing me as much" (10). She refers to his growing up as creating "what felt like a hole in the family" (11), a space that she feels could only be filled by another baby. In particular, she describes the moment when her son is ready to move out of the nursery into a "big boy room", a turning point that gives rise to much despair and a deep sense of loss, a loss that is specifically related to the need for a second child (69). This corresponds with Simons' comment that, where an existing child is embroiled in a case of secondary infertility, "every developmental step is greeted with the realization that this stage will not come again" (106). As a result of the ongoing struggle with secondary infertility, the mother's relationship with the first born is disrupted and comes to be associated with feelings of maternal failure rather than maternal plenitude or, as Simons terms it, "a grief for the loss of the future child that she will not have" (17) and "a fear that you will never experience a new-born again" (19).

Having teased out the key similarities between the experiences of primary and secondary infertility in relation to the negotiation of non-motherhood while simultaneously indicating some of the inherent distinctions between the two conditions, the following section will further probe the unique characteristics of secondary infertility that, I argue, vindicate the need to acknowledge this complex subjectivity as a figuration of the non-mother. In particular, this section will interrogate the way in which being a mother who cannot conceive a second or subsequent child complicates the negotiation of non-motherhood in that it leads to a sense of non-entitlement to the grief that arises from secondary infertility, thereby exacerbating or even doubling the feelings of non-existence.

Secondary Infertility, Silence and Invisibility

If the woman experiencing secondary infertility is made to feel like she is frozen in time and forced to occupy a form of non-identity in which her original maternal status is rendered worthless and void due to her inability to produce additional children, this sense of 'nothingness' is augmented by the fact that that there is almost complete cultural and societal silence surrounding the condition. As Isabel Andrews (2010) notes in her study of secondary infertility among birth mothers, the phenomenon is predominantly shrouded in secrecy (84) and the distinctness of this particular form of suffering (not being able to have further children) is frequently unacknowledged, not only by society at large but also by close friends and family. The author-narrator of *More Love to Give* refers to her secondary infertility as "a dirty big secret" (70) and feels that she has no right to talk about it with others. This, in turn, leads to the awkward and painful situation of regularly being subjected to questioning from unknowing friends and colleagues as to when she is going to have more children (29). When those around her eventually do learn that she is struggling to conceive a second child and that she has had to engage in fertility treatment, the possibility for a more open discussion of the pain and suffering does not necessarily present itself in the way that it should.

According to Simons, unfortunately, secondary infertility is often met "with a lack of understanding of the enormousness of the loss and […] a tendency to minimise the accompanying depression" (17). In *More Love to Give*, the author-narrator, therefore, encounters an overall lack of empathy from others due to the fact that she is already a mother, and this causes her to feel that her trauma is invalid and misplaced. Instead of being supported by friends and family, the author-narrator is shamed into a position of ungratefulness and reminded that she is "already blessed" with the existence of her son (16). She writes, "It was hard to talk to anyone openly and honestly about the pain I was feeling by now. Those around me would always try to cheer me up or make me feel more positive by referring to Zac, how gorgeous he was, kind, great, cute and so the list went on of Zac's attributes that I was apparently blind to. I knew I had a fabulous kid! I knew I was lucky! I just wanted to scream sometimes that I wasn't daft, I knew he was great, that's why I want more! It was futile. Too few people understood" (181). Davies comments on this again through her remark that "when you already have a family but would like another child, there is a level of understanding that is absent from society […]. You have a child, […] you should be happy that at least you have one, or that's how others see it" (233). Well-meaning comments such as "at least you have Zac" (her son) and "don't put yourself through it" (fertility treatment) offer little solace (107). On the contrary, they lead the author-narrator to further bury her suffering (to which she feels unentitled) and retreat into a space of increased silence and non-existence.

In *Childless Voices*, Lorna Gibb (2019) discusses the importance of having access to a safe-space, for example, belonging to a group or association, when suffering from the pain, anxiety and stigmatisation associated with infertility. However, in *More Love to Give*, the invisibility and lack of recognition experienced by the author-narrator among friends and family persist even within the very spaces where she might expect to find support. In her attempt to engage with therapeutic online reading material and infertility fora, she senses a division between her status as a woman with secondary infertility and those with primary infertility. Whereas primary infertility is seen to be more tangible, "secondary infertility is unfamiliar and unrecognised and, consequently, unsupported" (Simons, 39). As Davies laments in *More Love to Give*, "the IVF community seemed to focus on couples trying for a first child, which only sought to ram home my feelings at that time, of guilt, greed and shame at wanting another" (viii). Hence, in both the 'real' world (among friends and family) and the 'virtual' (internet sites, blogs), the author-narrator is reduced to the status of interloper. There is no place for her to belong and seek comfort given that she already has a child, hence her experience of non-motherhood goes unheard and unacknowledged.

Davies describes her in-between position as "a lonely place; almost a No Man's Land. You feel so isolated and distant from the fertile, baby world that you long to be a part of and yet you are cast aside from the infertile community who shun you as they seek a little of what you already have" (x). Davies elaborates on this, revealing that she felt like a fraud, "a cheat [...] like I shouldn't be there, that I didn't belong [...] The odd one out. The greedy one who had come back for more" (53). Agarwal concurs with this account of secondary infertility, revealing that she too "[...] felt guilty for wanting more" (146) and berating herself for "this desperate need and desire to be a mother again" (200) when she already has what so many other women long for. For Simons, it is precisely this 'out-of-placeness' that captures the crux of the secondary infertility dilemma. She writes, "Women experiencing secondary infertility are uniquely isolated. Although you are infertile, you are not childless; although you are a mother, you are not currently fertile" (57). Subsequently, as is the case for the author-narrator of *More Love to Give*, there is no natural support network for those suffering from secondary infertility: it is difficult for both the childless and other parents to empathise with the feelings of loss that occur.

However, what is perhaps most surprising in Davies' account of her journey through secondary infertility is that this sentiment of non-belonging and being an imposter extends to the medical environment. During her various appointments, she admits that "telling the clinic I already had a little boy felt wrong. Like it was a secret I should keep to myself" (116) and is apprehensive of negative judgement and perhaps also the possibility that her case will be deprioritised. Davies develops this point in more detail, wondering, "Would they look at me any differently knowing that I had a child? Would they wonder why I was here in the clinic and would they think I was being greedy at going through so much treatment when I was lucky enough to already have a child? [...]. Saying I had a child seemed to be a sort of cheat, a shameful admission" (116). It is not just the medical staff among whom she feels uncomfortable but also the other couples that she encounters in the waiting room of the clinic, "couples longing for a child, many of whom, despite the best treatment, will never be a parent. Yet here I was, crying about my next cycle of treatment, when already I had what so many of them longed for" (116). Despite having a legitimate reason to be at the clinic, the author-narrator feels guilty for taking up the medical practitioners' time and is fearful of being treated as an outcast by the other couples undergoing treatment. Davies astutely points out that "nobody questions whether a desire for another is reasonable when you try to conceive naturally" (181) but that the issue of secondary infertility and the need for medical intervention seem to delegitimise this need and label it as greedy and selfish thereby causing the sufferer to experience feelings of guilt and shame. From the perspective of society, once "you have a child, [...] you should be happy that at least you have one" (233). Added to this is the fact that, as Davies points out, even though the World Health Organization defines infertility as a disease of the reproductive system, treatment is not as readily available as it is for other diseases, especially if you are trying for a second child (238). In fact, where there may be some allowances in most Western countries for the covering of expenses in instances of primary infertility, this is categorically not the case for secondary infertility and, subsequently, the right/ability to have another child becomes controlled by financial status and cultural privilege (238).

When considered in conjunction with one another, the various silences that pervade at the family/community level and the medical level engender a situation where the woman experiencing secondary infertility is deprived of both a voice and a recognised identity. As the author-narrator remarks, "secondary infertility has become a taboo, a shameful condition, one that sufferers feel guilty about having or talking about" (233). There is neither the space for frank discussion of the condition nor a willingness to listen on the part of others. Indeed, when the sufferer attempts to speak, the articulation of her personal experience is invalidated through responses that try to convince her that she should be satisfied with her lot in life and the fact that she already has a child. Secondary infertility, therefore, causes the sufferer to feel stigmatised and marginalised, women suffer alone and in silence (238). This, in turn, reinforces the sense of nothingness and insignificance that has come to characterise secondary infertility, all of which feeds into a more nuanced definition of the non-mother.

THE INCOMPLETE MOTHER AS NON-MOTHER

The final layer of the experience of secondary infertility as a form of non-motherhood that I wish to explore in relation to *More Love to Give* relates to the stigma of the only child and the negative impact that this has on maternal status. As Adriean Mancillas (2006) comments, "it is commonly assumed that for a child to develop normally, he or she should have siblings and that, in itself, the position of being an only child has detrimental effects on an individual's adjustment, personality and character" (268). Injurious stereotypes of the only child as lonely, deprived of social skills, over-protected, over-indulged and selfish (among others) abound. What is more, according to Mancillas, they have "permeated cross-cultural thought so thoroughly that they have become accepted as fact" (269). Simons makes a similar point, stating that the desire to provide a sibling is both a powerful motivating factor and a major cause of suffering where secondary infertility is concerned. This desire to have more than one child emanates from "internal forces, such as fantasies about the ideal family [...] but is also shaped by external forces, such as public opinion about the desirability of siblings and the stigma that is still attached to being or having an only child" (97).

It is quite clear in *More Love to Give* that the author-narrator has interiorised many of the negative stereotypes surrounding the only child to the extent that she feels like a failed and incomplete mother when confronted with secondary infertility. That her son will not have other children in his family to play with is a source of great upset and distress and perceived as "a huge injustice and a massive frustration" (19). The author-narrator projects feelings of loneliness and discontent onto her son, without actually knowing whether or not this is his lived experience. The following quotation reveals the depth of her anxiety which is a direct consequence of her struggle to conceive a second time. Davies writes:

> I'd watch other neighbours' children playing, two brothers and one boy, an
> only child. Of course they all got on well, but it would literally feel like my
> heart was breaking to see the young boy on his own when the brothers had

gone in for tea [...]. I never had reason to think that he felt lonely, or that he felt isolated in any way as they always looked like they had enormous fun. I never spoke to his Mum or to him to know whether he did indeed feel any loneliness, yet knowing my child didn't have a sibling to fall back on, rely on, play with when nobody else was playing out, used to fill me with horror and dread. (19)

The author-narrator feels that it is her responsibility as a mother to provide a sibling for her son and, subsequently, that her inability to do so positions her as a failed mother, an imperfect mother, and, to a certain extent, a 'non-mother' in that she has not fulfilled her role. She spends hours imagining her son as an older brother and is utterly convinced that this is both what he needs and longs for himself. This unwavering belief that it is her duty as mother to provide her son with a sibling engenders "an overwhelming desire to apologise [...]. I had done so much, it had all hurt so bad and yet still, I hadn't managed to give him a brother or a sister" (104). That she is struggling to get pregnant a second time is, therefore, interpreted by the author-narrator as her own personal failing, a fault in her mothering. Both she (as a mother) and her family are perceived as incomplete and imperfect. Davies describes becoming obsessed with the idea of having a second child and thereby rescuing her existing son from the fate of a solitary childhood. She reveals: "The thought that he might be the only child that I could ever have was increasingly bearing heavy on my mind. I simply couldn't shake it" (190). That she considers her secondary infertility as having an adverse effect on her son and not just her further heightens the feelings of maternal worthlessness, loss and lack that have previously been discussed.

As Simons informs us, "women with secondary infertility more often than not state that they are failing their children as mothers by not providing them with siblings" (97). Not only does this complicate their guilt but it also leads them to question the legitimacy of their family (and, indeed, their own maternal status) and mourn for the intended children who have not arrived as expected (Simons, 93). In the case of *More Love to Give*, it is extremely difficult for the author-narrator to accept that her family might differ significantly from the family that she fantasised about. However, the sense of loss experienced from the failure to produce a second child extends beyond the longed-for baby itself and becomes entangled with the author-narrator's desire to perpetuate the mothering role which has become central to her identity and daily existence. To return to the scene referenced earlier when the author-narrator reluctantly moves her son into his new 'big boy' room, it becomes apparent that she equates the latter's growing independence with an erosion of her own identity as a mother. Davies writes, "Then it hit me. We were moving Zac out of the nursery. We had an empty nursery, a situation I had been trying to avoid [...] it was like someone was stripping my house of my baby [...]. I wasn't ready. [...] our family dynamic was moving further and further away from babies" (146).

A similar distress arises when her son no longer asks for his baby blanket. The author-narrator reveals, "I was desperately trying not to cry but it felt like the final act in saying goodbye to my baby. He didn't want his comforter anymore and we had nobody else who would love it" (146). Once again, it is clear that a substantial part of her pain is intertwined with the fact that she feels she is losing her maternal status and, in some ways, morphing into a non-mother. It is significant, therefore, that when she talks about her son, she refers to him in the past tense, as if he no longer exists: "I missed my baby boy [...] he was gone from us" (147). This preoccupation with having a second baby as well as her internal psychic alignment of motherhood and caring for a new-born leads to an ambivalent relationality with her existing son whereby, despite already having the opportunity to be a mother, she struggles to derive pleasure from this role. She confesses, "Here I was, with my beloved child, who was fit, healthy and hilarious and who was gushing to tell me about his lovely day and yet I wasn't enjoying his moment" (94). Regardless of her keen awareness of her own distraction and inattentiveness, the author-narrator seems unable to recentre her energies on her living child. Davies writes, "My poor baby [...]. He couldn't have my time but some unknown, unborn, chance of a second child could. I was angry with myself for not giving my existing child my time. I was angry at my selfishness and guilty at my focussing in other directions away from him" (208).

The woman suffering from secondary infertility is, therefore, caught in a double-bind. Although already a mother, such knowledge is of little consolation to her and even the company of her existing child serves as little more than a painful reminder of what she may never enjoy again. Secondary infertility thrusts the mother into two diametrically opposed positions at once, that of having a child but also that of being without a child. It is the irreconcilability and incongruity of this phenomenon that muddles the definition of the non-mother, for in the case of secondary infertility, it would seem that a woman can experience both motherhood and non-motherhood simultaneously.

CONCLUSION

As this chapter has demonstrated, defining non-motherhood as a singular and absolute state is both impossible and counterproductive. Becoming and being a non-mother can present as a much more fluid state. A woman's relationship with the phenomenon can assume many shapes and forms and, what is more, has the potential to shift and fluctuate. In the case of secondary infertility, as I have evidenced here, the sense of non-motherhood that is experienced is complexly layered and interwoven with multiple factors, internal and external. First and foremost, there is the overwhelming sense of loss and lack that is associated with the failure to conceive a second child. Secondly, there is the pervasive silence that surrounds secondary infertility and the dearth of opportunities for women to articulate the particularities of their suffering, and if they do, they risk being judged as greedy or ungrateful for wanting another child. Thirdly, there is the persistent cultural belief that families with an only child are defective which, in turn, generates acute feelings of maternal deficiency and incompleteness for the mother concerned when she cannot produce a sibling. Finally, there is the feeling of liminality, being trapped between two states (mother and non-mother), and, moreover, having no recognised status in society. All of these factors combined lead to an experience of non-existence, nothingness, maternal invalidity and, I argue, a composite form of non-motherhood.

In the concluding pages of *More Love to Give*, Davies reiterates the overwhelming social isolation that women with secondary infertility are subjected to and describes her desire to create a legacy through writing for others who, like her, are struggling/struggled to conceive another child. She proclaims, "I see it as my mission to help bring better understanding, far greater empathy and much wider knowledge of the term Secondary Infertility and all its complexities. We need to help bring the subject and its sufferers out of the dark and into a society where it's ok to say 'I want another child'" (234). Her text, therefore, becomes a space of consciousness-raising, of frank discussion of the suffering, of community building and, potentially, healing. Davies is correct, it is absolutely vital that we improve our awareness, culturally and medically, of secondary infertility and its consequences for maternal identity. *More Love to Give* is a text that opens up the possibility for better understanding, increased dialogue and greater empathy. Furthermore, it is a text that provides a meticulous and insightful account of the specificities and uniqueness of the suffering attached to secondary infertility and, most significantly, its interconnections with the experience of non-motherhood despite the woman already being a mother.

It is important, however, to mention that by the end of *More Love to Give*, the author-narrator, after repeated failures, manages to conceive and birth twins through assisted reproduction. Thus, despite the many merits of the text in alerting us to the trauma of secondary infertility, in some ways, the narrative can also be interpreted as part of a body of infertility story-telling that promotes 'positive perseverance', provides inspiration and perpetuates the idea that a successful outcome can and will be achieved (Feasey, 69). *More Love to Give*, then, perhaps inadvertently plants the seed of another dilemma in relation to infertility more generally, that is, whether it is only possible to discuss the experience freely in a retrospective manner and in the context of an eventual pregnancy. Throughout *More Love to Give*, it is clear that the narrative is building towards a catharsis, and eventually it becomes a case of secondary infertility that is resolved. Therefore, it is impossible to know if *More Love to Give* would have materialised as an autobiographical account of secondary infertility had the author-narrator not been able to transition from the stasis of incomplete non-motherhood and back into the comfortable position of beatific mother.

REFERENCES

Agarwal, Pragya. 2021. *(M)otherhood: On the Choices of Being a Woman*. Edinburgh: Canongate.

Andrews, Isabel. 2010. Secondary Infertility and Birth Mothers. *Psychoanalytic Inquiry* 30: 80–93. https://doi.org/10.1080/07351690903200184.

Augé, Marc. 1992. *Non-Lieux. Introduction à une anthropologie de la surmodernité*. Paris: Seuil.

Blackstone, Amy. 2019. *Childfree by Choice. The Movement Redefining the Family and Creating a New Age of Independence*. New York: Dutton.

Cain, Madeline. 2002. *The Childless Revolution. What it Means to be Childfree Today*. New York: Perseus.

Cummins, Helene, Julie Rodgers, and Judith Wouk, eds. 2021. *The Truth About (M)Otherhood. Choosing to be Childfree*. Bradford: Demeter.

Daum, Megan. 2015. *Selfish, Shallow and Self-Absorbed. Sixteen Writers on the Decision Not to Have Kids*. London: Picador.

Davies, Helen. 2017. *More Love to Give*. York: Townbridge Press.
Edwards, Natalie. 2015. *Voicing Voluntary Childlessness: Narratives of Non-Mothering in French*. Bern: Peter Lang.
Feasey, Rebecca. 2019. *Infertility and Non-Traditional Family Building. From Assisted Reproduction to Adoption in the Media*. Cham: Palgrave Macmillan.
Gibb, Lorna. 2019. *Childless Voices. Stories of Longing, Loss, Resistance and Choice*. London: Granta.
Greil, Arthur, Kathleen Slauson-Blevins, and Julia McQuillan. 2010. The Experience of Infertility: A Review of Recent Literature. *Sociology of Health & Illness* 32 (1): 140–162. https://doi.org/10.1111/j.1467-9566.2009.01213.x.
Heti, Sheila. 2018. *Motherhood*. New York: Henry Holt.
Joubert, Lucie. 2010. *L'Envers du landau*. Montreal: Triptyques.
Mancillas, Adriean. 2006. Challenging the Stereotypes About Only Children. *Journal of Counselling & Development* 84: 268–275. https://doi.org/10.1002/j.1556-6678.2006.tb00405.x.
Notkin, Melanie. 2014. *Otherhood. Modern Women Finding a New Kind of Happiness*. New York: Seal Press.
Raque-Bogdan, Trisha, and Mary Ann Hoffman. 2015. The Relationship Among Infertility, Self-compassion and Well-being for Women with Primary or Secondary Infertility. *Psychology of Women Quarterly* 39 (4): 484–496. https://doi.org/10.1177/0361684315576208.
Simons, Harriet Fishman. 1995. *Wanting Another Child. Coping With Secondary Infertility*. San Francisco: Jossey-Bass Publishers.
White, Lynn, and Julia McQuillan. 2006. No Longer Intending. The Relationship Between Relinquished Fertility Intentions and Distress. *Journal of Marriage and Family* 68: 478–490. https://doi.org/10.1111/j.1741-3737.2006.00266.x.
Yoldemir, Tevfik, Mahmut Yassa, and Kemal Atasayan. 2020. Comparison of Depression Between Primary and Secondary Infertile Couples. *Gynecological Endocrinology* 36 (12): 1131–1135. https://doi.org/10.1080/0951359 0.2020.1807503.

CHAPTER 7

Pregnancy Loss in Contemporary Italophone Literature

Laura Lazzari

INTRODUCTION

Pregnancy loss is a form of grief frequently experienced in Italian society where it is estimated that one in five pregnancies ends up in miscarriage (Mattalucci and Raffaetà 2020, 9). Even though perinatal loss is still rarely studied and discussed, in the last decade autobiographical narratives considering this societal taboo have emerged. Stories of spontaneous abortion

This project has received funding from the European Union's Horizon 2020 research and innovation programme under grant agreement No 952366.

L. Lazzari (✉)
Sasso Corbaro Foundation for the Medical Humanities, Bellinzona, Switzerland

Georgetown University, Washington, DC, USA
e-mail: lazzari.laura@sasso-corbaro.ch

© The Author(s) 2025
J. Björklund et al. (eds.), *Negotiating Non-Motherhood*,
Palgrave Macmillan Studies in Family and Intimate Life,
https://doi.org/10.1007/978-3-031-66697-1_7

121

address the topic from a variety of perspectives and with different aims: process the experience, create memories, and educate society about a silenced but recurrent event. Despite its frequency, health care providers, family members, colleagues, and friends are often not prepared to offer the required support and fail to provide emotional and practical assistance to grieving parents. People do not usually know how to empathically address the topic and end up expressing well-meaning but inappropriate comments. Similarly, hospital staff fail to offer all the alternatives and information to the families affected. Even feminism—focusing more on abortion, contraception, and, overall, on the right not to have children—has paid little attention to this trauma, leaving women who experience miscarriage alone and excluded.

In 1996 Rosanne Cecil noted that "pregnancy loss has rarely been portrayed in any detail within literature" (3) and observed the following: "Where a pregnancy loss is mentioned, it tends to be given little prominence within the text and is rarely portrayed as an event of any great significance to either the narrative or the characters involved. To a very large extent, pregnancy loss appears not to have been considered to be a subject worthy of literary attention" (5).

Since Cecil published her contribution however, the topic has progressively gained prominence around the globe: narratives focusing on spontaneous abortion and stillbirth have dramatically increased across languages and genres in both literature[1] and films.[2] By removing the veil of silence, writers and filmmakers help to normalize the experience of miscarriage and change the way pregnancy loss is addressed and discussed. Furthermore, for some authors, storytelling becomes a form or therapy to process and overcome their own personal grief. The emergence of accounts of pregnancy loss, therefore, plays a significant role in reshaping the narrative of pregnancy, birth, and maternal identity. These stories—written from the mothers' point of view and, in some cases, from a feminist perspective—clearly reflect a maternal standpoint: the protagonists who have lost a child (not an embryo or a foetus) consider themselves as grieving mothers and want to be acknowledged as such by others. Through journaling and

---

[1] Berger Gross 2007; Roy 2011; Zerbini 2012, 2016, 2018a, 2018b; Sparaco 2013; Garavello 2014; Heineman 2014; Kimball 2015; Latino 2015; Howard 2016; Koehler Sanaysha 2018; Maraini 2018; Gianatti 2018; Barra 2020; Fraser 2020; Rademacher 2020; Micozzi 2021; Zucker 2021; Grover 2022.

[2] Hanish 2014; Mundruczó 2021.

storytelling, they effectively break an uncomfortable taboo and play a part in normalizing the feelings of grief and loss, while sharing their own personal experiences.

The difference between motherhood and non-motherhood is not clear-cut in the context of pregnancy loss and "the subject [...] is a site of struggle over the construction of identity" (Layne 2003, 26). Women experiencing spontaneous abortion are either labelled as childless by society or considered only as mothers of the number of children who were born alive. However, despite how they are defined by others, the identity of these women is usually much more intertwined with motherhood. Through a close reading of a corpus of texts discussing perinatal loss, this chapter will help to build a more inclusive picture of how the experience of non-motherhood is negotiated, by encompassing women who did not have children or did not have the desired number of alive children due to episodes of miscarriage and stillbirth. By doing so, I contribute to providing knowledge about a phenomenon that, although widespread and recurrent across societies and cultures, is still under-researched.

This chapter will focus on a series of books that discuss miscarriage and perinatal loss in contemporary Italophone culture and society, published in Italy and Italian-speaking Switzerland: Giorgia Cozza's *Goccia di vita* ('Drop of Life', 2010) is an autobiographical essay that addresses the topic of miscarriage and investigates how the experience is perceived by the author and her entourage. The writer discusses her excruciating feelings of loneliness and shows people's inadequate response to her grief as well as their lack of understanding and empathy towards this kind of loss. Eleonora Mazzoni's novel *Le difettose* ('The Defectives', 2012)—a work of fiction inspired by personal occurrences—narrates Carla's ups and downs through her infertility journey, by devoting some pages to the upsetting experience of miscarriage. Erika Zerbini's memoirs *Questione di biglie* ('A Matter of Marbles', 2012), *Nato vivo* ('Born Alive', 2016), *Chiamami mamma* ('Call me Mom', 2018a), and *Sembrava una promessa* ('It Seemed Like a Promise', 2018b) retrace—as a form of scriptotherapy—the challenges and anxieties related to a new pregnancy after two subsequent miscarriages. Finally, Angela Notari's book titled *Quello che ci unisce. Dalla levatrice Lucia al nostro e vostro parto* ('What Unites Us. From Midwife Lucia to Ours and Yours Childbirth', 2019) tells a positive and empowering childbirth story that ends with the narration of a later extrauterine pregnancy. The autobiographical text, written with a feminist intent, in the spirit of sisterhood, aims at breaking a taboo about how miscarriage is told, perceived, and experienced.

Italy and Italian-speaking Switzerland are particularly interesting for our investigation since, in these contexts, the level of assistance and support in the event of pregnancy loss are not always adequate (Ravaldi 2016, 18) and the first communities of parents affected by perinatal loss were created with a significant delay compared to other American and European countries (Mattalucci and Raffaetà 2020, 126). In Italy, CiaoLapo[3] was founded to fill a gap in assisting bereaving parents during pregnancy and after child-birth, providing both scientific resources and suggesting effective guide-lines for health care providers (Ravaldi 2016, 65–66).

The books taken under scrutiny in this chapter pertain to different genres and tell distinct stories of pregnancy loss: Cozza already has two children when she discovers that the embryo she had been carrying for 11 weeks is no longer viable; Carla's experience in *Le difettose* comes after years of infertility and failed IVF treatments; Erika Zerbini—already mother of two—shares the experience of two late miscarriages and the successive delivery of a child born alive; and Angela Notari discusses the life-threaten-ing condition of a subsequent ectopic pregnancy, after a first successful and empowering birth experience. Despite various similarities in the way preg-nancy loss is perceived, each account is personal and distinctive. Therefore, the writings selected for this analysis are not meant to be representative but show, rather, how miscarriage is finally becoming a topic that deserves to be acknowledged and discussed in both literature and society.

While some texts share literary intent, others are the result of therapeu-tic and expressive writing, primarily inspired by the urge to heal and share personal journeys. Considering these peculiarities, the methodology adopted here does not focus on literary style, but, rather, uses a combina-tion of qualitative descriptive analysis and close reading to address relevant topics present in the narratives. In this chapter, I highlight the way in which recurrent tropes emerge across various experiences, and I show how the authors aim to break taboos by acknowledging, validating, and nor-malizing personal experiences of loss and grief from the point of view of the mother. Recurring aspects mentioned in the texts will be subjected to

---

[3] CiaoLapo is a non-profit association founded in 2006 by Claudia Ravaldi, psychiatrist and psychotherapist, and Alfredo Vannacci, pharmacologist. The association provides psycho-logical support and assistance to families who face the death of a child during pregnancy or after birth, for any reason and at any gestational age (CiaoLapo n.d.).

close scrutiny: particular attention will be given to how pregnancy loss is perceived and depicted by the protagonists, how others address the topic, how maternal identity is defined, and the potential of their stories to instigate change in society and hospital protocols.

Pregnancy Loss Revealed and Perceived

Nowadays pregnancy tests can detect a gestation even before a missed period and ultrasounds may identify a heartbeat just a few weeks later. In contrast with the past, the perception of pregnancy and pregnancy loss has dramatically changed. Two lines on a stick are now considered as a rite of passage towards motherhood, whereas sonograms allow parents to bond with their babies from a very early stage (Layne 2003, 89). Advances in technology have rendered the presence of embryos and foetuses in the womb as real and visible entities long before a woman shows to be expecting and feels any other symptoms. Likewise, "women who experienced early miscarriage as late menstruation are now more likely to experience it as the loss of a pregnancy" (Kilshaw and Borg 2020, 85). Miscarriages are more common in the first twelve gestational weeks. Therefore, in our culture, the announcement of a pregnancy is usually kept for later, and rarely shared with others before the end of the first trimester in order not to "jinx it" (Aquien 2021). When a loss presents in the early weeks of pregnancy, deception and pain can be particularly excruciating and solitary. Since friends and relatives did not know that a pregnancy had occurred, women and their partners usually grieve and mourn alone and in silence.

This section of the chapter offers an overview of how miscarriage is revealed and perceived by the protagonists of the books. Feelings of powerlessness and lack of control over their own bodies—that failed to bring the pregnancy to term and showed no symptoms of what was happening—are frequently mentioned, and so are other forms of loss, equally painful, entailed in these experiences. Women, in fact, grieve and mourn more than just the death of their embryo/foetus/baby. Technology plays an important role in how pregnancy loss is discovered. If in the past women learned that they were "losing a baby" by physiological changes in their bodies, in many of today's experiences miscarriages are discovered by professionals through the routine use of devices such as sonograms (Layne 2003, 85). The stories discussed in this chapter make no exception and follow a similar pattern: the news of pregnancy loss comes unexpectedly, and it is conveyed by a health care provider after an ultrasound has been performed. When Giorgia Cozza goes to her first doctor's appointment she expects to see a viable pregnancy. Yet, by surprise, the sonogram cannot detect a heartbeat: "It's been years, but it's like it's now, and it still hurts my heart. So much. 'Where is the heartbeat?' And, for a moment, my heartbeat too remains suspended. The longest ultrasound of my life begins. The doctor moves the probe, applies a little pressure, tries a little more to the right, a little more to the left. But the heartbeat is nowhere to be found" (2010, 40).[4]

Cozza is upset because her body failed to acknowledge the loss of her baby and, therefore a D&C[5] had to be performed: "He died in my womb. Who knows why?! And now they must tear him away by force because my body hasn't noticed anything and continues, blissful, to be pregnant" (61–62).

Conception through IVF is usually observed from an earlier stage and, therefore, pregnancy and pregnancy loss are frequently discovered through blood tests and ultimately confirmed by a sonogram. The evolution of Carla's pregnancy and the subsequent miscarriage is monitored by regularly checking the level of Human Chorionic Gonadotropin[6] in her blood: "After two days HCG level is 350 [...] I have it checked again, and it is 470. [...] The week after it is 2740. It grew but did not double [...]. The day after the HCG level is 3100. After two days 4340. After a week 10750. [...] On Monday 15000. On Wednesday 21220. On Friday 29825. There's nothing to do. The heart should beat now but instead it shows no sign" (Mazzoni 2012, 80–82).

As is the case in Cozza's narrative, Carla's body fails to acknowledge that a miscarriage has indeed occurred: "But I have all [pregnancy] symptoms. How is it possible?" (Mazzoni 2012, 81). The role played by technology in conveying the news is also present in Erika Zerbini's story. As

---

[4] All translations from Italian are mine.

[5] "Dilation and curettage (D&C) is a procedure to remove tissue from inside [the] uterus. Health care providers perform dilation and curettage to diagnose and treat certain uterine conditions—such as heavy bleeding—or to clear the uterine lining after a miscarriage or abortion" (Mayoclinic 2023).

[6] "HCG (*Human Chorionic Gonadotropin*) is often called the pregnancy hormone because it is made by cells formed in the placenta, which nourishes the egg after it has been fertilized and becomes attached to the uterine wall. Levels can first be detected by a blood test about **11 days after conception** and about **12–14 days after conception** by a urine test. Typically the HCG levels will double every 72 hours. The level will reach its peak in the first **8–11 weeks of pregnancy** and then will decline and level off for the remainder of the pregnancy" (American Pregnancy Association 2023).

usual, the loss of her baby is confirmed by a health care provider while performing a sonogram:

> I showed my belly while lying on the bed and, the moment the probe rested on it, I looked at the monitor: the image I expected to see was not there.
> The doctor asked me when I had my last sonogram. "Last month". I replied, I caught her gaze, my eyes in her eyes, and I asked her "There is no heartbeat, is it?"
> She shook her head without taking her eyes off me.
> "Unfortunately not."
> I closed my eyes and I shed the first of a long series of tears. (Zerbini 2012, loc. 105)

Following a similar pattern, Angela Notari's extrauterine pregnancy— detected by her OB during a routine visit—comes by complete surprise: "On my first visit at nine weeks, the doctor had first to ascertain that there was no pregnancy in my uterus, and a few days later—thanks to her scrupulous attention—that an ectopic pregnancy, no longer viable was implanted in my tube and had to be removed urgently" (2019, 129). As in the previous stories, her body does not realize that something is wrong: "I usually listen to my body, which suggests me what I need. Have I ignored its signs? If not, how come I did not notice anything?" (131).

In addition to losing a desired child during gestation, other forms of loss are usually intertwined with the experience of miscarriage (Layne 2003, 173). As mentioned by Layne, "[m]any bereaved parents report [...] a loss of innocence as well" in the way subsequent pregnancies are perceived (173). This is confirmed by some of the accounts analysed in the present chapter: if the first miscarriage comes by surprise, without women acknowledging it, expecting another baby after a loss is usually faced with fear and emotional distress. As a matter of fact, Cozza welcomes the news of her later pregnancy with far less optimism, the two events being closely intertwined in her mind: "At the end of the summer, I was pregnant again. And a great joy timidly appeared in a heart already tired of so much suffering. But it wasn't easy. For me, these two pregnancies were inextricably linked for a very, very long time. First, in fear. Fear, or rather panic, that something would go wrong again" (2010, 114).

Similar feelings of entanglement and confusion among pregnancies are also mentioned by Erika Zerbini: "I try to keep you apart, but I can't... you are linked to each other... you are linked by the same desire that hasn't materialized yet" (2012, pos. 698). After experiencing two consecutive miscarriages, the writer laments "her loss of innocence" (2012, pos. 1188) and emotionally withdraws from engaging with a baby who may not survive (Layne 2003, 108). Likewise, while dealing with an extrauterine pregnancy, Notari tries to overcome "the invasion of a surgical operation" and the loss of a tube that also needs to be mourned (2019, 130).

Women connect themselves to motherhood at different stages of their pregnancy. However, it has been noted that those "seeking fertility treatments engage with and commit to parenting long before becoming parents" (Kilshaw and Borg 2020, 98). The recourse to ART may involve the perception of a loss in an earlier stage of pregnancy, since "some would-be mothers begin the social construction of their 'baby' even before implantation" (Layne 2003, 83). In Carla's last IVF attempt, all five embryos are transferred in her womb. After two failed artificial inseminations and two miscarriages, the protagonist's desire for a child has become so obsessive that "even the idea of giving birth to an entire army was appealing" to her (Mazzoni 2012, 157). While staring at the pictures of her embryos, she comments that "they had already split in multiple cells" and observes with surprise that "life multiplies so widely" (156). However, when her period eventually comes, she realizes in dismay that the embryos will never result in actual children (164). For women who struggle with infertility, stories of unsuccessful inseminations are closely linked with those of miscarriage. In fact—as in Carla's account—each failed attempt may be experienced as a pregnancy loss even before implantation has occurred (Layne 2003, 83).

Language Matters

The role of language in how pregnancy loss is perceived is twofold. First, in addition to the feelings of pain and loneliness, this condition lacks vocabulary to describe it, and women find themselves in a liminal space where they do not fully belong to the realm of motherhood or to the childless community. However, even though a child is missing, people experiencing miscarriage usually consider themselves as fully-fledged mothers. Second, the authors regularly refer to how other people address the topic: typically, by lack of empathy and frequently expressing inappropriate and offensive comments to the grieving mother and her partner. This section will investigate the role of language from a dual perspective: how the lack of definition shapes the identity of a woman who experiences pregnancy loss, and how a communication that acknowledges this loss as real and valid may better support women in their negotiation of miscarriage.

Unlike the terms "widow" and "orphan", as noted by Elise Hugueny-Léger and Julie Anne Rodgers in their study of bereaved parents in literary texts, there are no words to define the heartbreaking condition of the mother or father who experience the unthinkable loss of a child (Hugueny-Léger and Rodgers 2019, 4). Indeed, such parents are faced with a veritable aporia when it comes to articulating and recording their experiences (4). By contrast, when a person was born alive, the issue of formal documents, customary rituals, and rites of passage such as death certificates, funeral arrangements, wakes, and greeting cards are usually in place to acknowledge the existence of the deceased person and express condolences to the grieving family. In the "culture of silence" we live in (Layne 2003, 68) none of this happens in the occurrence of miscarriage and stillbirth, de facto defining the event as irrelevant to society and denying parental status to all people involved. This constitutes a paradox if we consider that the same entourage contributed to active construction of babies-to-be as real individuals during gestation (105). In our culture, pregnancy loss occupies a limbo where there is "no recognized space or place" for either the foetus or the woman (Kilshaw and Borg 2020, 356). As a means of finding a legitimate space and validate a silenced experience and identity—not yet acknowledged by society—women who have miscarried usually claim for themselves the status of "real mothers" (Layne 2003, 105).

Regardless of the fact that they already are the mother of other children—alive or not—the maternal identity of the writers is specifically asserted in relation to the babies lost during pregnancy, and so is their deep affection towards them. Giorgia Cozza dearly loves her child, born and dead in the first trimester, emphasizing her role: "I am his mom" (2010, 49) because "if three months of pregnancy are not enough to 'make' a dad, they suffice to feel a mother" (99). The very same maternal identity and fondness are expressed by Erika Zerbini: "I have always been their mother and they will always be my daughters, who lived only for a short period, but long enough to be loved" (Zerbini 2012, pos. 1295).[7] In keeping with this culture of silence and denial that revolves around

---

[7] The importance attributed by Erika Zerbini to her maternal identity is further confirmed by the title chosen for one of her books addressing perinatal loss: *Chiamami mamma* ['Call me Mom'] (2018a).

pregnancy loss, relatives, friends, colleagues, and health care providers often react to the event as if nothing has happened or diminish the importance of the occurrence by expressing inappropriate comments (Layne 2003, 69). Words have the power to hurt and therefore insensitive, cold remarks can be very upsetting to hear, as frequently reported by the authors discussed in this chapter. Inappropriate comments can be divided in three main categories: a series of remarks meant to console but which, instead, aggravate the situation; sentences that banalize the event, expressing the pressure to "get over it" in a short period of time; and the use of medical terminology to define the loss. Since this peculiar loss is not acknowledged by society, the reaction to it tends to be expressed through non-empathetic communication. Angela Notari reports well-meaning sentences that did not bring any comfort but instead upsets her even more (2019, 130). Cozza lists a series of inappropriate and painful comments, such as: "[t]hank goodness you were only three months pregnant", "it happens to a lot of women", "[y]ou already have two children" (2010, 80), or "you will have other kids" (113), which "made her so mad" (80) because they did not acknowledge her actual grief (113). To protect herself, Erika Zerbini "erected a high wall made of silence with all those whom [she] feared would say something inappropriate and banalize her bereavement" (2012, pos. 607).

Not being considered a real loss, the grieving mother is supposed, and sometimes pressured to overcome the event in a short period of time: "Now was the time to react, right? Well, maybe that was the worst part. If you try to talk about it again, you realize that you are starting, not exactly to bore people, but at least to surprise them a little. One day a friend asked me why I was so down. And when I mentioned my lost child, she came out with an 'again?' which rumbled in my heart like a cannonball" (Cozza 2010, 79–80).

The grieving process needs time and cannot happen overnight. As Angela Notari puts it: "to overcome pain you don't have to pretend it didn't happen [...] you need to give yourself time before being ready to deal with it" (2019, 132). Early miscarriages are often banalized by society. However, research shows that the pain is not proportional to the time of the loss, but to the woman's emotional investment in her gestation and the imagined baby (Mattalucci and Raffaetà 2020, 112). Moreover, not acknowledging or downplaying the experience of miscarriage does not help to heal but instead can lead to depression and stymie a faster recovery.

The use of medical terminology by caregivers is also frequently mentioned as an example of non-empathetic communication. If during a healthy pregnancy, embryos and foetuses are regularly anthropomorphized by physicians—who refer to them as babies and print their pictures (sonograms) for the family album[8]—once they are no longer viable, they suddenly become "retained products of conception" (Cozza 2010, 65), "histological waste" (Zerbini 2012, pos. 50), or "abortive materials",[9] as in Carla's story: "It's a good sign, this way you will *expel* all the *abortive material*—says the nurse. That's exactly what she says. 'Material'. And then 'abortive'. Yet, it does give an idea of the horror" (Mazzoni 2012, 41).[10]

In medical terms, childbirth resulting from a miscarriage is regularly referred to as "expulsion".[11] Like Erika Zerbini puts it: "the choice of *words matters* [...] According to science, I didn't give birth to my daughters who died prematurely, I *expelled* them... as if they were waste... precisely *histological waste*. How much sadness is there in the cruelty of every single definition?" (2012, pos. 60).[12] From the choice of words carried out by health care providers who interact with patients and write medical reports, both maternal identity and childbirth experience are erased: "when children happen to die during pregnancy, social expectations are activated for their removal, as if they never existed; that child is no longer defined as a child, but abortive material or clot of cells; they establish that one cannot give birth to a clot of cells, but expel it, they establish that whoever expelled it is not a mother, but an IFD"[13] (Zerbini 2018, 18).

The way miscarriage is treated provides an important opportunity to interrogate how motherhood is interpreted in our society (Kilshaw and Borg 2020, 96). In this regard, it is important to note that our culture only tends to consider the woman who is expecting a viable foetus as a mother, thereby erasing the maternal element from any experience of

---

[8] "The OB who gives you the picture of the sonogram with the 'close-up for the album' at 10 weeks of gestation, considers that baby alive. However, in my experience, that baby will live just as long as his heart beats, then it will become a histological waste to be analysed with no hurry" (Zerbini 2012, pos. 50).

[9] "It is written here: 'abortive materials weighing an estimated of 30 grams'. What child can weigh thirty grams? Mine: you" (Zerbini 2018b, 8).

[10] Emphasis mine.

[11] See also Cozza 2010, 50.

[12] Emphasis mine.

[13] Intrauterine Fetal Demise.

pregnancy loss: "When the pregnancy ends without a baby to bring home, the very people who have encouraged the mother-in-the-making to take on this role and may have participated with her in the social construction of her 'baby' often withdraw their support […] The cultural denial of pregnancy loss challenges the validity of the social and biological work already undertaken in constructing that child and belittles the importance of the loss" (Layne 2003, 17).

On the other hand, despite not having an actual child to care for, women who miscarry perceive their babies as tangible and motherhood constitutes an integral part of their identity. For these reasons, they want to be acknowledged as fully-fledged mothers, not as non-mothers, and advocate for a change of paradigm.

WRITING ABOUT PREGNANCY LOSS

For the authors of the texts analysed in this chapter, sharing personal stories via writing has various purposes: they process a traumatic experience, break the silence about a taboo topic, support other women, and, overall, educate and instigate change in society. Some go even further, by taking a radical feminist stand, denouncing mainstream feminism which has failed to support women who miscarry. This section investigates the reasons for sharing autobiographical accounts of pregnancy loss and the desired effects on the readers.

Conveying traumatic experiences verbally or in writing is recommended by mental health care professionals and may be beneficial to women navigating miscarriage and stillbirth, since "the act of telling or writing one's story […] helps to vent and release the emotions that have remained unexpressed up to that moment" (Foà 2014, 70). This is confirmed by Cozza who "was desperate to talk", for "[e]xpressing all that suffering" and "releasing it in words was probably the only chance to ease [her] pain" (2010, 78). Many grieving families find support by joining self-help groups where they can express their feelings in a safe environment, while others—like the protagonist of Mazzoni's novel—seek help anonymously in online communities. Expressive writing is another technique used by Zerbini who, besides publishing her autobiographical texts, runs scripto-therapy classes for people who encounter pregnancy loss.[14]

---

[14] As mentioned on Zerbini's website, expressive writing teaches techniques that facilitate the expression of the events of one's life linked to disruptive emotions (Lutto Perinatale Life 2023).

In addition to their healing potential, conveying personal stories can break the silence about a taboo topic such as miscarriage and validate a recurrent experience that is still denied in our society. Furthermore, in the spirit of sisterhood, these accounts provide useful information and resources to other women. When Notari breaks the silence, she receives numerous testimonies from readers who identify with her and manage to fully acknowledge their own grief through her book (2019, 133). By talking about her experience, Cozza tempers her own loneliness (2010, 108) and hopes that her story will help other grieving women too (127). As noted by contemporary scholars, feminists—having focused their attention on abortion—have not yet provided an appropriate framework for pregnancy loss and therefore infertile women and those who miscarry feel marginalized and excluded (Kimball 2015, 2019; Layne 2003, 244–245). As Layne has shown, breaking the silence is the first necessary step to set a feminist agenda and a women-centred discourse of pregnancy loss (2003, 239). Since most women learn about miscarriage only post facto, when it happens to them, it is imperative to provide realistic information and resources so that women do not "continue to be uninformed and unprepared for this not uncommon eventuality" (238). A further move is to develop specific feminist rituals of pregnancy loss that "focus on the woman and provide scripted ways for friends, relatives, and colleagues to offer support, acknowledge her loss, reaffirm her connection to others, and her sense of belonging and identity" (247). A similar feminist stand is taken by the authors analysed in the present chapter: as suggested by Layne, they help to challenge the taboo surrounding pregnancy loss, take care of their "abandoned" sisters by supplying information, support, and available resources, and, overall, contribute to the creation of a women-centred discourse of pregnancy loss (238).

As well as reshaping the narrative, these writings also have the potential to improve how pregnancy loss is experienced in our society as a means to "provide a fuller understanding of the experience of loss for contemporary […] women and their social networks and to seek ways in which this experience could be ameliorated" (Layne 2003, 21). In fact, by offering suggestions and expressing their dissatisfaction, writers have the capacity to introduce concrete change in society and medical protocols. For example, research has shown that "it would be good to set up a separate delivery area, so that the crying of other children and the vision of mothers caring for their newborns do not exacerbate the pain and frustration of the parents" who encounter pregnancy loss (Mattalucci and Raffaetà 2020, 119).

Such distress is confirmed by Carla when, after her miscarriage, she goes to the hospital to have a D&C performed and is disturbed by a throbbing noise coming from the opposite room. When she discovers that it is the amplified sound of a baby's heartbeat monitored next door, Mazzoni's alter ego feels the urge to run away (Mazzoni 2012, 40). After the same medical intervention, Cozza expresses similar feelings: "They take me back to my room. Now it's over. My pregnancy is over. […] In the corridor of the ward, I see newborns wrapped in their blankets; they are taken to their mothers to be breastfed. I will go away empty-handed. I will leave the ward with nobody, with nothing. I suffered a lot; I also deserve a beautiful child. These are my thoughts when, around eleven in the evening, my OB lets me 'flee' home" (2010, 64–65).

By telling their own stories, these writers, therefore, have the potential to educate their readers about pregnancy loss and make suggestions that could eventually improve the way women are supported. Authors recommend introducing routinely psychological counselling to all women who miscarry (Cozza 2010, 86) and advocate for the supply of updated and detailed information about women's options before, during and after birth, even in the event of spontaneous abortions. As Zerbini puts it: "I hope that things can improve and that my experience can help to bring change" (2012, pos. 88). In the same way that pregnancy loss support organizations "have been instrumental in changing hospital protocols, especially in the case of stillbirth or neonatal death" (Layne 2003, 78), so too can women writers instigate actual change in both society and the medical domain by breaking the silence about a taboo topic such as miscarriage and expressing their actual needs through storytelling. In this way, they invite clinicians to consider women's preferences and to address pregnancy loss in a more sensitive and holistic manner (Kilshaw and Borg 2020, 230).

Accounts of pregnancy loss show how miscarriage is perceived as a devastating experience with long-lasting repercussions on the quality of the lives of the women involved. Pregnancy loss followed by inadequate support can easily give rise to depression, trauma, and PTSD. Women ought not be left alone while coping with it. Doctors, family, and the whole society should be prepared to address the needs of such women, by routinely providing information and by recommending support groups and counselling. Moreover, addressing such a taboo topic has the advantage of educating people on the effects that pregnancy loss has on women's lives, by promoting a more effective and empathetic communication.

CONCLUSION

This chapter has discussed a selection of contemporary texts pertaining to different genres that address the topic of spontaneous abortion in Italian-speaking literature and society from the point of view of the mother and—in some cases—from a feminist standpoint. Through the prism of writing, these authors process their personal traumatic experiences and challenge the culture of silence that hovers over pregnancy loss so as to fully acknowledge, validate, and normalize personal occurrences of pregnancy loss and bring about actual change in society and medical protocols. Women who experience pregnancy loss are usually considered as involuntary non-mothers or only as mothers of the children who were born alive. This specific maternal identity—related to the imagined baby who was carried in their womb but was not born alive—is poorly acknowledged by society. These writings help to change the narrative by asserting a fully-fledged maternal identity even in the event of pregnancy loss. They show that motherhood and non-motherhood are not clear-cut where miscarriage is concerned. Women navigate their own experiences to find a suitable space and place that can encompass and acknowledge their specific identities by going beyond strict definitions. The texts considered in the present chapter hope to build a more inclusive picture of how the experiences of motherhood and non-motherhood are negotiated, encompassing women who found themselves in liminal, in-between spaces. It should be noted, however, that the writings analysed are not meant to be representative and do not claim to convey every woman's story. In this regard, it is important to mention that these personal accounts are all written by cisgender women from the middle-class who are in a stable heterosexual relationship and pertain to the Italian and Swiss-Italian socio-cultural contexts. In addition to this, the present study focused on miscarriage only, and does not touch on other relevant experiences such as stillbirth, neonatal death, voluntary abortion, and therapeutic abortion, among others. Further research should compare different experiences of loss from a transnational and intersectional perspective to investigate how motherhood and non-motherhood are negotiated in a broader context.

REFERENCES

American Pregnancy Association (Website). 2023. https://americanpregnancy.org/getting-pregnant/hcg-levels. Accessed 1 February 2024.

Aquien, Judith. 2021. *Trois mois sous silence. Le tabou de la condition des femmes en début de grossesse*. Paris: Payot.

Barra, Francesca, ed. 2020. *Gli indimenticabili*. Independently Published.

Berger Gross, Jessica, ed. 2007. *About What Was Lost. 20 Writers on Miscarriage, Healing, and Hope*. New York: Penguin.

Cecil, Rosanne. 1996. Introduction: An Insignificant Event? Literary and Anthropological Perspectives on Pregnancy Loss. In *The Anthropology of Pregnancy Loss. Comparative Studies in Miscarriage, Stillbirth and Neonatal Death*, ed. Rosanne Cecil, 1–14. London and New York: Routledge.

CiaoLapo (Website). n.d. http://www.ciaolapo.it/. Accessed 24 February 2024.

Cozza, Giorgia. 2010. *Goccia di vita*. Rome: AVE.

Foà, Benedetta. 2014. *Dare un nome al dolore. Elaborazione del lutto per l'aborto di un figlio*. Turin: Effatà.

Fraser, Janet. 2020. *Born Still. A Memoir of Grief*. North Geelong, Mission Beach: Spinfex Press.

Garavello, Alessandra. 2014. *Pagine di un dolore*. Independently Published.

Gianatti, Silvia. 2018. *Se tu vai via porti il mio cuore con te*. Rome: Leggereditore.

Grover, Carmen. 2022. *A Diary to My Babies. Journeying Through Pregnancy Loss*. Coe Hill: Demeter Press.

Hanish, Sean, Director. 2014. *Return to Zero*. Cannonball Production.

Heineman, Elizabeth. 2014. *Ghost Belly*. New York: The Feminist Press.

Howard, Karin. 2016. *Wild Mourning*. Parker CO: Outskirtpress.

Hugueny-Léger, Elise, and Julie Anne Rodgers. 2019. Untimely Mourning: Representing Child Death and Parental Mourning in Contemporary French and Francophone Literature and Culture. *Irish Journal of French Studies* 19: 1–10. https://doi.org/10.7173/164913319827945783.

Kilshaw, Susie, and Katie Borg, eds. 2020. *Navigating Miscarriage. Social, Medical and Conceptual Perspectives*. New York and Oxford: Berghahn.

Kimball, Alexandra. 2015. Unpregnant: The Silent, Secret Grief of Miscarriage. *The Globe and Mail*. December 3. https://www.theglobeandmail.com/life/parenting/unpregnant-the-silent-secret-grief-of-miscarriage/article27576775/. Accessed 1 February 2024.

———. 2019. *The Seed. Infertility is a Feminist Issue*. Toronto: Coach House Books.

Koehler Sanaysha, Anita. 2018. *Perché non sono nata*. Lulu.

Latino, Elisa. 2015. *A braccia vuote*. Irda Edizioni.

Layne, Linda L. 2003. *Motherhood Lost. A Feminist Account of Pregnancy Loss in America*. New York and London: Routledge.

Lutto Perinatale Life (Website). 2023. https://www.luttoperinatale.life. Accessed 1 February 2024.

Maraini, Dacia. 2018. *Corpo felice*. Milan: Rizzoli.

Mattalucci, Claudia, and Roberta Raffaetà, eds. 2020. *Generare tra la vita e la morte. Aborto e morte perinatale in una prospettiva multidisciplinare*. Milan: Franco Angeli.

Mayo Clinic (Website). 2023. https://www.mayoclinic.org/tests-procedures/dilation-and-curettage/about/pac-20384910. Accessed 1 Februray 2024.

Mazzoni, Eleonora. 2012. *Le difettose*. Turin: Einaudi.

CHAPTER 8

Infertility, Desire for Motherhood and Surrogacy in Miguel de Unamuno's *Dos madres*

María Sebastià-Sáez

One way of overcoming non-motherhood and fulfilling the desire to be a mother is through surrogacy. While commercial and medicalised surrogacy has gained traction as a way to deal with infertility during recent decades, surrogate motherhood is not a new practice, though it has not received much scholarly attention. This chapter will explore non-motherhood and surrogacy in a century-old text, Miguel de Unamuno's

This project has received funding from the European Union's Horizon 2020 research and innovation programme under grant agreement No 952366.

M. Sebastià-Sáez (✉)
Vilnius University, Vilnius, Lithuania
e-mail: maria.sebastia@flf.vu.lt

© The Author(s) 2025
J. Björklund et al. (eds.), *Negotiating Non-Motherhood*,
Palgrave Macmillan Studies in Family and Intimate Life,
https://doi.org/10.1007/978-3-031-66697-1_8

Spanish novella-play[1] *Dos madres* ('Two Mothers'), included in his work *Tres novelas ejemplares y un prólogo* ('Three Exemplary Novels and a Prologue', 1920). As one of the most recognised Spanish writers, Miguel de Unamuno (1864–1936) may seem like an odd choice for exploring surrogacy, as the extensive scholarship on his work has mostly been concerned with literary, philosophical, theological and psychoanalytical perspectives (see, for instance, Portilla Durand 2019; Stenstrom 2007; Sáenz de Zaitegui 2006; Cifo González 1996; Franz 1994). However, some of Unamuno's work does indeed deal with motherhood and non-motherhood,[2] as researchers have acknowledged (see, for instance, Estébanez Calderón 2015; Sáenz de Zaitegui 2006; Lázaro Carreter 1956).

This chapter explores non-motherhood and how the desire to become a mother is dealt with and given a solution through surrogacy in *Dos madres*. As it analyses a literary text from the 1920s, this chapter contributes a historical perspective to the volume. At first glance, the novella-play seems to confirm and reproduce some of the stereotypes about infertile women, but, as I will argue, *Dos madres* ends up subverting those stereotypes. Surrogacy is represented as something beyond a cure for infertility since it produces more than a baby; it makes possible queer desires, subverted gender roles, and new ways of imagining family formations.

As such the novella-play can be said to reflect and respond to some of the developments in post–World War I Spain. *Dos madres* was written in the early twentieth century, a period of forward-thinking changes in Spanish history. The 1920s was a vibrant period in Spain in many areas (Serrano and Salaün 2006), but this chapter focuses on two important aspects: (1) the general social changes regarding women's rights, their role in society and changing paradigms of femininity and masculinity in Spain; and (2) the specific Basque Country idiosyncrasy concerning the so-called *matriarchy myth*.[3]

In Spain, the first decades of the twentieth century were a period of social change that particularly involved women's rights. In contrast to the established gender roles, different feminist movements proposed several theoretical approaches with the aim of promoting work and educational

---

[1] A *novella-play* is a short story with long dialogue that uses the visual structure of a drama script, little action and a text that invites reflection.

[2] *Soledad* ('Solitude', 1920), *Raquel encadenada* ('Rachel Bound', 1920) and *La tía Tula* ('Aunt Tula', 1921).

[3] Unamuno's intrinsic and academic connection to the Basque Country might indicate that his cosmovision and his female character's literary—and philosophical—conception was deeply influenced by the Basque culture and folklore.

rights for women as well as legal and political equality, especially regarding women's suffrage (Aguado 2010, 132, 145). Finally, the right to vote for women was approved in 1931 (Montero 2011, 86).[4] Another relevant social change in Spain was the dilution of traditional gender identities. Despite the neutral position of Spain in the First World War, the war had strong economic and social consequences in the country. One of these consequences was the destabilisation of the masculine and feminine established roles.[5] The young Spanish women were influenced by the English and American *flappers* and the French *garçonnes*. The result was an archetype of a modern woman, gendered ambiguously and defiant in the face of the traditional gender feminine assumptions (Aresti 2012, 2–3).

In parallel to the changing Spanish society, there was the specific case of the Basque Country, with its own particularities concerning feminine roles. Feminine supremacy is at the heart of Basque mythology. In traditional Basque folklore women were a substantial cultural, religious, and social symbol, mainly displayed as a *woman-mother* totem (Boguszewicz and Gajewska 2020, 37). Starting in the nineteenth century, a feminine model based on women's procreative function had gained importance (Sabadell Nieto 2011, 44–45), and this is well reflected in Unamuno's literary works. In addition, women in the Basque Country were much more educated than the average Spanish women (Montero 2009, 138).

Dos madres

The *Dos madres* plot starts from the same core leitmotiv as the biblical passage it is inspired by, the story of Rachel and Jacob (Gn. 30: 1–6).[6] There are three main characters: Raquel, don Juan, and Berta. Raquel is a widow

---

[4] This right was removed as a consequence of the Spanish Civil War (1936–1939) and the subsequent Francoist dictatorship (1939–1975). It was approved again with the Spanish Constitution of 1978 (Ramos 1988; Cuenca Gómez 2008).

[5] Due to WWI women had to take on traditional masculine jobs, as the men had to assume military obligations. Also, women had to contribute to these military tasks.

[6] "When Rachel saw that she failed to bear children to Jacob, she became envious of her sister. She said to Jacob, 'Give me children or I shall die!' In anger Jacob retorted, 'Can I take the place of God, who has denied you the fruit of the womb?' She replied, 'Here is my maidservant Bilhah. Have intercourse with her, and let her give birth on my knees, so that I too may have offspring, at least through her'. So she gave him her maidservant Bilhah as a consort, and Jacob had intercourse with her. When Bilhah conceived and bore a son, Rachel said 'God has vindicated me; indeed, he has heeded my plea and given me a son'. Therefore, she named him Dan" (Gn. 30: 1–6). The punctuation of this passage has been adapted by the author from the original text of *The New American Bible* (2002).

who could neither have a child with her husband nor with her younger lover, don Juan. Raquel is desperate to become a mother and makes a plan to achieve her goal. She encourages don Juan to marry a young woman, Berta—who is supposed to be fertile—and have a child with her but then give the child to Raquel, who will raise the baby as her own. Indeed, Berta and don Juan get married and conceive a child. When the child is born, Raquel becomes the godmother, an important figure for the child in Catholic and Spanish culture.[7] Soon Raquel moves in with don Juan and Berta, taking charge of the house and the baby, and the three of them form a household. One day, while Berta and Raquel are arguing about who really is the baby's mother, don Juan escapes and drives to the mountains, where he is involved in a car accident and subsequently dies.

Suddenly, Berta finds herself in a situation of helplessness. As a widow she should inherit her husband's fortune and have a good income, but she discovers that Juan has left his fortune to Raquel before dying. Berta comes to the conclusion that the only solution for her and her family is to let Raquel support them financially and, in exchange, give the baby to her. Ultimately, Berta loses the battle for the baby's motherhood, and Raquel accomplishes her profound desire to become a mother. However, as a final plot twist, it is revealed that Berta is pregnant again, and she will give birth to don Juan's posthumous child. Raquel decides to support this child and provide for Berta's future.

THE GOOD FERTILE WOMAN AND THE BAD INFERTILE WOMAN

Initially, *Dos madres* seems to reproduce conventional stereotypes about women through the juxtaposition of the two main female characters: Raquel, who represents the *bad* infertile woman, and Berta, who represents the *good* fertile woman. Both characters are inspired by two biblical figures: Rachel, Jacob's spouse, and Bilhah their maidservant. Raquel and her biblical namesake are both women who are driven to desperation by their non-motherhood and find in surrogacy a balm for their pain. Berta seems to be inspired by Bilhah since Berta gives birth to a child, conceived with Raquel's lover, who would be raised by Raquel. Nonetheless, despite this apparently conservative textual foundation, Unamuno provides

[7] Especially before Spain became a secular state in 1978.

Raquel with a mindset that allows her to break the traditional gender structures.[8]

Forming a family and having children could be considered adulthood rites of passage (Archetti 2019, 176; Feasey 2019, 2). Accordingly, Raquel is the *incomplete* non-normative woman, as opposed to Berta, who is the fully developed archetypal mother/woman. Traditionally, Western culture has produced more depictions of women as mothers than as childless (Benninghaus 2014, 2). In addition, there is a tendency to create representations of childless women as linked to disordered life (Archetti 2019, 182). Raquel is not an exception to this tendency. She is don Juan's lover, and because of this, she is contravening one of the most crucial rules of Catholic doctrine: having sex without the sacred mission of forming a traditional family under the blessed sacrament of marriage. She is completely aware of this, which inflicts additional pain to her barrenness:

> RAQUEL: What's the point of being married by the Church and the Civil Law? Marriage was established, as we learned in catechism, for being married, blessing the married couple, and to provide children for heaven.
> With these words, her voice was faltering and in her lashes liquid pearls were trembling, where the bottomless blackness of her pupils was reflected. (De Unamuno 1920, 32)[9]

In this respect, Raquel's widowhood and non-motherhood (as a result of infertility) are depicted as inherently negative. In fact, in *Dos madres* there is a correlation between infertility, death, and passion: "In love? Was he, don Juan, in love with Raquel? No, he was absorbed by her, submerged in her, lost in the woman and in her widowhood. Because Raquel was, don Juan thought, first and foremost, the widow, the childless widow. [...] Her love was furious, with a taste of death. [...] And don Juan felt dragged by her to someplace deeper than the ground. 'This woman will kill me!'" (31)

From the beginning, Raquel is referred to as a 'childless widow', and these two words define her. She brings with her two main features: infertility and death. These two features are closely connected: she is a woman

---

[8] The equilibrium between traditional values and progressive ideas is one of the most particular characteristics of Unamuno's thinking, which is reflected in his works (Delgado 1988, 9; Guy 1988).

[9] All the translations from Spanish to English by the author. Ángel Flores's (1956) translation into English (edited by Ángel de Río) has been consulted.

unable to bring life, and she bears with her the unconceived children and
the dead husband. Hence, there is a dichotomy between the ideal woman
who should represent life and fertility—especially in the first half of the
twentieth century in Spain—and Raquel, who represents infertility and
death. Indeed, she brings a terrible fate with her, marked by don Juan's
prophetic words: "This woman will kill me!" In contrast, Berta serves as
Raquel's counterpoint. Miss Berta Lapeira is the perfect young virgin
woman, who will become the perfect mother after marriage: "RAQUEL: I
have already found a woman for you… I have already found the future
mother of our child… No one searched more carefully for a wet nurse
than I did for this mother" (35).

Since don Juan knew Berta since childhood, her virtue is assured.
Moreover, according to Raquel, Berta might be truly in love with don
Juan: "Berta is in love with you, hopelessly in love with you! And Berta,
who has the heroic heart of a virgin in love, will accept the role of redeemer,
she will redeem me, for I am, according to her, your damnation and hell"
(36). Berta represents all the valuable features of a canonical woman that
Raquel lacks. She has a 'heroic heart', she is 'a virgin in love', and her
purity is so radiant that she even will be able to redeem Raquel's sins with
don Juan. On the contrary, Raquel embodies damnation; she has the
power to carry don Juan with her to hell. Raquel's is a devastating unstoppable force; Berta has the grace of healing. The text presents goodness
confronting devilishness, the *good woman* against the *bad woman*.

When Berta marries don Juan and, in fact, has a baby, Raquel's alterity
is reinforced. As Gayle Letherby (2002, 10) argues, women without children represent 'the other' in societies that value motherhood. Unamuno
points directly to this matter when Raquel proposes to Berta: "Should I
give my Quelina[10] to you, so that you can make of herself another like you,
another Berta Lapeira? Another like you, an honest wife?" (De Unamuno
1920, 77). This passage emphasises the juxtaposition between the 'honest
wife', the category to which Berta belongs, and 'the other' Raquel, the
unconventional woman who contravenes the law and sacred rules. In this
respect, an inner tension can be found in Raquel's portrayal. She rejects
the Spanish social conventions and decides not to be a decent married
woman. In opposition to this, she needs to be a mother to feel fulfilled and
have a meaningful existence. This suggests an iconoclastic image of a

---

[10] The newborn is named after Raquel, "Quelina" is the diminutive for "Raquel" and
implies affection. At times, don Juan refers to Raquel as "Quelina".

woman that above all wants to be a mother, but she does not need—nor want—a husband to accomplish her purpose. Instead, she finds her way to surrogate motherhood, where don Juan is only a procreative tool, objectified by Raquel. The representation of Raquel as a woman who defies norms of respectable femininity but still, eventually, reaches her goal to become a mother subverts the stereotype of the infertile woman as linked to death. Therefore, Raquel breaks this connection between infertility and death, becoming a mother through surrogacy and consequently a carer, linked to life.

SURROGACY AS A WAY TO OVERCOME NON-MOTHERHOOD

The representation of Raquel also subverts the stereotype of the infertile woman as incomplete. At first sight, Raquel seems to fulfil this stereotype as she suffers with deep emotional pain from not being a mother; she feels unfulfilled, and her relationship with don Juan cannot be completely meaningful as she is not able to have children. Raquel is at a point in her life, after being married and widowed, where she does not believe in marriage anymore, at least for herself, though she says, "[t]here are very sincere pretences and marriage is a good school for learning them" (De Unamuno 1920, 60). This alterity of being a non-married woman but a lover defines her (De Boer et al. 2022, 14). Despite this, Raquel is not going to let this stop her from motherhood. She does not want marriage but needs to be a mother—otherwise she feels incomplete.

At first, don Juan comes up with a different solution: he suggests that they should take one of Raquel's sister's children and raise him/her as her own. As don Juan and Raquel are wealthy, he thinks that her sister will certainly give to them one of her children, as the child would have a good life and a prosperous future. It is worth mentioning the fact that for a substantial part of the twentieth century, adoption was not a transparent, nor a legal, process in Spain (Ingenschay 2021); therefore, the option that don Juan suggested was viable in the epoch the novella-play was written. However, Raquel is not happy with don Juan's solution. She associates motherhood with suffering and thinks that without it, motherhood is not real and worthy: "Oh, I can't give birth! I can't give birth! And die in labour!" (De Unamuno 1920, 33).[11] Furthermore, she thinks that an adoptive child—even if he/she would be her sister's child with a biological connection to Raquel—will never be a real son/daughter for her: "An adopted child, adoptive, will always be an orphan" (33). In this sense, in the novella-play 'real motherhood' is linked to an embodied motherhood, which implies physical pain. Raquel professes that other forms of motherhood that do not involve giving birth are 'not real'.

Breaking with ideals of passive femininity, Raquel rejects don Juan's ideas and takes charge of the process, suggesting a different kind of surrogacy arrangement. Raquel would consider as her own a child conceived by her lover don Juan and another woman, in this case, Berta. This option is connected with the Rachel and Jacob biblical passage (Gn. 30, 3) and the Hebrew ritual through which the adoptive mother achieved the parental rights and the biological—surrogate mother—lost all the rights regarding the baby (Cantera Burgos and González 1979, 34). The biblical connection is made explicit when Raquel explains to don Juan: "I almost made your Berta, our Berta, give birth upon my knees, as it was said in the Holy Scriptures" (De Unamuno 1920, 75). The use of the possessive in reference to Berta ('our Berta') has ambivalent meanings and interpretations: it could imply the 'real' possession of Berta, like the Hebrew mistress with their slaves/servants; and it could connote the passionate and emotional link between the three of them.

Raquel does not dare to make Berta give birth on her knees, but she accomplishes two other rituals to take ownership of the motherhood and establish some rights over the baby. Raquel's first performed ritual is to name the baby after her. When the baby is born and is proclaimed a girl, Raquel shouts: "Her name will be Raquel!" (68). With this action, through the power of words, Raquel assumes the motherhood of the newborn. This can also be explained as in line with traditional Spanish practices common until the twenty-first century that the first-born of a family used to take the name of their father or mother (depending on the sex of the baby). Raquel's second ritual is becoming Quelina's godmother. With this action, Raquel becomes the sacramental mother of the child and a sort of

---

[11] This idea of motherhood closely linked with physical pain also appears in one of the most representative Spanish literary works about infertility: Federico García Lorca's *Yerma* (1972, act. I, sc. 1), premiered in 1934; possibly, the strong Catholic Spanish background has a great influence on this association of ideas regarding motherhood: "I will intensify the pangs of your childbearing; in pain shall you bring forth children" (Gn. 3:16).

co-mother. This situation allows Raquel to share parenthood with Berta and don Juan.

Berta does not really take part in this decision consciously. She accepts it after a difficult birth, exhausted after having lost a lot of blood, and she seems unable to oppose it: "As you wish!" (70). In fact, she is not acknowledged in Raquel's plan from the beginning; she just keeps accepting Raquel's wishes. Thus, Raquel has planned a *forced surrogacy*. Raquel does not care about the future surrogate mother or her emotions; she only thinks about her unrestrained desire for motherhood. She expresses clearly to don Juan that her infertility is like hell for her:

> RAQUEL: Do you know what heaven is? Do you know what hell is? Do you know where hell is?
> DON JUAN: In the center of the earth, they say.
> RAQUEL: Or maybe in the center of a sterile womb. (35)

At first, when Raquel moves to Berta and don Juan's home, Berta thinks that Raquel is only trying to help. Soon Raquel takes charge of the house and the baby. She even finds a wet nurse for her, arguing that it will be the best for Berta and the baby. However, this can also contribute to breaking the mother-daughter connection established by breastfeeding (Krol and Grossmann 2018). When Berta realises that Raquel's true plans are to separate her from her baby, a confrontation between the two women begins:

> RAQUEL: I'm the real mother, me! […]
> BERTA: But no! I'm the mother, me, me… […] Give me my daughter, return my daughter to me!
> RAQUEL: What daughter?
> BERTA: My… my… my…
> The name was burning her lips. (De Unamuno 1920, 77)

The two women claim the motherhood of the baby for different reasons. Raquel claims it because the baby's birth has been carefully planned by her; therefore, the baby was born because of her will. In addition, she has been taking care of Berta's pregnancy and the baby during recent months. On the other hand, Berta is sure she has maternal rights over the baby, as she is the biological—and also the legal—mother. This dispute is solved with don Juan's death and the need to find a new household model.

SURROGACY AND A QUEER FAMILY MODEL

In *Dos madres*, non-motherhood and surrogacy are closely linked to alternative ways of making a family, as they facilitate a kind of queer family model. The queer family model is made possible through a love triangle between the protagonists and through the death of don Juan. In order to delve into how the relationship between the three protagonists operates, two additional aspects need to be analysed: the gender role subversion in Raquel and don Juan's characters and the lesbian desire between Berta and Raquel. These relationships create an inversion of the classical love triangles in literature. The love triangle is a common trope used to schematise erotic relations in Western intellectual tradition (Kosofsky Sedgwick 2016, 21). However, while traditional love triangles are formed by two male characters who share a desire for a female character, in Unamuno's novella-play there are two female characters, Raquel and Berta, who desire a male character, don Juan, which also creates an erotic bond between the two women.

Therefore, despite the fact that it was common to employ the erotic triangle in different cultural expressions from the end of the nineteenth century (Lönngren 2012, 207), it is rarely used to depict love triangles involving homosocial female desire; the most common is the display of male homosocial desire (Kosofsky Sedgwick 2016). Kosofsky Sedgwick argues that there is a continuum between male homosocial desire and male homosexual desire (1). In this sense, the same continuum can be found between female homosocial and homosexual desire and, accordingly, in the relationship between Raquel and Berta. In addition, as stated by René Girard (1961, 7–28), in any erotic rivalry between the two active members of an erotic triangle, the bond that links the two rivals is as powerful as the bond that links either of the rivals to the beloved, as rivalry and love in many cases are equivalent (Kosofsky Sedgwick, 21).

Therefore, in this case Raquel and Berta are bonded not only by rivalry—first for don Juan's love, but then for Quelina's motherhood, a more intense and potent love—but also by lesbian desire. In this sense, the attraction between the two women destabilises the love triangle, making it collapse and overshadowing don Juan (Castle 1993, 83). When Berta gets pregnant, it seems clear that don Juan does not want to get involved in family arrangements and that the future newborn will be only a matter for the two mothers. From the beginning, the idea of the wedding, which involved starting a family, appals him: "The arrangement of the wedding soned the foundations of poor don Juan's soul" (De), 49).

r family model is made possible through Raquel's struggle for motherhood, the subsequent surrogacy, and the triangular relationship of the protagonists. The key actors in the novella-play are Raquel and Berta, while don Juan seems only to be alive in the novella in order to allow Raquel and Berta to be mothers. He has no clear will and, most certainly, does not have an inherent desire to become a father: "But he hadn't any hunger of parenthood...! Why would he bring someone like him into the world?" (41). This reflects how traditionally the desire of having children and parenting was associated with female roles.

A point of departure for understanding how this love triangle and queer family model works in *Dos madres* is in the way Raquel and don Juan exchange traditional gender roles. While Berta meets the feminine standards throughout the novella-play, performing the virgin/mother role, Raquel possesses some inherent features traditionally associated with male characters. And while Unamuno's don Juan is a clear allusion to the popular Spanish literary character and archetype of a womanising man, this character is the antithesis of what his name suggests.

While at first it might seem that in *Dos madres* don Juan is a seducer, as he is pursuing romantic and sexual relationships with two women at the same time, he is actually pushed into this situation by Raquel's desire to become a mother, even though it is not a desirable situation for him. In fact, don Juan gets overwhelmed by this triangular relationship and anguished with the idea of marriage and parenthood. He perceives his wife and his lover as two chains that hold him prisoner and feels he has lost his free will. He did not even want to get married in the first place: "When finally, one autumn morning, Berta announced to her husband that he would become a father, he felt over the flesh of his tortured soul the painful brush of the two chains that were grabbing him. And he began to feel the sorrow of his dead will" (63).

Another issue to take into account is that in the 1920s the don Juan masculine model was obsolete and considered weak and effeminate (Aresti 2012, 4–6) and this is reflected in the way in which Unamuno's don Juan is represented as lacking in virility. Indeed, at some points, Raquel behaves like a maternal figure for him: "My son...my son...my son... I saw you searching for what can't be found...I was looking for a son...And thought I found him in you" (De Unamuno 1920, 52).[12]

For her part, Raquel is the pivotal point in the threesome relationship. She is always desired by the other two. Thus, she is not a passive object of desire; she is a natural seductress, and she always achieves what she wants from the infatuated don Juan and Berta. In this sense, Raquel breaks the rules of the feminine standards: she is an empowered and not a submissive woman. Hence, she performs the new *masculine women* model of the 1920 and also is a paradigmatic cliché of the strong independent Basque woman.[13] Indeed, Raquel becomes a 'father' for Berta's children; Raquel does not intervene in the gestation process or giving birth but becomes the provider of the household.

The marriage, which makes possible the future of shared motherhood between the two women, only brought joy to Raquel and Berta. And although don Juan is an intermediary between them both, Berta and Raquel have a clear attraction between them. A priori, it would seem that Berta's attraction to Raquel is more evident than Raquel's to Berta. Berta's love for Raquel begins before she is married: "The person with whom Berta was hopelessly in love was Raquel. Raquel was her idol" (De Unamuno 1920, 43). After the wedding, Berta and don Juan start visiting Raquel. During these visits, Berta's love and admiration for Raquel goes further:

> RAQUEL: Yes, when you came to visit me the first time, with that almost ceremonial visit, I observed she was analysing me...
> [...]
> DON JUAN: She is infatuated with you; you captivate her...
> Raquel bowed her face to the floor, which was suddenly intensely pale and she raised her hands to her breast, pierced by a breathless stab. (56)

Raquel's reaction to don Juan's words reveals that the attraction seems to be mutual. In addition, Raquel chooses Berta as the perfect woman with the perfect attributes to be the surrogate mother for her future child,

---

[12] Don Juan is an orphan and lived in a state of loneliness since he was very young (De Unamuno 1920, 39). This situation could have contributed to his maternal dependence on Raquel. For this reason, Sáenz de Zaitegui (2006, 98) compares Raquel to Iocasta, Oedipus's mother.

[13] Unamuno's Raquel also can be linked with some classical literary paradigms of 'bad' non-submissive women with 'masculine' features (Lewis 2011; Lefkowitz 1986; Pomeroy 1975).

demonstrating her admiration—which could be considered one of the main principles of romantic love—for Berta. Even before the three of them live together, they start to become a sort of household, and the two women share some intimacy though conversations about their emotions, their 'new family' and their man in common. Gradually, a certain process of symbiosis between the two future mothers develops: "And it was true that Berta was preceiving from Raquel the way to win over her husband and, at the same time, the way to win over herself, to be her, to be a woman. And so she allowed herself to be absorbed by Juan's master and she was discovering herself through the other [woman]" (59).

For that matter, Berta's choices and actions are always subordinate to Raquel's desires. This is not a relationship of servitude, as is the case in Rachel and Jacob's biblical passage, but there is an emotional submission, for Berta is in love, with the deepest admiration for Raquel. Therefore, in part, Raquel is in a role of power in relation to Berta. Additionally, what seems clear is that Berta and Quelina complete Raquel and don Juan's relationship, and the four of them form a real family: "And that lonely home, outside of the law, was like a cell of a couple in love in a monastery" (31). Their home was a 'lonely home' because there were no children. It was like a "cell [...] in a monastery", they lived isolated 'outside of the law', as they were not married. Berta and Quelina completed the family with children under the institution of marriage.

When don Juan dies, the family model they have constructed changes dramatically. Berta is left without financial resources. It should be recalled that in 1920s Spain—and for much of the twentieth century—a decent woman, especially after marriage, should not have a job; the man had to provide for the family. However, Raquel becomes the head of the family, taking care of Berta and the children—the one who is already born and the one with whom Berta is pregnant. She even assumes a paternal role with regard to Berta, offering a dowry in case she would like to marry again: "Raquel: If you get married again—Raquel said to Berta—I will give you a dowry. Think it over. It is not a good situation to be a widow" (80). At the same time, at the end of the novella-play, there are no suitors in sight, and Raquel and Berta are in a relationship that resembles 'conventional' lesbian relationships (Cook et al. 2013, 163; Levitt and Hiestand 2005), based on two roles: masculine/active (Raquel) and feminine/passive (Berta). They have a daughter whom they both mother, and they are expecting another child. In *Dos madres*, non-motherhood and the surrogacy Raquel initiates thus produces more than just a baby; it produces queer desires, subversions of gender roles and traditional stereotypes about infertile women, as well as new ways of imagining family formations.

CONCLUSION

Unamuno's *Dos madres* raises an uncommon and complex discussion about non-motherhood and surrogate motherhood, using literature as a basis to present an accurate and bold social analysis. The author puts on display the tension between certain conservative ideals, rooted in Spanish society, versus more radical dimensions, which denote the progressive cultural and sociopolitical era the country was experimenting with in the 1920s. The point of departure for this novella-play is a biblical passage from *Genesis*, the story of Rachel and Jacob, which could be seen as an obsolete text. Nonetheless, Unamuno takes the universal core of the text and adapts it to his contemporaneous time, performing within his novella-play surrogate motherhood—or 'delegated motherhood'—*avant la lettre*. At first glance, *Dos madres* seems to reproduce stereotypes around women and infertility, such as the connection to death and the woman as incomplete. However, Unamuno's work reveals forward-thinking ideas regarding surrogacy and new family models.

The most important way this text pushes against conventions is undoubtedly the path by which surrogate motherhood is achieved: a love triangle, where don Juan and Berta are subordinated to Raquel's will. Therefore, their arrangement is not supported by religious law that allows surrogacy as there is the Hebrew biblical text, nor is there even a socio-medical context that could assist with surrogate motherhood. In addition, there is no economical transaction with which a woman—or a couple—in a wealthier position could take advantage of a woman with lower income. It is don Juan's and Berta's emotional dependence on Raquel that allows her to become a mother. For that matter, surrogacy goes beyond being a remedy for infertility and creates an unconventional family formation.

A dichotomy between motherhood and non-motherhood is the backbone of the drama. The two female protagonists are constructed in relation to the polarisation of the *good fertile mother*—Berta, the virgin, the wife, the Christian woman paradigm—and *the bad infertile woman*—Raquel, the lover, the Machiavellian widow, the sinner. The strong Spanish Catholic influence is always present but not as an unbreakable prerogative.

On the contrary, Unamuno shows the desire of motherhood in a disruptive way; it is an unstoppable passion that drives all Raquel's actions. Consequently, motherhood is not represented as the result and the central piece of a heteronormative and Christian family. It is represented as individual and intimate desire, which leads to a queer household structure.

Finally, the subversion of gender roles that takes place in the novella-play can be highlighted as a reflection of the changing gender roles in Spain in the 1920s. Raquel displays ambivalence regarding gender expectations. On the one hand, she is anchored partially to the traditional female role: she must be a mother, and she will devote all her resources to achieve this goal. On the other hand, she has features that are traditionally coded as masculine: she does not give up on her desires, she imposes her will on others, and she fascinates and subjugates the other two protagonists. Furthermore, there is an exchange of gender roles between Raquel and don Juan. She is revealed as the true don Juan, and she becomes the paterfamilias who provides for the woman and the children of her household. In contrast, don Juan is ultimately shown as a weak man, almost superfluous in the story, who only is valuable for his reproductive capacity. For her part, Berta represents the traditional feminine archetype throughout the story, submissive and dependent. Even so, she breaks the established social gender expectations when she gradually changes her subordination from don Juan to Raquel.

Consequently, this change of paradigms allows the formation of a non-heteronormative family by Raquel and Berta, whereby Raquel can find a solution to her non-motherhood. In this sense, the *Dos madres* surrogacy not only facilitates motherhood for a barren woman but also brings about new outcomes and kinship perspectives. Consequently, in Unamuno's novella-play, surrogacy is more than a remedy for infertility; it becomes a pathway into an unconventional queer family model, disrupting gender role expectations.

References

Aguado, Ana. 2010. Cultura socialista ciudadanía y feminismo en la España de los años veinte y treinta. *Historia Social* 67: 131–153. https://doi.org/10.2307/23228639.

Archetti, Cristina. 2019. No Life Without Family: Film Representations of Involuntary Childlessness, Silence and Exclusion. *International Journal of*

Media & Cultural Politics 15 (2): 175–196. https://doi.org/10.1386/macp.15.2.175_1.

Aresti, Nerea. 2012. Masculinidad y nación en la España de los años 1920 y 1930. In *Género, sexo y nación: representaciones y prácticas políticas en España (siglos XIX–XX)*, ed. Ana M. Aguado and Mercedes Yusta Rodrigo, 55–72. Madrid: Casa de Velázquez.

Benninghaus, Christina. 2014. 'No, Thank You, Mr Stork!': Voluntary Childlessness in Weimar and Contemporary Germany. *Studies in the Maternal* 6 (1): 1–36. https://doi.org/10.16995/sim.8.

Boguszewicz, Maria, and Magdalena Anna Gajewska. 2020. El matriarcado gallego el matriarcado vasco: revisión del mito en *Matria* de Álvaro Gago y *Amama* de Asier Altuna. *Madrygal* 23: 35–50. https://doi.org/10.5209/madr.73603.

Cantera Burgos, Francisco, and Manuel Iglesias González, eds. 1979. *Sagrada Biblia: Versión crítica sobre los textos hebreo, arameo y griego*. Madrid: Biblioteca de Autores Cristianos.

Castle, Terry. 1993. *The Apparitional Lesbian. Female Homosexuality and Modern Culture*. New York: Columbia University Press.

Cifo González, Manuel. 1996. Algunos antecedentes del personaje de *La tía Tula*. *Cuadernos de la Cátedra Miguel de Unamuno* 31: 23–35.

Cook, Jennifer R., Sharon S. Rostosky, and Ellen D.B. Riggle. 2013. Gender Role Models in Fictional Novels for Emerging Adult Lesbians. *Journal of Lesbian Studies* 17 (2): 150–166. https://doi.org/10.1080/10894160.2012.691416.

Cuenca Gómez, Patricia. 2008. Mujer y constitución: los derechos de la mujer antes y después de la Constitución española de 1978. *Universitas* 8: 73–103.

De Boer, Marjolein Lotte, Cristina Archetti, and Kari Nyheim Solbraekke. 2022. In/Fertile Monsters: The Emancipatory Significance of Representations of Women on Infertility Reality TV. *Journal of Medical Humanities* 43 (1): 11–26. https://doi.org/10.1007/s10912-019-09555-z.

De Unamuno, Miguel. 1920. *Tres novelas ejemplares y un prólogo*. Madrid/Barcelona: Calpe.

Del Río, Ángel, ed., and Ángel Flores, trans. 1956. *Miguel de Unamuno. Three Exemplary Novels*. New York: Grove Press.

Delgado, Buenaventura. 1988. Introducción. In *Cincuentenario de la muerte de Unamuno*, 7–9. Barcelona: De set a nou.

Estébanez Calderón, Demetrio. 2015. Introducción. In *Miguel de Unamuno. Tres novelas ejemplares y un prólogo*. Madrid: Alianza.

Feasey, Rebecca. 2019. *Infertility and Non-Traditional Family Building. From Assisted Reproduction to Adoption in the Media*. Bath: Palgrave Macmillan.

Franz, Thomas R. 1994. *La tía Tula* y el cristianismo agónico. *Cuadernos de la Cátedra Miguel de Unamuno* 29: 43–53.

García Lorca, Federico. 1972. *Teatro Mayor: Bodas De Sangre; Yerma; La Casa De Bernarda Alba*. La Habana: Instituto Cubano del Libro.

Girard, René. 1961. *Mensonge romantique et vérité romanesque*. Paris: Grasset.

Guy, Alan. 1988. Unamuno, signo de contradicciones y hombre de todas las cosas. In *Cincuentenario de la muerte de Unamuno*, 55–74. Barcelona: De set a nou.

Ingenschay, Dieter. 2021. Tener presente a los desaparecidos, narrar lo inenarrable. Adopciones forzadas y niños robados en la novela española actual (2012–2018). In *Decir desaparecido(s) II. Análisis transculturales de la desaparición forzada*, ed. Albrecht Buschmann and Luz C. Souto, 31–45. Berlin: Lit.

Kosofsky Sedgwick, Eve. 2016. *Between Men. English Literature and Male Homosocial desire*. New York: Columbia University Press.

Krol, Kathleen M., and Tobias Grossmann. 2018. Psychological Effects of Breastfeeding on Children and Mothers. *Bundesgesundheitsblatt, Gesundheitsforschung, Gesundheitsschutz* 61 (8): 977–985. https://doi.org/10.1007/s00103-018-2769-0.

Lázaro Carreter, Fernando. 1956. El teatro de Unamuno. *Cuadernos de la Cátedra Miguel de Unamuno* 7: 5–29.

Lefkowitz, Mary R. 1986. *Women in Greek Myth*. Baltimore: Yale University Press.

Letherby, Gayle. 2002. Childless and Bereft?: Stereotypes and Realities in Relation to 'Voluntary' and 'Involuntary' Childlessness and Womanhood. *Sociological Inquiry* 72 (1): 7–20. https://doi.org/10.1111/1475-682X.00003.

Levitt, Heidi M., and Katherine R. Hiestand. 2005. Gender Within Lesbian Sexuality: Butch and Femme Perspectives. *Journal of Constructivist Psychology* 18 (1): 39–51. https://doi.org/10.1080/10720530590523062.

Lewis, Sian. 2011. Women and Myth. In *A Companion to Greek Mythology*, ed. Ken Dowden and Niall Livingstone, 443–458. Oxford: Wiley-Blackwell.

Lönngren, Ann-Sofie. 2012. Triangular, Homosocial, Lesbian: A Queer Approach to Desire in August Strindberg's Novel A *Madman's Manifesto*. *Contagion* 19: 205–229.

Montero, Mercedes. 2009. *La conquista del espacio público. Mujeres españolas en la Universidad, 1910–1936*. Madrid: Minerva.

———. 2011. Mujer, publicidad y consumo en España: Una aproximación diacrónica. *Anagramas* 9: 83–92. https://doi.org/10.22395/angr.v9n18a6.

Pomeroy, Sarah B. 1975. *Goddesses Whores Wives and Slaves: Women in Classical Antiquity*. New York: Schocken Books.

Portilla Durand, Luisa. 2019. *La tía Tula*, de Miguel De Unamuno, y la quinta identificación de un yo insatisfecho. *Acta Herediana* 62: 110–119. https://doi.org/10.20453/ah.v62i2.3613.

Ramos, Maria Dolores. 1988. Luces y sombras en torno a una polémica: la concesión del voto femenino en España (1931–1933). *Baetica* 11: 563–573.

Sabadell Nieto, Joana. 2011. *Desbordamientos. Transformaciones culturales y políticas de las mujeres*. Barcelona: Icaria.

Sáenz de Zaitegui, Ainoa Begoña. 2006. Metafísica de la maternidad: estudio comparativo de *Dos madres* y *La tía Tula* de Miguel de Unamuno a la luz de *Génesis* 29–30. *Cuadernos de la Cátedra Miguel de Unamuno* 42: 93–108.

Serrano, Carlos, and Serge Salaün. 2006. *Los felices años veinte: España crisis y modernidad.* Madrid: Marcial Pons Historia.

Stenstrom, Monika. 2007. Acercamiento al pensamiento de Unamuno: *La tía Tula* y la lucha entre fe y razón. *Revista de Filosofía* 25 (43): 35–54.

United States Conference of Catholic Bishops. 2002. *The New American Bible.* Washington: United States Conference of Catholic Bishops.

CHAPTER 9

Autonomy, Autocreation and Agency: Radical Non-Motherhood in Amandine Gay's *Une poupée en chocolat* (2021)

Jasmine D. Cooper

The white fathers told us: I think, therefore I am.
The Black mother within each of us—the poet—whispers in our dreams:
I feel, therefore I can be free.
—*Audre Lorde* (Poetry Is Not a Luxury, in *Your Silence Will Not Protect You*, 2017, 9–10)

This project has received funding from the European Union's Horizon 2020 research and innovation programme under grant agreement No 952366.

J. D. Cooper (✉)
Girton College, University of Cambridge, Cambridge, UK
e-mail: jdc52@cam.ac.uk

© The Author(s) 2025
J. Björklund et al. (eds.), *Negotiating Non-Motherhood*,
Palgrave Macmillan Studies in Family and Intimate Life,
https://doi.org/10.1007/978-3-031-66697-1_9

157

INTRODUCTION

To negotiate non-motherhood is to negotiate systems of power: how bodies and identities are stringently regulated by pronatalist economies and institutions. It is to negotiate a range of adjacent reproductive justice issues, including the ongoing management of sex and gender, and how these intersect with race, sexuality, class, age, disability, fantasies of nation and futurity. Finally, to negotiate non-motherhood requires a reckoning with challenging ethical and existential questions which disrupt the "biologic paradigm" (Brakman and Scholz 2006, 56): from the grounds of one's subjectivity, and more widely, what it means to be (legible as) human, to new forms of (extra-familial) kinship; from rethinking the conditions and shape of care, to questions of relationality with other human animals, non-human animals and the non-human/natural world.

A text which reflects on many of these issues is the book-length essay, *Une poupée en chocolat* ("A Chocolate Doll," 2021) by French author and filmmaker Amandine Gay. This work marks a departure from Gay's primary medium of cinema; she is perhaps better known for her documentary films *Ouvrir la voix* ("Speak up: Make Your Way," 2017) and *Une Histoire à Soi* ("A Story of One's Own," 2021).[1] Gay's auto-theoretical essay treats, first and foremost, the politics and violences of transracial and transnational adoption, both within and beyond France, a highly personal topic given that Gay herself is a transracial adoptee. But the intimacy of this text extends to Gay's elaboration of her own lack of desire to become a biological mother or to partake in traditional family-making. In Gay's focus, we see how the link between reproduction and family-making are embedded within colonial and racialised logics, enhanced by the French republican model of assimilation. Also specific to discussions about non-traditional family-making within France—including recent debates elsewhere regarding assisted reproductive technologies for queer couples and single women—her discussion of (transracial) adoption reveals the particularity of the French laws of *filiation* ("legal kinship" [Rye 2018, 100]). Thus, in this rageful and impassioned tract, Gay reveals the multiple ways in which violence is done to the Black, cisgender woman's body. She highlights the repeated infantilisation and disempowerment she

---

[1] This latter film, released in the same year as *Une poupée en chocolat*, deals with many of the same themes and would offer an interesting textual counterpoint to many of the discussions this chapter raises.

experiences at the hands of the French state, both as an adoptee in search of her origins and in her quest to obtain a hysterectomy in her mid-thirties.

In this chapter, I argue that Gay's story, both as a transracial adoptee and as a woman in pursuit of autonomy over her body, permits for a reflection on the violence of the (French) state's hand in family-making and the paternalistic pronatalism which structures medical spheres and discourses. With the biological family already contestable from her position as a pansexual, transracial adoptee, and considered alongside her refusal to be a biological mother, I suggest that Gay's work offers a meditation on autonomy, autocreation and agency. By refusing the glorification of biological kinship, I will show how Gay negotiates new ways of conceptualising care, love and connection beyond the heteronormative family, and, in turn, offers innovative ways of negotiating and understanding non-motherhood.

As discussed in the introduction to this volume, the terminology around non-motherhood is imperfect. As I explore elsewhere (Cooper 2020), the language and various labels denoting non-motherhood (e.g. maternal refusal, in/voluntary childlessness; child-free; "rich auntie"[2]) is full of pitfalls, often masking or flattening out what is a complex matrix of (self-)determination, and often obscures other groups' relationship to non-maternity other than cisgender women. Such complexity is evidenced in the case of Gay, a "transracial adoptee and a woman without a uterus," who also considers herself "the mother of a child that I met when he was 7 and who has been brought up by four adults, including me (the latest arrival)" (Gay 2021, 105–06).[3] She emphatically divests the notion of "mother" of its biological primacy, has no desire for biological children and yet does not explicitly identify anywhere as a "non-mother." Notwithstanding, her multifaceted relationship to questions of non-motherhood, other-motherhood and, indeed, being adopted is productive when thinking through care, ethical connection and reproductive justice more widely. In relation to care and ethical responsibility, I dispute referring to proto-familial care as "mothering," principally because it upholds

---

[2] "Rich auntie" is a term coined by author, commentator and anti-racist campaigner Rachel Cargle to denote, "a space to celebrate and be in community with those women who choose a journey of being child-free and indulgence in the villages around them." See Cargle (n.d.).

[3] All translations, unless otherwise stated, are my own; page numbers refer to the original French edition.

a gendered and family-centred primacy of maternal care, one which is extremely difficult to extricate from patriarchal and essentialist traditions. I hold that there is power in thinking through the pluralised ways in which care is being undertaken. In short, I argue that not all mothers care and not all caring should be understood as a form of mothering (Cooper 2020). American author Sheila Heti in her 2018 book-length auto-theoretical essay, *Motherhood*, articulates the ways in which we are all necessarily entangled in different relationalities of care which normally fall under the auspices of "mothering," preferring the elliptical label "to be not 'not a mother'" (157). She states: "To be *not not* is what the mothers can be, and what the women who are not mothers can be. This is the term we can share. In this way, we can be the same" (158, original emphasis). Such gestures of parity rather than enmity between non-mothers and mothers are echoed in Gay's work, where the very absence of biological motherhood opens up more radical ways to think about how care, community, kinship and love are understood beyond the shadow of the family, liberating mothers and non-mothers alike.

Breaking Blood Ties: Towards "Anti-Genealogical Fugitivity"

As stated, negotiating non-motherhood or anxieties around not being able to become a (biological) mother are closely entwined with adjacent reproductive justice issues, not least adoption and surrogacy.[4] In France, Gay argues, "adoption is firstly a solution to the problem of infertility" (2021, 82). Yet, the rise in assisted reproductive technologies (ART)—recently opened to lesbians and single women in France—has seen adoption become the third option taken by involuntarily childless couples. This preference for biological reproduction over adoption largely reflects what Gay terms the obsession with having "a child of one's own." As Sarah Vaughan Brakman and Sally J. Scholz isolate, "the emphasis on biological reproduction carries with it certain assumptions about maternity...constitut[ing] the 'biologic paradigm'" (2006, 56). For Gay, this is reflected in the current language around family-building and mothering,

---

[4] This chapter does not have space to fully address the nuances of surrogacy; see Sophie Lewis 2019 for important and critical discussions about surrogacy and its ties to colonial, capitalist and patriarchal logics, many of which find mirror in Gay's critique of transnational and transracial adoption.

which is "founded on the notion of parental exclusivity and biological kin-ship" (57). This paradigm situates reproduction less as a choice, but closer to an imperative which governs idealised femininity amongst cisgender (especially white, middle-class) women given that it suggests that maternal instinct is a feature inherent to female sex and latent in her embodied experience of pregnancy. As philosopher Paul B. Preciado (2020) states, "femininity is defined bio-politically (by women's obligation to give life)" (273). Importantly, it may also "obscure the very important physical or embodied connections between *all* parents and their children" (Brakman and Scholz 2006, 56; my emphasis), thus siloing women's bodies and lives for domestic, affective and caring labour.[5] It is precisely the overdetermi-nation of the biological connection between mothers and their children in both pregnancy and birth that often sees "infertile women utilize repro-ductive technologies" (56), because this narrative reinforces—or is at the origin of—the myth of maternal instinct and "the care that goes under the name of maternal instinct" (58). The myth of maternal instinct obscures the vast numbers of cisgender women who have no desire to reproduce or those who experience dysphoric or traumatic pregnancies; it also over-writes the real perils of childbirth, especially for women of colour (Mahase 2020; McLemore 2019; Randone 2020) and ignores the increasing num-ber of women experience maternal regret (Donath 2017; Thomas 2022).

Whilst such technological advances are not unilaterally bad in and of themselves, they are indicative of Preciado's (2013) theory of the pharma-copornographic regime, where biopower now extends into the very fabric of the body. These technologies issue from racist, capitalist and paternalis-tic medical foundations (a point I return to) and feed into upholding a biologised underpinning of the Family, which is often supported by romanticised and, paradoxically, heavily naturalised discourses on preg-nancy.[6] Such discourses delineate which bodies constitute birthing bodies, thus mediating the ways in which we understand care, attachment and embodiment. As such, women who choose not to reproduce are often seen as selfish, shallow, unnatural, self-absorbed, immature and failed women (Cooper 2020; Badinter 2010; Daum 2015; Debest 2014); for those who cannot conceive naturally, the language is also couched in

---

[5] Indeed, it is telling that many ethical models—from The Buddha to Levinas—are fre-quently based on holding the other with the same 'unconditional love' as a mother holds their baby. For a critique of Levinasian ethics to this regard, see Lisa Guenther 2006.

[6] For a thoroughly de-romanticised account of pregnancy, see Sophie Lewis 2018.

failure and inadequacy, giving concomitant rise to feelings of shame, inferiority and loss (Cooper 2020); and those subjectivities who desire to be pregnant but who fall outside the idealised reproductive subject—namely transmen, other marginalised queer subjectivities, disabled people, racial minorities or migrant bodies—see their desires cast as unnatural, anti-social, even morally reprehensible. Finally, the biologic paradigm continues to undermine long legacies of queer family-making and alternative non-Western kinship practices, namely those by indigenous communities and black feminist models of care.

The tyranny of a "strictly biological conception of family-making" (Gay 2021, 56) is thus crystallised through discussions of non-motherhood and adoption—and in particular France's adoption policy of *adoption plénière* ("plenary adoption") (the route which terminates all links between biological parent and child and sees the adoptive parents become the sole recognised parents of the child), and the recent debates around ART. The confluences of power enacted on and through the body in order to uphold the primacy of biological *filiation*—or as Gay calls it, "the myth of blood ties" (56)—emerge strongly to reveal the colonial and privatised roots of this model which, as Janet Farrell Smith's (2005) work on adoption shows, ensures that "biological reproduction is prized as the primary normal condition and primary, normal condition and foundation for parenting" (112). In particular, the question of ownership and exclusivity inherent to this model perhaps typifies the embeddedness of colonial and capitalist logics of the Family. Gay cites Farrell Smith's assertion that the "child of one's own" model suggests that "the child is somehow one's natural property or possession" (112). Adoption in France, and more widely in the Global North more widely, privileges involuntarily childless parents' feelings and desires to reproduce. Indeed, examining "the history of adoption in France, whether national or international," we can see that, "what has always prevailed is the interest of the State (and its natalist and familialist policies) and the private interests (of the candidates for adoption, of the adopting parents and of the adoption agencies or institutions)" (Gay 2021, 91). As Sophie Lewis (2019) also conveys in relation to surrogacy, adoption is directly linked to state and private interests, not least profit.

Gay outlines how the desire to emulate biological kinship models undergirds plenary adoption. She asks, "Why, in the twenty-first century, do legislators and public opinion agree on the need to make adoptive parenthood as similar to biological parenthood as possible?" (59). The first answer to her own question is that this "legal lie" reveals the "impossibility

of thinking kinship outside of genetic continuity, but also the need to create orphans on paper so to avoid any risk of pluralised approaches to parenting" (59). Indeed, the distinctive French notion of *filiation* "determines
who can or cannot be a parent, who can or cannot have parental authority
over a child" (Rye 2018, 100). The laws of *filiation* hold that children
"have only two parents, one of each sex" (100), historically proscribing
both the queer couple and non-coupled people from becoming legal parents until recent amendments to the law.[7] But such a proprietary relationship between parents and children is particularly freighted for adoptees—in
particular transnational and transracial adoptees—and produces vexed
questions of belonging and legitimacy: "If our parents are not our *real*
parents, whose children are we? Who do we belong to?" (Gay 2021, 57).
Such precarity informs Gay's own creative projects as part of an autocre-
ational impulse permitting her to become the daughter of her own works,
as I explore later in this chapter.

The second part of Gay's question is linked fundamentally to race, culture and questions of nation. Gay details how infertile couples desire "a
tabula rasa baby: with no past, no history, no previous affiliations, no risk
that the birth family will try to gain visiting rights one day" (61). The
"*tabula rasa* baby" captures an anxiety not only about forms of kinship
which exceed heteronormative models or risk muddying the proprietary
links ensured by the strict two-parent rule of *filiation* but also about ensuring cultural and racial transplantation of the (transnational and/or transracial) adoptee within the Family/Nation. If, as Judith Butler (2002) argues,
French *filiation* is linked to the idealised reproduction of "the fantasy of
the nation" (23), then a *tabula rasa* Child ensures securing cultural assimilation by way of total erasure of origin. It not only confirms Butler's assertion that the Child is, "a dense site for the transfer and reproduction of
culture, where 'culture' carries with it implicit norms or racial purity and
domination" (22), but mirrors colonial logics of the appropriation and
theft of non-white bodies and, "reveals in particular the one-sided nature
of assimilation of racialised children into white families" (Gay 2021, 44);
the reverse is extremely rare. This strategy feeds into "an institutional

---

[7] Although the Sénat have approved amendments to the *filiation* laws to be expanded to
include 'two mothers' or 'two fathers' (see 'Bioéthique' 2020), the insistence on including
parents' genders will naturally lead to the exclusion of non-binary and trans people seeking
to become parents. Indeed, this is likely to be the next chapter in the ongoing bioethical
debates.

fabrication of the incompetence of poor mothers [from the Global South]"
(90) in which "the civilising argument has been replaced by a humanitar-
ian argument, and the need to manage mixed children in the colonies
replaced by the need to save children from the poverty of the third world"
(138), thus confirming a proto-civilising, neo-colonial mentality, one
which is tacitly white supremacist and permits a narrative of white saviour-
ism to persist.

The violent extraction and deracination of non-white (transnational)
children who are then grafted into societies which ignores birth language,
culture and heritages causes often untold trauma. The prioritisation of
safeguarding the "assimilationist orientation of French republican univer-
salism" (224) results in an affective gulf between the motivations of the
state/the adopting families and those primarily affected (the birth mothers and fostered or adopted children), whose "rights, wellbeing and emotional, mental and cultural equilibrium […] are systematically ignored"
(138). This results in deep and embodied fragmentation in the adoptee,
such that "many adopted and indigenous teenagers come to believe that
their only real power is to make their bodies disappear" (134). Worse still,
the adoptee is expected to be grateful for the privilege of having been
chosen; as Gay argues, "it's time to reverse the burden of gratitude" (111).

For these reasons, Gay enacts what Sophie Lewis (2022) terms, "anti-
genealogical fugitivity," that is, "ways of negating, pre-dating, ignoring,
and/or provincializing the private nuclear household" (45). For Gay, this
constitutes recentring adoption to privilege the interests of the child and
birth mothers, supplanting the model of parental exclusivity. In particular,
she turns towards alternative modes of kinship, care and relationality. In so
doing, she refuses the colonial, racialised and patriarchal modes of networks of care, suggests that we need a new ethics that "it is our entire
relationship with the other that we must deconstruct" (Gay 2021, 93) and
discovers powerful ways of re-casting and re-securing her agency.

THE BANYAN TREE, SPIRALS AND WATER

Gay's experience as a pansexual, transracial adoptee, cisgender woman
without a uterus and stepmother to a child means her relationship to
(non-)motherhood is complex and complicates the model of kinship upon
which heteronormative kinship is based. Following the violence of her
experiences as a transracial adoptee, she adumbrates alternative modes of
kinship which in turn permit her to re-explore her hybrid identity. She

does this through mobilising the image of the banyan tree which serves as a powerful metaphor which embraces plurality, multiplicity and potentiality in collective and compassionate horizonal or rhizomatic care beyond biological motherhood. She situates an analysis of relationality before any in-depth discussion of her own horror of pregnancy and total rejection of biological maternity.

The image of the banyan tree is a motif which takes on enormous significance in this work: "the banyan tree is a tree which does not respect the codes; it blurs boundaries and it is for this reason it is my tree" (Gay 2021, 162). On the cover of the first edition is an illustration by Maya Mahindou of "this magical tree with thousands of root-branches" (162). As Gay herself outlines, trees or roots are part of the lexicon which are used to metaphorise the experience of being adopted; but it is the banyan tree which speaks to her own particular rejection of biological motherhood. Citing Marie-Andrée Ciprut's (2014) work on banyan identity in the Caribbean, we read of the sacred place that the banyan tree holds in various traditions, symbolising moving against established boundaries, borders and hegemonies: "it extends to and therefore opposes any idea of confinement, of reductive nationalism that would incite racism, hatred and exclusion" (36; translation mine). Édouard Glissant's work on the rhizome—which, along with René Despestre, informs Ciprut's analysis of the banyan tree—encourages us to think about the rhizome as less linked to national identity and Nation, but rather as expanding us beyond borders and binary systems, into Relation. For Glissant, "the poetics of Relation is never bi-something, it is always multiple-something" (Hantel 2013, 110–111, citing Édouard Glissant; translation mine). Max Hantel concludes from this description of the poetics of Relation that this is a "spiral retelling […] the movement out to the multiple from this economy of the One, but it is rhizomatic in the sense of producing a rootedness in the world" (111).

The use of the rhizomatic and spiral retelling is useful insofar as, read through this Glissantian lens, it opens up "a different model […] to articulate the possibility of *une nouvelle sensibilité* [a new awareness]" (111). For Gay, spiralling and spirals are usually evidenced in relation to her slides into deep depressions, blackouts from alcohol and autodestructive tendencies from her adolescence onwards (as I explore later). It is sufficient to say at this point that much of this embodied agony arises in part due to the racism she endures at school, in her small rural town, being cut off from Black culture and communities, and then, when she finally encounters other Black people in her adolescence, feeling like an imposter,

struggling to find her place in relation to Blackness. The resultant existential fragmentation in the adopted subject, resulting in "spirals of questioning" (Gay 2021, 57) and spiralling moods and behaviours, as Gay
elaborates throughout the novel, bear witness to the violence of the language around adoption but also family-building more widely. For her, the
banyan tree has enabled her to think beyond the rigidity of what she
understood Black identity to signify: "to be or not to be a *real* Black
woman, that is not the question" (162). Drawing on the multiplicity of
influences in her life, she sees herself as radiating the expansive, multidirectional influences: "synthesizing my life experiences in order to become
who I wanted to be" (163). In this way, her work and her life are a testament to the "spiral retelling" that is possible when dispensing with bina-
ries borne of colonial logics and geographic delineations. The spiral in this
sense is a powerful vector not dissimilar from Christina Sharpe's (2016a)
notion of "trans*" which is a way of thinking "the range of trans*formations
enacted on and by Black bodies [...] a range of embodied experiences
called gender and to Euro-Western gender's dismantling, its inability to
hold in/on Black flesh" (30). Such afro-/Black feminist critical material-
isms permit a going beyond established models and understandings of the
body, family, kinship, nation and ethics. In its excess, its multifariousness
and multidirectionality, such spiralling permits *une nouvelle sensibilité* to
emerge, both inwardly, in relation to self, and outwardly to the encounter
with other(s), the natural world, histories, memory and the archives to the
extent that, such that we are "transformed into being" (Sharpe 2016a,
citing Dionne Brand).

Gay's own description of rebuffing biological motherhood and calls for
alternative forms of kinship sits within another wider Black feminist tradition, one which "black communities put in place forms of resistance to the
racist and capitalist appropriation of their children" (2021, 100). In particular, she draws on Patricia Hill Collins's notion of "othermothering"—
not necessarily a gendered term, as Gay argues—which allows children "to
find parental figures in cases where their birth parents are not able to fulfil
this function full time" (101). Indeed, this collective approach to upbringing is highly important in opening up modes of kinship and belonging
where, "in France, certain children are lesser, or not seen as children at all"
(302). The recuperation of those that have fallen victim of the systems of
exploitation is part of her imagined future: "My lack of interest in biological parenting is matched only by my passion for symbolic kinship—whether
that be with individuals or works" (348). Fundamentally for Gay, her

experience of kinship "is that of encounter, the taking into account of difference, the non-glorification of biological kinship and the importance that the first parents are allowed to exist" (92). She sees this as a collective responsibility: "If our children are the community's children, we are all responsible for fighting for their emancipation and for the dismantling of systems of exploitation which wants to appropriate them" (100).

Thinking about non-motherhood, maternal refusal and non-traditional modes of intergenerational (and interspecies) care through nature metaphors of relation emerging from anti-colonial, critical material feminisms might serve to replace the stultifying ways in which returns to nature have stymied discussions around alternative forms of relationality. These have historically been (and arguably continue to be) imputed and interpolated to reinforce essentialised discourses around womanhood and, indeed, gestational politics (Badinter 2010). If the rhizomatic, expansive and plural is typified by the banyan tree, then this posthumanist and feminist model permits "[t]he self-regulating and expansive nurturing trajectory of its roots encourages us to embrace its symbolism beyond prohibitions, stereotypes and prejudices, to trace identity" (Ciprut 2014, 36).[8] Ideas of multiplicity are particularly useful, as it is still a form of relationality with questions of care and community which exceeds the family, and itself cannot be divorced from wider senses of holding and containment which are so often and narrowly aligned with mothering/maternalised modes of imagining care, including beyond human paradigms. Non-mothering, like other forms of relationality which do not simply rely on the established ways of being understood, breaches the boundaries of ways of legislating care. While the language of care undertaken by women is so often ensconced within highly maternal language and, even, in the language of sweetness, gentleness and softness (Dufourmantelle 2013), then the visions of non-mothering and co-existence emergent in image of the banyan tree imagine relationality differently. It is not always soft, gentle or sweet, but *radical—radicelle*, even—and caring while necessitating certain forms of rupture. A rootedness in the world, then, for Gay is a spiral retelling, paradoxically, of

---

[8] A similar vision is elaborated in the watery gestationality by Mielle Chandler and Astrida Neimanis. For Chandler and Neimanis, gestationality is a model of care which exceeds "human, female, reprosexual experience" (Chandler and Neimanis 2013, 63), drawing upon fluid ecologies and relationalities. Gestationality is in many respects indebted to anti-racist black feminist models of "othermothering" and the "banyan identity" adumbrated by Gay, albeit through a different geographical cipher. Like these models, Chandler and Neimanis see gestationality as "providing the conditions for an unpredictable plurality to flourish" (62).

her displacement, dispossession and disillusionment within a world that sees her birth *herself* into being through her work. She moves from dispossession and autodestruction into relation through autocreation; this autocreation, however, is possible precisely because of the multiplicity—the hybridity—of her identity, seeing her become the daughter of her own texts, rather than a proto-mother to her proto-textual-offspring.

DAUGHTERS OF CREATION: AGENCY, ACTIVATION AND ACTIVISM

Reclaiming the Body

At various points throughout the text, Gay refers to the various "autodestructive tendencies" (2021, 121) that she attributes to being a Black, transracial adoptee. She states that since her adolescence, "to make the noise in my head stop and wanting everything to stop are two feelings that it has been difficult for me to distinguish between" (121). For Gay, this psychic agony is a deeply embodied experience, where the body politic and the environment converge in the body of the individual:

> My body is the manifestation of the social stigma that my birth mother suffered, it is the evidence of the mistake she made or the horrors she suffered. My body is a Black woman's body in a white, patriarchal society. My body constantly betrays me, I am Black to white people and white to Black people […] my body has no history because it is not part of a genealogy. My body speaks but everything it says is nonsense. My body taunts me and also deprives me of my agency. I am 13 years old and there is only one option left to me: to separate myself from my body. (122)

The separation from the body results in a series of downward spirals towards the oblivion that she finds through drinking in order to: "stop everything, forget everything, drink myself into oblivion" (122). This cycle continues for many years, well into her twenties. Gay references that adoptees are four times as likely to attempt suicide, something which haunts her own writing of her story—the proximity to risky and destructive behaviour is reflective of the multiple embodied traumas that she carries as detailed above. Alongside the experiences of racism and alienation, she also experiences horror at the idea of pregnancy: "For as long as I can remember, pregnancy has always horrified me and monogamy for me is an aberration" (168). Such alienation is compounded by the fact that throughout her adolescence and adulthood, she experiences excruciating pain during her menstrual cycle. After years of being ignored or gaslit by medical professionals, she is eventually diagnosed as having fibroids.

Her discussion of the bodily and psychic pain she experiences is accompanied by a critique of the paternalism and racism she endures within medical contexts: "The strength of patriarchy is to make people believe that it doesn't exist [...] 'All women have pain during their period,' and we don't care" (322). This "racist paternalism" (324) continues when she seeks out voluntary sterilisation by having a hysterectomy; she is repeatedly refused this procedure, stating, "I underestimated the amount of energy the medical world puts into forcing women with a uterus to give birth" (327). She eventually turns to Twitter, asking for help to find a surgeon, ending the tweet in all capitals: "I DON'T WANT TO GIVE BIRTH AND THAT IS MY RIGHT. The End" (328). The refusal of voluntary sterilisation by the medical domain reveals not only just how medicalised and essentialised the cisgender woman's body remains, but also, as Gay herself acknowledges, that "to affirm the non-desire to give birth remains difficult if not taboo with the public [...] care providers are still unable to hear the lack of desire for motherhood" (327). Gay makes clear that "medical racism kills us, infantilises us and ensures that we are not listened to or believed" (323). Her accounts in medical topoi reveal the pressures that are enacted upon the body under compulsory cis-heteronormativity, recalling Preciado's (2018) description of the body's ensnarement within biopolitical management: "But the organs considered as part of the reproductive system (breasts, womb, penis, testicles) are still subject to the theologico-patriarchal regime. Put in terms of the social labels ascribed to the body, then, the nose, lips, buttocks are the software, while the genitals are the hardware" (para 2). But, like Gay, Preciado (2021) also ascribes power in rejecting the reproductive imperative, signalling the womb as a site of rebellion and resistance: "And so it must have been in my rebellious, non-reproductive uterus that all the other strategies were conceived: the rage that made me mistrust the norm, the taste for insubordination [...]" (24). For Preciado, this is linked to his trans struggle; for Gay, this is linked to a conscious, afrofeminist rejection of maternity, pregnancy and the biologisation of kinship and care. However, there is one further way in which Gay comes to understand her total rejection of pregnancy. She eventually learns that she was the product of a rape and her birth mother claims she had no idea that she was pregnant. Gay says: "I spent nine months glued to Naïma's spine, unknowingly vampirizing her. The disinterest, even disgust, that pregnancy has always inspired in me makes sense beyond my materialistic Afrofeminism; it is also, on an unconscious level, the anguish of undergoing what my birth mother experienced with me" (2021, 345). That non-motherhood might be Gay's beginning—that is, the non-motherhood of her mother, foreclosed to her by the violence of Gay's conception, and the various material reasons and (structural) violences which led her to give Gay up for adoption—is suggested to both subliminally haunt Gay and yet is also a source of her conscious liberation and rejection of maternity. In this way non-motherhood—understood here as a non-biological motherhood—is also an end in itself, a way of enacting agency and self-determination. This "end" however is less one of finitude, but part of an ongoing project of negotiating relationality and self-actualisation.

"La recherche, la création et le militantisme": From Autodestruction to Autocreation

The fragility that we read in Gay's adolescence, and which continues into her twenties, is eventually balanced by her work as a filmmaker, author and activist. These pursuits offer her a different outlet to channel these "autodestructive tendencies" and, by contrast, become modes through which she finds agency. She moves from disempowered autodestruction to empowered autocreation: "This book is part of my process of healing-acceptance emerging from the hidden depths of my strength" (110). In discourses surrounding non-mothers and their creativity, products of creation are often couched in terms which would suggest them to be proxy children or reproductive acts. This follows a particularly masculinist and patriarchal understanding of creative acts standing in for—or a masculinised version of—procreative acts. However, there are significant limitations in such a reading of non-mothers' works. Firstly, very few cisgender women without children refer to their works in this way; this reading is often made by readers of their work, resulting in reductive and highly gendered appraisals of creative output. Moreover, such an approach repeats a model of propriety and ownership often subtended by anxieties about legacy and posterity—namely: who will remember me? As Gay speaks of at length in her work, the emphasis on ownership and possession is inherently linked to the ways in which adoption is linked to patriarco-colonial conceptions of family-building, where children *belong* to their parents: "It is possible to move from a biological and capitalist vision of the family, in which the children figure as the exclusive property of their biological parents" (106).

Gay has a strikingly innovative way in which she positions herself in relation to her work: she suggests that she is the daughter of her artistic creations (rather than their mother). She says, "To be a daughter of one's work, to give birth to oneself and to discover one's agency: this is what I aspire to above all else" (169). In this sense, there is an opening up of the relationship of the author to one's work—one which is not about posses-sion or arrival, but rather about the awakening of agency. As gestured to above, Gay's model of kinship is about a *rencontre*: a meeting, an encoun-ter. Through her writing, activism, filmmaking and research, she comes into better contact not only with herself, and thus new ways of narrating herself and negotiating her story. Birthing oneself is to realise one's agency: becoming the source and beneficiary of the "self-full" (Downing 2019) act of self-actualisation. But the creative act should not be understood as leading to possessing the work, but rather it is the work which contains within it the multiplicity of beings, actors and contacts that have contrib-uted to making self-actualisation possible. As Gay seems to articulate, she is a vessel through which creativity moves and connection is made. This does not negate the particular positionality from which she creates, rather they are all part and parcel of her creative position: "I became an artist as it is the identity which contains all the others and allows me to be the daughter of my work" (Gay 2021, 170). In an important way, this text is a narrative and self-conceptualisation about *dis*possession as much as creation.

In the epigraph to this chapter, I employ Audre Lorde's beautiful asser-tion that there is feeling in freedom, and freedom in feeling. Lorde figures the ways in which we have been historically dispossessed of feeling and freedom through the narratives given to us by the world, by the "white fathers." Gay's narrative is a testament to the dispossession that she experi-ences—as a Black woman in France, as a person without a uterus, as a transracial adoptee: "I was born under the sign 'X'" (2021, 8), she tells us. The immense feeling that Gay writes with—rage being a predominant affect, which she learns to negotiate—is testament to the power of feeling and, in many ways, being totally dispossessed by it. And in her disposses-sion, she moves towards an agency which is not conditional on ownership or being said to "have," but rather the changed and changing state that

creativity, resistance work and research allow her to experience and witness. Butler (2013) argues poignantly that "we do not simply move ourselves, but are ourselves moved by what is outside us, by others, but also
by whatever 'outside' resides in us" (3). The porous boundaries between
self and other, between self and the world might be a powerful way of re-
casting agency both through maternal refusal and through artistic creation—and without merely creating consolatory proxies for children or
approximations to supposed intimacy and unconditionality that undergirds ethical models based on mother-child ties. If the narrative and political critique that Gay mounts reminds of anything, it is perhaps as Butler
puts it: "The dispossessions of grief, love, rage, ambition, ecstasy [...] call
into question whether we are, as bounded and deliberate individuals, self-
propelling and self-driven. Indeed, they suggest that we are moved by
various forces that precede and exceed our deliberate and bounded self-
hood. As such, we cannot understand ourselves without in some ways
giving up on the notion that the self is the ground and cause of its own
experience" (4). The myth of possession, of having, dogs the ways in
which we perceive non-mothers, maternal refusal, childlessness (the lack
inherent in the suffix); it dogged Gay throughout her life, and all those
like her who were born and dispossessed of their histories, their cultures,
their languages. But rather than seek out possession or to partake in the
repetition of dispossession through endless accumulation, non-
motherhood and other-motherhood offer models of dispossession which
is to say participation and encounter: "[w]e can only be dispossessed
because we are already dispossessed. Our interdependency establishes our
vulnerability to social forms of deprivation" (5).

CONCLUSION

In February 2023, a report by two historians from the University of
Angers revealed the shocking and illegal practices of international adoption undertaken in France over the last thirty years, seeing transnational
adoptive strategies partaking in what could more readily be named child-
trafficking—all in the name of family- and nation-building (Le Cam
2023). What Gay reveals so poignantly through her discussion of adoption
is how reproductive justice more widely—including the right to refuse to
be a mother, which bodies are permitted to reproduce (safely, legally), the
right to abortion, to sterilisation, to contraception—are bound up in
questions of power frequently ignored by mainstream feminisms (2021,

77). Indeed, they reveal "systemic and institutional violence against women in vulnerable situations, isolated minors, adoptees, Black communities and, by extension, all marginalized groups" (47). To take up Sharpe's powerful articulation, "[s]lavery is the ghost in the machine of kinship. Kinship relations structure the nation. Capitulation to their current configurations is the continued enfleshment of that ghost" (2016b).

As should be clear, discussions around reproductive justice and the body politic must be understood intersectionally, given the convergences of race, gender, class, age and disability. Discussions of non-motherhood, adoption, infertility and alternative forms of kinship must always take into account the transnational networks of exploitation and (neo-)colonial logics which are alive and well in the contemporary. In the case of adoption, we must recognise "their impact on the primary mothers in the Global South and on racialised and precarious women in the Global North, whose children are made available for adoption" (Gay 2021, 46). If, in her own words, "speaking out itself is a political act" (175), then Gay's work is a radical statement which disrupts—ragefully—to "refuse colonial taxidermy" (134), to refuse any "continued enfleshment" (Sharpe 2016b) of its ghost. Gay's work cites the radical, active love by bell hooks as inspiration and recalls Lorde's reminder that our silence will not protect us, but merely limit feeling and freedom. In Gay's own words: "I have seen the consequences of silence and isolation on our paths and I will not be silent any longer" (2021, 25). The non-mother/other-mother finds powerful voice in this text, and not a moment too soon, negotiating the pitfalls of her painful anonymity and ignominy, thus flourishing through creative, radical dispossession.

REFERENCES

Badinter, Élisabeth. 2010. *Le Conflit: la femme et la mère*. Paris: Éditions Flammarion.

'Bioéthique'. 2020. *Senat.*, 5 Feb. https://www.senat.fr/espace_presse/actualites/201912/bioethique.html. Accessed 15 Jul 2020

Brakman, Sarah-Vaughan, and Sally J. Scholz. 2006. Adoption, ART, and a Re-Conception of the Maternal Body: Toward Embodied Maternity. *Hypatia* 21 (1): 54–73.

Butler, Judith. 2002. Is Kinship Always Already Heterosexual? *differences: A Journal of Feminist Cultural Studies* 13 (1): 14–44.

———. 2013. Aporetic Dispossession, or the Trouble with Dispossession. In *Dispossession: The Performative in the Political. Conversations with Athena Athanasiou*, 1–9. Cambridge, UK, and Malden, MA: Polity Press.

Cargle, Rachel. n.d. Our Story. *Rich Auntie Supreme.* https://www.richauntiesupreme.com/our-story Accessed 1 Sept 2023.

Chandler, Mielle, and Astrida Neimanis. 2013. Water and Gestationality: What Flows Beneath Ethics. In *Thinking with Water*, ed. Cecilia Chen, Janine MacLeod, and Astrida Neimanis, 61–83. Montreal: McGill-Queen's University Press.

Ciprut, Marie-Andrée. 2014. Identité banian de la Caraïbe: formation, transformations et expansion dans les diversités. *Sens-Dessous* 13 (1): 35–48.

Cooper, Jasmine. 2020. *An End in Herself: Narratives of Non-Motherhood in Contemporary French Women's Writing.* Unpublished doctoral thesis:. University of Cambridge.

Daum, Meghan. 2015. Introduction. In *Selfish, Shallow, and Self-Absorbed: Sixteen Writers on the Decision Not to Have Kids*, ed. Meghan Daum, 1–10. New York: Picador Paperback.

Debest, Charlotte. 2014. *Le choix d'une vie sans enfant.* Rennes: Presses Universitaires de Rennes.

Donath, Orna. 2017. *Regretting Motherhood: A Study.* Berkeley, CA: North Atlantic Books.

Downing, Lisa. 2019. *Selfish Women.* Abingdon and New York: Taylor & Francis.

Dufourmantelle, Anne. 2013. *Puissance de la douceur.* Paris: Payot.

Gay, Amandine. 2021. *Une poupée en chocolat.* Paris: La Découverte.

Guenther, Lisa. 2006. *The Gift of the Other: Levinas and the Politics of Reproduction.* New York: SUNY Press.

Hantel, Max. 2013. Rhizomes and the Space of Translation: On Edouard Glissant's Spiral Retelling. *Small Axe* 17 (3): 100–112. https://doi.org/10.121 5/07990537-2378955.

Heti, Sheila. 2018. *Motherhood.* London: Harvill Sacker.

Le Cam, Morgane. 2023. Adoptions internationales en France: une étude révèle l'ampleur des dérives. *Le Monde*, February 9. https://www.lemonde.fr/international/article/2023/02/09/adoptions-internationales-en-france-un-rapport-choc-revele-l-ampleur-des-derives_6161090_3210.html. Accessed 21 May 2023.

Lewis, Sophie. 2018. 'Labour Does You': Might thinking through pregnancy as work help us radicalise the politics of care?. *New Socialist*, December 26. https://newsocialist.org.uk/labour-does-you-might-thinking-through-pregnancy-work-help-us-radicalise-politics-care/. Accessed 2 Feb 2021.

———. 2019. *Full Surrogacy Now.* London: Verso.

———. 2022. *Abolish the Family: A Manifesto for Care and Liberation.* London: Verso.

Lorde, Audre. 2017. Poetry Is Not a Luxury. In *Your Silence Will Not Protect You*, 7–11. London: Silver Press.

Mahase, Elisabeth. 2020. *Black Babies Are Less Likely to Die When Cared for By Black Doctors*. US study finds: *BMJ*. https://doi.org/10.1136/bmj.m3315.

McLemore, Monica R. 2019. To Prevent Women from Dying in Childbirth, First Stop Blaming Them. *Scientific American*, May 1, 2019. https://www.scientificamerican.com/article/to-prevent-women-from-dying-in-childbirth-first-stop-blaming-them/. Accessed 6 May 2019.

Preciado, Paul B. 2013. *Testo Junkie*. Trans. Bruce Benderson. New York: Feminist Press.

———. 2018. L'opération. Libération, November 2. https://www.liberation.fr/images/2018/11/02/l-operation_1689546/. Accessed 15 Jul 2020.

———. 2020. *An Apartment on Uranus*. Trans. Charlotte Mandell. London: Fitzcarraldo Editions.

———. 2021. *Can the Monster Speak*. Trans. Frank Wynne. London: Fitzcarraldo Editions.

Randone, Amanda. 2020. Black Mothers Are Five Times More Likely To Die During Childbirth. That Needs To Change. British Vogue, July 25. https://www.vogue.co.uk/beauty/article/black-maternal-mortality. Accessed 14 Sept 2020.

Rye, Gill. 2018. Mums or Dads? Lesbian Mothers in France. In *Motherhood in Literature and Culture: Interdisciplinary Perspectives*, ed. Emily Jeremiah, Adalgisa Giorgio, Abigail Lee Six, Victoria Browne, and Gill Rye, 98–110. New York and Abingdon: Routledge.

Sharpe, Christina. 2016a. *In the Wake: On Blackness and Being*. Durham, NC: Duke University Press.

———. 2016b. Lose Your Kin. *The New Enquiry*, November 16. https://thenewinquiry.com/lose-your-kin/. Accessed 21 May 2023.

Smith, Farrell, and Janet. 2005. A Child of One's Own: A Moral Assessment of Property Concepts in Adoption. In *Adoption Matters: Philosophical and Feminist Essays*, ed. Sally Haslanger and Charlotte Witt, 112–131. Ithaca NY: Cornell University Press.

Thomas, Stéphanie. 2022. *Mal de mères: Dix femmes racontent le regret d'être mère*. Paris: Points Documents.

CHAPTER 10

Choosing Childlessness: Familial and National Acts of Resistance in Preti Taneja's *We That Are Young* (2017)

Orlagh Woods

INTRODUCTION

Preti Taneja's debut novel *We That Are Young* (2017) adapts Shakespeare's *King Lear* to explore the entanglement of motherhood and nationhood in contemporary India. More specifically, the novel interrogates the cultural investment of the mother as bearer of future citizens that leads to the

This project has received funding from the European Union's Horizon 2020 research and innovation programme under grant agreement No 952366.

O. Woods (✉)
Maynooth University, Maynooth, Ireland
e-mail: Orlagh.Woods@mu.ie

© The Author(s) 2025   177
J. Björklund et al. (eds.), *Negotiating Non-Motherhood*,
Palgrave Macmillan Studies in Family and Intimate Life,
https://doi.org/10.1007/978-3-031-66697-1_10

conflation of the woman with the womb of the nation. Signe Hammer (1976) maintains that cultural investment in the motherhood ideal weighs heavily upon all women, whether they choose to have children or not: "Not all women become mothers, but all obviously are daughters, and daughters become mothers. Even daughters who never become mothers must confront the issues of motherhood, because the possibility and even the probability of motherhood remains" (xi). As a British-Indian writer, Taneja's work is responsive to the presiding cultural presence of Shakespeare in a post-colonial context, and the adaptation becomes a way to critically engage with her own ideological heritage.[1] While Taneja maps her plot almost directly onto *King Lear*, *We That Are Young* breaks from its Shakespearean urtext by presenting voluntary non-motherhood as means of covert resistance to the hetero-patriarchal structures of the nation, characterised and maternalised in the novel as the "motherland". In what follows, I explore the novel's family dynamics, the rights and memories of stories, especially maternal ones to demonstrate how *We That Are Young* revises its ur-text to contest cultural ideas of non-motherhood.

Before moving to the analysis of the novel, it is important to explore the dynamics of the play text it is adapting. The plot of *King Lear* is initiated by Lear's decision to divide his Kingdom between his three daughters: Goneril, Regan and Cordelia. To determine their individual inheritance, Lear demands that each of them articulate their devotion to him and this "love test" sets the paternalistic tone of the play. Indeed, although Shakespeare's *Lear* opens with a blunt conversation about Edmund's conception, there are no mother figures in the play, and no explanation of their absence. However, Coppélia Kahn (2011) productively reads the "maternal subtext" of the play as the imprint of the mother on the psyche of the characters (242). Kahn interprets Lear's particular obsession with his youngest daughter Cordelia and his longing for respite in her "kind nursery" (1.1.124) as evidence of his desire for a daughter-mother (2011, 248). Where Kahn argues that this maternal desire propels the drama, Janet Adelman's work (1992) suggests that the fantasy of *annihilating* maternal desire is at the heart of the play. Ultimately though, the fantasy of maternal "annihilation" is not realised

---

[1] Taneja elaborates: "Shakespeare is a big part of [UK] language and culture, so I always wanted to explore his legacy through an Indian lens. It was my way of examining colonial legacies in the Indian part of my story, of tracing how patterns of violence repeat in nations and families over time and see if fiction can address that" (Borges 2017).

in *Lear*, and the uncanny returns of the "mother" throughout the play force Lear to confront his vulnerability and the futility of absolute paternal power. Preti Taneja adopts and adapts this "maternal subtext" in *We That Are Young* to show how constructions of motherhood are transferred and translated in different socio-cultural spaces. In this way, *King Lear* as ur-text, via its relegation of the mother to the non-place, provides Taneja with the form and method to demonstrate the persistence of such relegation across time.

Partially set in the border town of Kashmir, the violent repercussions of partition reverberate throughout *We That Are Young*. Taneja's Lear analogue is Devraj, known affectionately by his children and the nation as "Bapuji", or "father figure". Devraj is the billionaire owner of a thriving conglomerate, who intends to divide the lion's share of his company between his three daughters: Gargi, Radha and Sita. The director of the Devraj group and Devraj's second in command is Ranjit. He and his son Jeet assume the supporting roles of Gloucester and Edgar, and the return of Ranjit's illegitimate son Jivan initiates the plot. When Devraj announces his retirement, his youngest and most beloved daughter Sita absconds, refusing her share in the business and her arranged marriage. Devraj's company is run predominantly by men, an arrangement established and maintained by the broader patriarchal system, one in which "mothers, alive or dead, [are] not mentioned" (21). Taneja depicts a world so patricentric that the girls' late mother is prohibited even from the linguistic space where she is confined in the original play text. Jivan solemnly informs Gargi: "After your mother died [...] my dad banned Jeet or me from talking about her. Bapuji's orders, apparently" (153). Devraj's authoritarian command of language is enhanced by the fact that he is the only character who speaks in the first person, and his rambling interjections throughout the novel reveal his intention to usurp the delicate unfolding of his daughters' stories with his own patriarchal narrative. Despite his attempts to suppress their mother's memory, each of the women long for their mother, seek out surrogates for her and variously perform her maternal role for one other. Taneja's exploration of the sisters' individual acts of resistance— Sita's refusal to marry, Radha's revenge on her abuser and, most importantly for this chapter, Gargi's decision *not* to become a mother—belie an awareness of and a refusal to perpetuate patricentric corporate and national systems. However, despite the sisters' individual forms of protest, Taneja prescribes an ending bleaker than Shakespeare's. Charged with the brutalities of twenty-first-century life, overbearing cultural (and perhaps literary) forces condemn Gargi, Radha and Sita to violent, untimely deaths, and the future is alarmingly male-oriented with Jeet poised to inherit the company and become "a pure leader of all men" (552). This desolate conclusion can be read as an indictment of a certain kind of neoliberal feminism that casts women as individually responsible for overcoming systemic barriers. In this regard, this chapter argues that the bleakness of Taneja's ending might productively be understood as a call to *collective* arms against the backdrop of rising nationalist regimes across Europe and South Asia.

"IT IS THEIR MOTHERLAND": MATERNALISING THE NATION

This section traces the development of the national emblem, Mother India, and the ways it is culturally maintained and reified. It demonstrates how Taneja's novel interrogates residual cultural commitments to this national ideal before exploring covert means of resistance later in the chapter. In nations that reify the mother figure, all women's identities are attached to the domain of mothering, whether or not they decide to have children. Before turning to the specifics of the novel, it is important to initially trace the development of the mother as a cultural figure in India as it emerged from colonial rule. Ania Loomba (1993) points out that throughout the Indian nationalist struggle, "tradition" and "modernity" as well as "India" and "the West" were being debated via the question of Indian womanhood" (272). *We That Are Young* provides a narrative space to explore points of divergence and intersection between the conceptual legacies of Western and Indian feminism. Taneja explores the ways femininity and specifically motherhood are co-opted by nationalist regimes as means to solidify homogenous ideas about nationhood *and* motherhood. Patrizia Albanese (2007) has pointed out that "pure and virtuous mothers are believed—and expected—to reproduce the nation in body (blood/children/future nationals) and mind (preservation of past traditions, food and ritual, and 'mother tongue', to name a few)" (830).[2] This expectation on daughters to perpetuate the nation can be traced back to Lear's supposition that his daughters will faithfully reproduce his kingdom and him through their sons and heirs who will, literally and symbolically, carry on Lear's legacy. Moreover, Albanese's claim is particularly relevant in an

[2] Albanese further argues that at times of historical crisis, women are "expected to give up/sacrifice their bodies and shut down their minds, desires, needs etc. to be and do 'motherhood', for the sake of the invisible, seemingly homogenised collective—the nation" (835).

Indian context. The gendered discourse of nationalism that characterised India's emergence from colonial rule crystallised the establishment of a maternalised nation.[3] Much like the ageing personification of Ireland, Kathleen Ni Houlihan, the spiritually sanctioned national personification, Bharat Mata, or, Mother India is a figure to be guarded by her brave sons. Anthropomorphising the nation in this way consolidates the idea of the nation and propagates an image of essential womanhood and motherhood that is then culturally integrated. It reifies a prescriptive, normative vision of motherhood that renders any behaviour outside its own limited boundaries deviant and potentially dangerous.[4] Accordingly, at the beginning of the twentieth century, the leader of India's independence movement, Lala Lajpat Rai sought to establish a separate, non-Westernised version of womanhood, predicated on "the superiority and sanctity of [women's] mother function" (Malhotra 1994, 47, citing Lajpat Rai). Lajpat Rai promoted a highly pronatalist narrative, declaring: "Every woman is a mother in embryo. That is her supreme function in life. That is her social mission" (Malhotra 1994, 47, citing Lajpat Rai). *We That Are Young* emphasises the legitimising function of narratives like this in the process of nation building.[5] The novel provokes important questions about which narratives, and indeed, *whose* narratives, are validated by the wider cultural audience.

As the only character written from the first-person perspective, Devraj's interjections are structured around the delivery of *his* story. The first line of Devraj's first chapter seeks to establish an intimacy between the character and the reader: "My name is Devraj. Mine is a simple story, come closer if you can" (58). The tyrannical preoccupation with his own legacy offers a fleeting opportunity for Devraj to evade his own death and map the future; it takes precedence over everything else, including the memory of his late wife. He plans to open a luxury hotel on the grounds where his

---

[3] For in depth explorations of the emergence of gendered nationalism in India, see Chaudhuri (1999, 113–133).

[4] In 2017, Delhi University students' group Pinjra Tod who marched with the slogan "Hum Bharat Ki Mata Nahi Banenge" ("We Won't Be the Mothers of India") were accused of being "anti-nationalist" (Gupta 2020, 86).

[5] Taneja has written on the importance of foregrounding women's stories that have been "silenced" by nationalist regimes: "I believe in collective unconscious and historical memory. I know that such trauma is passed to women through generations. It is in our blood, running silent, looping in our veins. These stories have been silenced by at least three nations, by racial and gender hierarchies" ("A King Lear Sutra" 340).

wife and father-in-law were brutally murdered in Srinagar, figuratively overwriting their murder with the narrative of his own corporate success. Just as Lear treats his daughters as his possessions: "*my* flesh, *my* blood, *my* daughter[s]" (2.2.410), and he resents any relationship outside this central filial bond, Devraj attempts to separate his daughters, supplant their sisterly bond and overwrite Sita's silence with *his* story: "Come down now, I ask it, but there is no reply. Don't you want to come? Answer me. No? Still refusing to speak? Fine, I said. Listen little bird, and I will tell you another story" (267). His seeming endearment "little bird" has darker undertones via its allusion to Lear's fantasy of his incarcerated reunion with Cordelia: "Come, let's away to prison. We two alone will sing like birds i'th'cage" (5.3.8–9). The earlier call to heed his story, a narrative interpellation of the reader, is shown to be a mechanism of control. The novel explores tensions that emerge when women seek out a life that is different from the stories that have been projected onto their bodies.

We That Are Young explores the enduring cultural currency of this notion and highlights the consequences of making the female body, to quote Judith Butler (1993), an "inscriptional space of [...] phallogocentrism, the specular surface which receives the marks of a masculine signifying act only to give back a false reflection" (39). Butler cautions against the ways masculine narratives are inscribed onto the bodies of women, and how female power that is defined within the bounds of masculine authority is nothing more than a reflection of masculine inscription. Lending credence to this, Devraj's elderly mother, Nanu appears to hold some power over him insofar as she influences his decision making, however this power is shown in the novel to be futile, as she cannot ultimately prevent the tragic course of events from unfolding. As the novel develops, Nanu's identity is revealed to be wholly dependent on and under the protection of her son. As per Butler's assertion, she is assigned limited power in the novel for working within the masculinist structures of the company and the wider society. She frequently and harshly chastises her granddaughters for their unwillingness to follow her path and obey their father's command. Disturbingly, the most insidious forms of patriarchal control are passed through the only mother figure in the novel, and Taneja suggests that this is a much broader issue by incorporating images of inscribed female bodies throughout. In the markets in Srinagar for example, Gargi observes "old women" whose "bodies [are] written with the stories that end in fire and tears" (188). Like these nameless women, Nanu allows her story to be written by Devraj, in exchange for some—albeit limited—power and influence. Taneja contrasts these older women whose bodies have already been "inscribed" by masculinist rhetoric with the three younger female protagonists, to highlight the ways they attempt to write their own stories.

As the novel progresses, the façade of an elderly man recounting his "simple story" starts to falter and Devraj's alternative agenda becomes increasingly clear: "A statesman [...] understands the power of repeating, until his stories transcend to the level of mantra and myth, become the truth of what has passed, a blueprint for the future" (267). Towards the end of the novel, Devraj's deteriorating health means he is no longer able to differentiate his daughter and his mother: "He does not recognise (Sita) at all, and calls her Nanu instead" (480). Cordelia-like, Sita is forced to assume a mothering role for her father and nurse him through his illness. While Devraj "set[s] [his] rest/On her kind nursery" (1.1.123–4), the physical signs of sickness on his body create a corporeal cartography in Sita's mind: "Trying not to look at his body, she sees instead a crumpled map. She does not want to read it, but she has to. Now the tributaries of his veins swell blue beneath his skin then fade as if running dry" (466). Sita's cartographic reading of her father's body evokes Lear's "Give me the map there" (1.1.36), that initiates the disbursement of the kingdom to his daughters, revealing the play's "cartographic consciousness" as Valerie Traub describes it (2009, 43). As Traub elaborates, *King Lear* "participates in cultural logics that developed out of the material and conceptual interaction of anatomical illustrations of the human body and representations of human figures on maps" (45). Maps and bodies, and especially women's bodies, are objects for Lear to read and express dominion over. Lear's relentless desire to delimit geographical boundaries with his map is appropriated in the novel by Sita being forced to read the territory of her father's fading body. Laura Mulvey (1975) argues that within patriarchal culture, the woman remains "tied to her place as bearer of meaning, not maker of meaning" (7). As such, the maternalised land in *Lear* requires a masculine cartographic signature to delimit its boundaries and "mak[e] meaning". In a powerful inversion, through her reading of the father's feeble body, Sita becomes the maker of meaning just as Taneja asserts her right to (re)make via adaptation.

While the representation of Devraj's ailing body as a "crumpled" map signifies his waning influence on corporate and familial affairs, he attempts to consolidate his legacy by passing down stories to his cadre of riotous young businessmen, known collectively as Devraj's Hundred. The novel's call back to Lear's retinue of knights serves to ensure that the masculine narrative takes precedence even when women occupy positions of power within the Company. When Gargi temporarily assumes the Directorial role in Devraj's absence, she observes during a meeting with three independent directors of the Devraj group, that while "they are Serious Men—each of them with his story […] all [she] see[s] is the same face, repeated" (181). The men morph into a homogenised figure in Gargi's mind, solidifying the suffocating reach of her father's narrative legacy. Gargi's attempts to claim her own narrative are stifled by her "sense that someone […] might be writing *her* story, too, with a sure hand towards the promised end—she had never been sure she wanted that end at all" (129–30). There is metafictional dimension to Gargi's covert desire to write her own story, and write back to dominant patriarchal narratives that echoes Taneja's own re-writing of *Lear* and her assertion of validity in doing so. The pervasiveness of this homogenised patrilineal narrative that Devraj calls the "blueprint for the future" underscores the vital importance of matrilineal counter narratives (267).

Correspondingly, both Radha and Sita look to Gargi as the eldest sister to bequeath an alternative story that validates their experiences. Gargi's remembers "the feeling of Sita as a toddler […] sleepy heavy. Story, story, story she had wanted. She had always wanted" (210). Much later in the novel, when Radha discovers that she is pregnant, she turns to Gargi for comfort: "All she wants is to be told stories; stories from their mother, stories, stories, stories until she falls asleep" (534). At moments of vulnerability, the sisters long to reconnect with their lost mother; a reconnection that is only available through the oral histories passed down by their eldest sister. The mother here is not only remembered but proliferated through her association with storytelling. As such, Sita's attempts to resolve her mother's absence are revealed by her commitment to "excavat[e], debat[e] and discuss […] her own mother's history" which can also be read as the history of the nation, a history that, in turn, the novel suggests is comprised of many stories, many versions (131). Within a family and a broader social system where men control the narrative, Sita's desire to "excavate" her mother's identity by revising her history affirms Adrienne Rich's focus on revising inherited mythology to recover and reclaim overlooked female (hi)stories.[6] The metafictional dimension of the novel is itself enacting

[6] Rich posits, "until we can understand the assumptions in which we are drenched we cannot know ourselves. And this drive to self-knowledge, for woman, is more than a search for identity: it is part of her refusal of the self-destructiveness of male-dominated society" (1972, 18).

Sita's maternal excavation via Taneja's own unearthed authorial voice. Taneja writes: "As I wrote I became more conscious of trying to excavate my own authorial voice through years of conditioning and silencing by cultures in two homelands" (2022, 338). While the two younger sisters seek out their mother via storytelling, Gargi's most powerful evocation of her mother is through music: "[her] own mother sang her this lullaby [...] Gargi stands, tears sliding down her cheeks [...] There is comfort here, a dissolving language of sounds she cannot let herself recall" (167). Gargi's somatic response to her mother's lullaby, and the temporary relief of the dissolution of the language that has been so powerfully co-opted by masculinist, nationalist regimes, implies the possibility an alternative route, though music, to the maternal realm.

"Herself to Herself": Embracing Non-Motherhood

This section explores Taneja's depiction of patriarchal influence on women's fertility before considering the significance of Gargi's decision not to have children against the backdrop of a highly pronatalist society. The family is presented as the space where women's bodies are most scrupulously monitored and controlled and the investment in Gargi's fertility in particular is in part informed by the patrilineal desire to carry on Devraj's name. *We That Are Young* explores the myriad ways female bodies function as "material and discursive sites where nation [is] performed, values [are] contested, and borders and boundaries [are] policed and controlled" (Oza 2006, 80). Throughout the twenty-first century, technological innovation has opened up new avenues for "polic[ing]" and "control[ing]" bodies. In *We That Are Young*, Taneja employs technology to exacerbate Lear's scrutinous male gaze that is disturbingly concentrated on his daughters' sexual organs: "Beneath is all the fiends'; there's hell, there's darkness,/There's the sulphurous pit, burning, scalding,/Stench, consumption! Fie, fie, fie! Pah! Pah!" (4.6.123–25). Taneja signals the omnipresence of technology in the lives of the characters by introducing the three sisters in the novel as they are being watched on CCTV by Jivan and "half a dozen young men [who] sit tapping at the screens, faces backlit, flickering" (39). Through the plate glass of Devraj's security screens, Jivan treats the women's bodies as spectacles for him to consume, conflating them with the mediated, abstracted image of the female sexual ideal: "It's Radha! [...] In a stiff candy colored dupatta, over a low-necked pink kameez. It should be vulgar, but she looks like those flowers on the vine outside, fragile,

delicate, promising" (40). The women in the novel live in a world of per-
petual male surveillance; in Foucauldian terms, they operate like inmates
in a patriarchal Panopticon, in an induced "state of conscious and permanent visibility" (Foucault 1977, 201).

The advent of new reproductive technologies, particularly 4-D scan-
ning, has externalised the internal, making the womb an accessible space
for surveillance and control. Taneja evokes this sense of being intimately
monitored when Gargi feels like her own corporeal boundaries are being
breached by the men in the company, who seem strangely invested in her
reproductive capacity: "All the men in the room stare at her belly, as if just
by looking they can see through her skin to her womb and could plant a
seed in there" (207). Shame is an emotion that individualises and silences,
drives self-assessment and fosters desire to hide the self, and *We That Are
Young* interrogates shame as one of the most powerful tools of patriarchy.
Gargi explains the gendered onus on purity from the earliest point of her
development through to menstruation practices and the maintenance of
virginity until marriage: "[D]id your mother use the word 'sharam' to
you? Of course not, why would she? We girls are stalked by shame from
the moment we are born. We try to escape it. Then we are caught" (96).
From early adolescence, Gargi recalls the extent to which her reproductive
potential was monitored: "Through her puberty and into her marriage,
the cyclical weeks of the month when Nanu inspected her bed sheets? Her
clothes, her bras, her panties, each size change mulled over and measured"
(131). This habitual body monitoring is internalised by Gargi from a
young age, and she grows accustomed to a form of forensic self-monitoring
of her own body that becomes subject to constant revision and critique.

As the eldest daughter, Gargi is most heavily scrutinised for her childlessness. She reveals that her loveless arranged marriage to her husband
Surrendra has been a topic of public enquiry since their engagement: "The
excited, pre-wedding—*how many do you want?*—became, after Surrendra—
are you eating right, are you pleasing him, are you trying every month?—
then—*something is wrong. Here is the doctor*" (130). These lines of
questioning underscore that childbearing is the highest criterion of success
in her marriage, and, of particular frustration to the highly organised
Gargi, they patronisingly imply that she cannot be trusted to effectively
'manage' her own body. These invasive enquires are exacerbated when
Gargi assumes the directorial role of the Company in her father's absence.
A national magazine interviews Gargi about her new role and during the
interview, Gargi tries to evade questions pertaining to her fertility by

presenting herself as 'mother' of the business. When asked about employee numbers, Gargi responds: "You want numbers? No, it's not nice to talk about people in those terms. I prefer to think of us as one big happy family [...] I have a thousand children to look after" (148). While she uses language that accentuates her maternal capacity, the journalist is unsatisfied and pushes her to address her own fertility: "And yet no babies of your own?" (148). Taneja thus demonstrates how women's bodies, along with the choices they make, come to be public domain. As such, while the article lauds Gargi's business acumen, it is her fertility that makes the headline: "*Meet Mrs. Devraj Grover, a woman guarding the top: a dynamo dedicated to her country's growth, to her family and to the Company, hoping one day for a family of her own*" (149). The pernicious implication of this strange public interest in Gargi's reproductive capacity is that motherhood is not only the ultimate expression of successful marriage, but also successful femininity.

In response to Gargi's promotion, which Devraj reads as evidence of her disloyalty, he criticises her chances of succeeding in business by attacking her fertility, enhancing the disturbing sentiment that unruly women are unfit to bear children that is echoed throughout Shakespeare: "You are the one whose name is evil, the one who lies with disease upon your womb, who kills the embryo as it settles, as it rests, as it sets, who wishes to kill it before it is born [...] if you think you are going to be the great Mother of my whole company, you are wrong. You cannot be a mother to anyone" (209). The shift from Gargi being pressured to conceive by any means necessary to her father's explicit condemnation of her inability to mother 'anyone' underscores the patriarchal impetus not only on mothering but on so-called good mothering. As an ambitious career woman, determined to move up the company ladder, Gargi is perceived as fundamentally selfish, incapable of conceiving and caring for a child. Moreover, Devraj blames Gargi for her failure to conceive, and his conflation of her reproductive potential and the capitalist continuity of his business highlights his more generalised fear of the generative potential of matriarchal structure. The threat of female sexuality outside of procreation is regarded by Devraj throughout the novel with complete derision. Lear's reference to the "sulphureous pit" becomes Devraj's explicitly sexualised allusion to "the lips you hide between your legs, waiting to suck a man dry" (295). He denounces female liberation only as far as it disrupts patrilineal power structures, and in so doing he, like Lear, reifies his daughters' power over him as his sole means of transmitting his wealth to future generations.

Lending credence to this, early in the novel, Devraj usurps his daughters' biological capacity by declaring: "More than a woman, a man bears a child" (63), thus reducing the maternal body to a tool of masculine creation. As successful as his Company is, Devraj's only chance to 'live on', is exclusively through his daughters and their willingness to procreate which makes Gargi's decision not to have children all the more powerful. When Gargi sees herself reflected in a mirrored ceiling, she compares her naked body to "a mud flat—riddled with pale dried rivulets of stretch marks; the earth photographed from the air" (170). Gargi's identification with a "dried" mud flat subverts traditional associations between the fertile, regenerative earth and the female body and foreshadows her refusal to have children; "*Sex is for making babies* [...] *You have it, and them. They can inherit this earth. I don't want a single one*" (171). Her environmentally conscious decision not to procreate is fuelled in part by Devraj's exploitative corporate system of greed that stifles any sense of planetary responsibility.

While voluntary non-motherhood has garnered more visibility in Western context(s) in the twenty-first century, Amrita Nandy (2018) argues that "in highly pronatalist India, [voluntarily childless women] are rare, objectionable and therefore closeted" (2). As such, when a romantic relationship develops between Radha and Jivan, she attempts to quell his burgeoning interest in Gargi by telling him: "Gargi doesn't want children. Did you know that? I mean, how could she not?" (305). Her disbelief reflects broader cultural attitudes to motherhood as the fullest expression of femininity. By taking action to prevent herself becoming pregnant and producing a child to inherit Devraj's corrupt legacy, Gargi effectively removes herself from the phallocratic system: "Every three months she went to the dermatologist—a kind man, the best—who prescribed her the Pill (for her acne, of course)" (212). Gargi's covert procurement of contraception can be read in the context of the novel and the play text as a form of resistance to masculinist nationalist expectations, a going against unavailable to Cordelia for example. As a public figure, "It is a matter of national concern it seems, whether or not Gargi conceives" (207), so her decision is both personal and political. In *No Future,* Lee Edelman (2004) explores the extent to which political visions of the future hinge upon "the Imaginary form of the Child" (14). Edelman's work proposes a queer subversion of this child-centred futurism but crucially, Edelman adopts an expansive definition queerness that "names the side of those not 'fighting for the children', the side outside the consensus by which all politics confirms the absolute value of reproductive futurism" (3). Edelman coins the term 'sinthomosexual' to describe one who resists the seemingly irresistible social ethic of childbearing. As a heterosexual woman of childbearing age, Gargi can be understood as voluntary sinthomosexual. Even more radically, she refuses biological motherhood from the position of already performing mother-work for her younger sisters and also within the Company. Sara Ruddick (1995) defines this "mother-work" as "a kind of caring labour" that champions the value of domestic labour (19–21). Gargi, as the eldest sister, steps into the mothering role for her younger sisters at a young age and demonstrates her proficiency in mother-work: "Sita was only ten months old. She needed feeding [...] [Gargi] spooned food into her sister's mouth. Then went to check Radha was ready for school" (154). Ruddick's important conceptualisation of mothering as *practice* allows for more expansive definitions of motherhood that transcend biological determinism.

While Gargi performs the mothering role within her family and the company, in the bleak thematics of *We That Are Young*, she is simultaneously a daughter without a mother and a mother without a daughter and punished accordingly. The novel oscillates between traditional and contemporary expressions of gender within Indian culture, tracing a shift from the patrilineal 'dowry' system and towards the trappings of neoliberal feminism. *We That Are Young*, in its resolute focus on the three sisters, Gargi, Radha and Sita, born into markedly different generations of feminist thinking, emphasises how certain patterns of shame prove to be stubbornly long-lived. By envisioning Gargi and Radha as highly skilled, professional working women in the public eye, they are expected to embody the right balance of domestic and professional traits and condemned by their family and the nation if they fail. Moreover, by depicting the sisters as exceptionally wealthy and relatively influential, Taneja can explore the *perception* of female empowerment within the confinement of existing patriarchal matrix. Gargi and Radha's attempts to "lean in" to the professional sphere and self-regulate their personal lives are ultimately futile because they are consistently subject to criticism centred on their weight, appearance, sexuality and fertility.[7] This aspect of the novel reverberates with more recent iterations of neoliberal feminism that centre around the notion of "choice". Catherine

[7] Former Facebook COO Sheryl Sandberg's Lean In (2013) has been widely criticised for ignoring the reality of intersectionality and systemic obstacles that women face in the workplace.

Rottenberg observes that neoliberal feminism of this kind "maintain[s] a discourse of reproduction and care work while at the same time ensuring that all responsibility for these forms of labour [...] falls squarely on the shoulders of so-called aspirational women" (quoted in Banet-Weiser et al. 2020, 7). Accordingly, the burden of care work in the novel falls squarely on Gargi's shoulders, as she is expected to assume the mothering role for her younger sisters immediately after their mother's passing: "*Gargi, you are so dedicated, you will heal her.* What would their mother have done? This only. And so Gargi did it too" (160). Similarly, Gargi's attempt to put an end to Devraj's raucous weekly Company parties leads Nanu to accuse Gargi of "trying to replace [his] mother [...] instead of bearing [her] children [herself]" (207). For this reason, Gargi's decision to procure contraception is perhaps best characterised as voluntary *childlessness*, rather than voluntary non-motherhood, because she, like all women within this neoliberal ideological structure, is expected to shoulder the burden of emotional labour and care-work within the family and broader social structure.

Gargi's refusal to procreate fundamentally undermines her father's legacy-building project on a micro level and more broadly serves as a refusal to perpetuate the hetero-patriarchal structures of the nation. She also decides to cease her sexual relationship with Surrendra "even if they were the last married couple left at the end of time. With no mother and no child, she would be, simply, sister to her sisters. Herself to herself" (212). By opting for childlessness, Gargi thus confronts what Sarah Rainey (2013) has called "the final female taboo" in a highly pronatalist society. Despite the pervasiveness of what she calls 'mater-normativity', in North India, Amrita Nandy uncovers a range of "maternal outliers" who offer alternatives to patriarchal models of mothering and caregiving (136). By writing the character of Devraj's mother into the narrative, who enables and at times encourages her son's deplorable behaviour, Taneja creates a template of matriarchal power that can only be achieved vicariously through the son, that none of the younger women in the novel want to emulate. Taneja's portrayal of the ruthless and vindictive Nanu echoes Shakespeare's Volumnia, aptly described by Maria Álvarez Faedo (2002) as a mother "who has deliberately avoided open displays of feminine affection in order to make her son a better warrior" (29). *Coriolanus* becomes another facilitating text for the novel, implying that in order to thrive within this deeply patriarchal system, women must acclimate to the cruelty it engenders. In her refusal to perpetuate these cycles of subordination, Gargi represents a "maternal outlier". While she cannot undo her own arranged marriage, she wills her younger sister to push back against hetero-patriarchal pressure at an earlier age: "She hoped, fiercely, that Sita would come back and show them what women can really be. She hoped Sita had taken a lover, found more pleasure with him that she, Gargi, ever did in the marriage bed" (538–9). Following in Gargi's footsteps, Sita exercises her own form non-compliance by refusing to marry "until the law changes for the rights of women, and all are protected, from eyes, from the streets, from brothers, uncles, from husbands" (267). Sita's altruism is powerfully set against her father's insatiable greed, and her specific commitment to 'protect' women from "brothers, uncles [and] husbands" underscores that misogyny is perpetuated along the masculine lines of the family network. In this sense, we might read the sisters' acts of resistance: Radha's blinding of her uncle and abuser, Sita's refusal to accept her chosen husband, and most especially Gargi's unwillingness to become pregnant and carry on her father's toxic legacy, as protests against the most powerful harbingers of misogyny in their lives; uncle, husband and father.

Conclusion

In the foreword to *May We Borrow Your Country* (2019), Taneja criticises two-dimensional representations of South Asian women in mainstream Western media, typically stereotyped as "docile, servile, perfect daughters, sisters, brides and mothers: sensual not sexual, good for nothing but to be handmaids to patriarchy by making sons" (3). *We That Are Young* probes and challenges these superficial portrayals in its depiction of deeply complex female characters. Taneja characterises the three sisters to draw out and critique archetypal representations of women as whores, saints and crones. Despite this, the three sisters are nonetheless burdened by the literary heritage of their analogues. Lear's evil, "pelican daughters" Goneril and Regan and the template for dutiful daughterhood, Cordelia, provide idealised benchmarks that none of the women in Taneja's novel can reach (3.4.73). Moreover, by associating the Cordelia figure with the Hindu goddess Sita, celebrated throughout India for her purity and sacrifice, Taneja interrogates the ways these figures transcend the realm of literary and mythic significance and enter the culture as templates of appropriate femininity and/or motherhood.[8] Despite Sita's Cambridge education and relative freedoms, Taneja prescribes her an ending more tragic than Shakespeare's when Jivan conspires to trap her in a building in Srinagar. Inside, Devraj's pathological ramblings culminate in his command to have her killed: "Punj thought her beautiful, I could tell. He lifted her like a bridegroom but she struggled like a cat. What claws! No, no, Sita, I said, do not struggle. Punj just wants to help you fly and he is right, she is a beautiful bird. See how she spreads! Do not let her squawk!" (514). The description of Sita's murder signals the extent of Devraj's mental deterioration: "Heave! Dangle dangle […] See how she dances in the breeze? She looked so pretty, like a beautiful chandelier" (516). Curiously, in her final moment in the novel, she is uncannily animate in Devraj's perspective: "She looked down at me, wide-eyed, bulging tongue. Breasts drooping, legs bare, mouth gaping, no sound" (517). Even in death, she is all too corporeal—"bulging […] drooping […] gaping"—and refuses to occupy the spectral space where she might be eternally "pretty […] like beautiful chandelier" in her father's mind.

Taneja's disturbing portrayal of Sita's death is totally at odds to John Everett Millais' immortalisation of arguably the most recognisable female death in Shakespeare, in which Ophelia's porcelain skin and tranquil expression can be read as part of a long cultural tradition of representing the "beautiful dead girl", a figure who, according to Alice Bolin (2018), serves as "a neutral arena to work out male problems" (19). Powerfully resisting this trope, Sita's final expression, devoid of speech, is anything but beautiful. In a subversion of Lear hunching over Cordelia's lifeless body, Sita is positioned high above Devraj, looking down upon him, terrifying and vengeful. Adaptations such as Taneja's further highlight the challenge of remembering Shakespeare—what norms and privileging do we repeat, for instance, and to what extent might we remember the plays differently or more capaciously. Culminating in the violent and permanent silencing of Sita in the novel's final pages, Taneja explores the limits of female speech within the confines of heteropatriarchal societies. Devraj's conviction that *Everyone knows my story* (544) captures precisely why adapted Shakespeares are so important; they carve out spaces for alternative readings that highlight forgotten or overlooked maternal stories.

[8]As recently as 2012, a judge in Bombay high court told a woman unwilling to live with her husband that: "A wife should be like Goddess Sita who left everything and followed her husband Lord Ram into the forest and stayed there for 14 years" (quoted in Lodhia 2015, 406).

Taneja utilises the novel form to stress the importance of Arundhati Roy's (2020) claim that: "There's really no such thing as the 'voiceless'. There are only the deliberately silenced, or the preferably unheard". *We That Are Young*, in its exploration of Gargi's voluntary childlessness, privileges a narrative that is commonly and "preferably unheard" in India and the wider world.

Jasodhara Bagchi (2016) underscores the pervasiveness of motherhood in contemporary Indian culture: "Feminist understanding of motherhood has been central to the unfolding of Indian society from the moment of insertion into the global capitalist system through the colonizing process to the present day, when it is directly under the thumb of a market-driven neo-liberal regime of globalization" (xxvi). *We That Are Young* confronts this hegemonic mode of motherhood and the way(s) it is culturally and religiously reified in contemporary India. Through her nuanced characterisation of the three sisters, Taneja interrogates the persistence of what Amrita Nandy calls "mater-normativity" in a contemporary Indian context. The novel sheds light on the variety of reasons women might choose not to have children, and it positions voluntary non-motherhood as covert means of resistance within a suffocating hetero-patriarchal society. Moreover, the novel emphasises the extent to which, to borrow from Patrizia Albanese (2007), "one need not look long and hard, nor look into 'the deep past', nor point fingers at (or invade) this or that 'fundamentalist regime' to find examples of the archaizing and re-patriarchalizing tendencies found within nationalism" (828). An academic and activist, Taneja draws on her experience as a human rights reporter in her striking exploration of 'new India'.[9] Her novel is infused with elements of feminist dystopia and can be read as a powerful indictment of neoliberal feminism that promotes a certain kind of visibility, but ultimately stifles female collective action by promoting individual acts of resistance in the face of systemic violence and oppression.

There is a palpable desire by the youngest characters in the novel to return to the mother's place and by extension the mother's body. The Banyan tree is characterised in the novel as a potential portal to the

---

[9] Taneja explicitly addressed the political motivation for the novel in "A King Lear Sutra": "Fascism's resurgence is global and that means we cannot rest: if race and nation are the fault lines, women and women of colour, and minorities are ever more at risk, ever more to be the target of incendiary rhetoric, discriminatory policy, unaccountable, state-endorsed violence" (347).

characters' past lives. Jivan fantasises that the Banyan tree might provide a portal for him to "find his way" back to his childhood home, "where he was a boy with a mother and a brother and some kind of father sometimes" (56). The tree as metaphor for branches of family is a familiar one, but the sentence structure here further suggests Jivan's own privileging of matrilineal lines; the father is an added, conditional thought. His desire to return to his childhood home and his mother through the portal of the Banyan tree is mirrored towards the end of the novel when Sita seeks "to find her mother's house—and [...] see her sisters again" (471). While *We That Are Young* does not reintroduce a mother-figure directly, the sisters look to one another for 'stories' of their mother that roots them within a close sisterly bond, and they reach for one another in moments of crisis, "[Sita's] heart wants Gargi and Radha: her hands need to hold theirs" (501). In this regard, *We That Are Young* might be read as a subversive sister text. Though the death of the three sisters is a bleak indictment of patriarchal capitalist regimes, Gargi's final moments in the novel underscore that Devraj's manipulative desire to drive his daughters away from one another, to stifle their sorority, has failed: "Gargi thinks of her sisters standing tall around a table. She wants to be with them. She must help Sita. She trembles on the ledge. She thinks of her mother running somewhere through these streets [...] Sita and Radha and her mother are waiting. She reaches her hands towards the fire" (549). While the opportunity for maternal reconnection cannot be realised in the novel's bleak thematics, the glimmer of hope, for Taneja, "lies just beyond the text, in the reader's hands" (Anjum 2017). Taneja's desolate ending can be read as a call for forms of collective resistance; of a kind the three sisters were ultimately prevented from enacting. The novel is responsive to Cordelia's final words in the play, specifically her impetus for Lear, consumed by narcissism, to see others beyond himself. The novel implores its readership to "see these daughters and these sisters" and to see them with new eyes. Gargi, Radha and Sita's unwillingness to be "handmaids to patriarchy" to borrow Taneja's term, can be read via their refusal to inherit, marry and bear children. Taneja's novel serves to shed light on the pernicious grasp tradition still holds on women in contemporary Indian society and points out that in cultures where mothering is co-opted by nationalist or corporatist rhetoric, women are relegated to vessels for future industrious citizens and prevented from mothering, or indeed in many cases, living, on their own terms.

REFERENCES

Adelman, Janet. 1992. *Suffocating Mothers: Fantasies of Maternal Origin in Shakespeare's Plays: Hamlet to The Tempest.* London: Routledge.

Albanese, Patrizia. 2007. Territorializing Motherhood: Motherhood and Reproductive Rights in Nationalist Sentiment and Practise. In *Maternal Theory Essential Readings*, ed. Andrea O'Reilly, 828–841. Ontario: Demeter Press.

Álvarez Faedo, Maria. 2002. Re-visions of Volumnia's Motherhood. *Revista alicantina de estudios ingleses* 14: 23–37. https://doi.org/10.14198/raei.2002.15.02

Anjum, Nawaid. 2017. Preti Taneja: A Gaze at World's Darkness. *The Punch Magazine*, December 31. thepunchmagazine.com/the-byword/interviews/preti-taneja-a-gaze-at-world-amp-rsquo-s-darkness. Accessed 1 Sept 2023

Bagchi, Jasodhara. 2016. *Interrogating Motherhood: Theorizing Feminism.* Sage Publications.

Banet-Weiser, Sarah, Rosalind Gill, and Catherine Rottenberg. 2020. Postfeminism, Popular Feminism and Neoliberal Feminism? Sarah Banet-Weider, Rosalind Gill and Catherine Rottenberg in Conversation. *Feminist Theory* 21 (1): 3–24. https://doi.org/10.1177/1464700119842555.

Bolin, Alice. 2018. *Dead Girls: Essays on Surviving an American Obsession.* Harper Collins.

Borges, Jane. 2017. King Lear and I Are Old Friends, Says Writer Preti Taneja. Mid-Day, November 12. www.mid-day.com/amp/sunday-mid-day/article/king-lear-and-i-are-old-friends-says-writer-preti-taneja-18730186. Accessed 22 Sept 2023.

Butler, Judith. 1993. *Bodies That Matter: On the Discursive Limits of Sex.* Routledge.

Chaudhuri, Maitrayee. 1999. Gender in the Making of the Indian Nation-State. *Sociological Bulletin* 48 (1–2): 113–133. https://doi.org/10.1177/0038022919990107.

Edelman, Lee. 2004. *No Future: Queer Theory and the Death Drive.* Duke University Press.

Foucault, Michel. 1977. *Discipline and Punish: The Birth of the Prison.* Trans. A. Sheridan. Vintage.

Gupta, Paridhi. 2020. Art(s) of Visibility: Resistance and Reclamation of University Students by Women Students in Delhi. *Gender, Place & Culture* 27 (1): 86–103. https://doi.org/10.1080/0966369X.2019.1586652.

Hammer, Signe. 1976. *Daughters and Mothers: Mothers and Daughters.* Signet.

Kahn, Coppélia. 2011. The Absent Mother in King Lear. In *Critical Insights: King Lear*, ed. Jay L. Halio, 239–262. Salem Press.

Lodhia, Sharmila. 2015. Deconstructing Sita's Blues: Questions of Misrepresentation, Cultural Property and Feminist Critique in Nina Paley's Ramayana. *Feminist Studies* 41 (2): 371–408.

Loomba, Ania. 1993. Tangled Histories: Indian Feminism and Anglo-American Feminist Criticism. *Tusla Studies in Women's Literature* 12 (2): 271–278.

Malhotra, Anshu. 1994. 'Every Woman Is a Mother in Embryo': Lala Lajpat Rai and Indian Womanhood. *Social Scientist* 22 (1–2): 40–63.

Mulvey, Laura. 1975. Visual Pleasure and Narrative Cinema. *Screen* 16 (3): 6–18.

Nandy, Amrita. 2018. *Motherhood and Choice. Uncommon Mothers, Childfree Women*. University of Chicago Press.

O'Reilly, Andrea. 2009. 'I Envision a Future in Which Maternal Thinkers are Respected and Self-Respecting': The Legacy of Sara Ruddick's *Maternal Thinking*. *Women's Studies Quarterly* 37 (3–4): 295–298.

Oza, Rupal. 2006. *The Making of Neoliberal India: Neoliberalism, Gender and the Paradoxes of Globalization*. London: Routledge.

Rainey, Sarah. 2013. Helen Mirren Confronts the Final Female Taboo. *The Telegraph*, February 4. www.telegraph.co.uk/women/womens-life/9847642/Helen-Mirren-confronts-the-final-female-taboo.html. Accessed 1 Sept 2023.

Rich, Adrienne. 1972. When We Dead Awaken: Writing as Re-Vision. *College English* 34 (1): 18–30.

Roy, Arundhati. 2020. *Azadi: Freedom, Fascism, Fiction*. Penguin.

Ruddick, Sara. 1995. *Maternal Thinking: Towards a Politics of Peace*. Beacon Press.

Taneja, Preti. 2022. A King Lear Sutra. *The Arden Research Handbook of Shakespeare and Adaptation*, eds. Diana E. Henderson and Stephen O'Neill, 334–351. The Arden Shakespeare.

CHAPTER 11

Voluntary Childlessness in the Spanish Graphic Novel: Irene Olmo's *No quiero ser mamá* (2020)

Mercedes Carbayo-Abengózar

INTRODUCTION

Irene Olmo's *No quiero ser mamá* ('I do not want to have children') tells the story of a woman who chooses not to become a mother and how she reaches this decision. The cover artwork (Fig. 11.1) presents the protagonist in a friendly style: an almost child-like drawing simulating a manga character, with big, dark eyes, thick dark hair, rosy cheeks, and a red shirt,

This project has received funding from the European Union's Horizon 2020 research and innovation programme under grant agreement No 952366.

M. Carbayo-Abengózar (✉)
Maynooth University, Maynooth, Ireland
e-mail: mercedes.abengozar@mu.ie

© The Author(s) 2025
J. Björklund et al. (eds.), *Negotiating Non-Motherhood*,
Palgrave Macmillan Studies in Family and Intimate Life,
https://doi.org/10.1007/978-3-031-66697-1_11

197

Fig. 11.1   Cover of Irene Olmo's book

framed by a green/aquamarine background and surrounded by bright flowers. While the cover is visually endearing and cute, it is deeply meaningful and socially provocative in Spain, a country that suffered under a repressive Catholic dictatorship in the twentieth century. This dictatorship restricted women's experiences to those of marriage and motherhood.

Voluntary childlessness, abortion, and teenage or unmarried pregnancies signified noncompliance with normative moral codes and were heavily punished, sometimes with child removal from the mother as recent research has shown.[1] *No quiero ser mamá* (2020) (*NQSM* further in the text) is a graphic novel that explores the process of deciding not to be a mother and is illustrative of the recent turn in critical attention to the issue of non-motherhood, enabled and encouraged by what Leticia Blanco (2022) has called a "literary boom about other ways of being a mother"[2] in her review of Diana Oliver's book *Maternidades precarias* ('Precarious maternities', 2022).

NQSM is a bildungsroman that narrates, over the course of approximately hundred pages, the story of an unnamed Spanish woman from the present through the prism of autographic memoir. Living in the aftermath of a fundamentalist Catholic dictatorship, the protagonist struggles to conform with a society that expects her to become a mother. In this graphic novel, Olmo introduces a new visual language, a narrative drawing about motherhood that breaks with the repressive silence in Spain regarding women's desire not to be mothers. Graphic novels are hybrid forms that share features with other media but utilise them in a unique way. Drawing styles, combinations of words and visuals, the use of panels, and various page layouts are combined to create powerful stories, which is precisely what Olmo does here to communicate the full experience of voluntary non-motherhood. The key aim of this chapter is to examine how this graphic novel places the reader inside the quasi-taboo experience of a woman who voluntarily chooses non-motherhood, drawing the reader's attention to her feelings and sense of self leading up to and following this decision. Olmo utilises the graphic narrative to convey the protagonist's attempts to navigate social situations and spatial environments as she

---

[1] Research about the lost children of Francoism has been extensive and published mainly under the auspices of the Association for the Recovery of Historical Memory funded in 2000 with a wide media cover. This research shows how women labelled as 'bad mothers' had their children adopted at birth so that they may be raised by 'good mothers'. In Spain, such decisions were made by the *Patronato de Protección a la mujer* ('Women's Protection Centre'), a network of centres established by religious orders in 1941 and headed by Franco's wife as honorary president. Women who were identified as noncompliant with gender norms were usually sent to these centres by their families or authorities, although there were also cases of self-internment as revealed by the writer and activist Consuelo García del Cid Guerra in her book *Las desterradas hijas de Eva* ('The Exiled Eva's Daughters', 2012)

[2] All translations from Spanish in this chapter are my own.

struggles between society's expectations of women and mothers and her own, and Olmo invites us as readers to recognise the significant gap between expectation and reality in contemporary Spain.

Before analysing the text itself, it is fundamental that we understand the importance of taking graphic novels into consideration when trying to understand Olmo's subversive stance as non-mother. Graphic novels have "a peculiar relation to expressing life stories" (Chute 2011, 108) for their reliance on space to represent time. The space is made up of presences (the frames) and absences (the white spaces in between) where readers fill in the gaps looking for meaning and causes. As narrative form graphic novels have the ability to "spatially juxtapose (and overlay) past and present and future moments on the page" (Chute 2008, 453). As we will see, Olmo's narrative takes us from her past to her present and invites us to also visualise her imagined future. By the same token, for the Spanish writer Terenci Moix, graphic novels are comics that develop a unique theme following the structure of the bourgeois novel, even in the psychological development of the characters (2007, 108). The graphic novel resists the juvenile element of comics to create a denser and thematically wider adult form, and it is perhaps for its association with juvenile literature that the critical apparatus for graphic narrative from a literary perspective is relatively recent, despite the popularity of graphic narratives like Art Spiegelman's *Maus* (1991), Joe Sacco's *Palestine* (1996), Marjane Satrapi's *Persépolis* (2000), Alison Bechdel's *Fun Home* (2006), or Power Paola's *Virus Tropical* (2011).

In this chapter we will see how Olmo exploits the spatial and psychological potential of the graphic novel form to disrupt norms around motherhood in Spain and to open up alternative pathways for women whereby they can assert agency over how they themselves wish to live. The chapter is divided in three sections that discuss the relationship between femininity and motherhood, the issue of free choice and the creation of new spaces for non-mothers.

FEMININITY AND MOTHERHOOD

In this section we will discuss Olmo's innovative silence-breaking perspective on non-motherhood with a focus on the subjective experience of that choice. In the opening pages of *NQSM*, the novel interrogates the culturally engrained connection between femininity and motherhood. In the first three pages of Chapter 1, entitled *Juegos de niñas* ('Girls' games'), the story commences with a six-year-old girl introducing herself and playing 'house' with her sisters. Along with their dolls, they perform the nurturing routines learnt in the home: providing food (by pretending to breastfeed them), taking care of bodily functions (by pretending to change a nappy), and managing behaviours (by putting them to bed). They also pretend they are pregnant by putting a cushion under their shirts and discussing their imagined pregnancies in such a way that reveals their child-like ignorance about the reality of it: "I am already 14 months pregnant", "and I am 23 months", "I think I am ready to have my navel pulled" (Olmo 2020, 6). These games might easily be recognised as an ordinary activity for young girls, but Olmo intends to interrogate the supposed 'ordinariness' of these games. For her, the game serves as a kind of ideological training that shows motherhood as an acquired performance that works against the possibility of non-motherhood and claims that motherhood is essential to women (diQuinzio, 1999). For diQuinzio, essential motherhood "construes women's motherhood as natural and inevitable" (xiii). In the following two pages, when the sisters have grown up, they still imagine their future naturally and inevitably as mothers. These pages, with a simple background, white bubbles (oval for conversations, in a star-shape to express anger and with dots to show thoughts), position the graphic novel as working against entrenched notions of innate maternal instinct by presenting motherhood as a social construction.

This social construction of motherhood continues beyond childhood games and becomes evident in various pressures to be a mother, but only when motherhood happens in a 'legitimate', or essentialist way. The protagonist tells us that her idealised maternal play and her ideas about the importance of giving birth were questioned by two incidents; a debate about abortion in school and the fact that her friend María became pregnant. María's isolation, victimisation, and rejection, and the comments of her classmates (she was a *"puta"* and a *"guarra"* ('slut') (Olmo 2020, 11)) signals a swift departure from the idealised 'happy moms' of their childhood games.

On page 9 (Fig. 11.2), Olmo changes the visual structure of the page from the six equally sized vignettes with mainly white backgrounds to two vignettes at the top of the page, with white backgrounds that show comments of teenagers at the school playground about early pregnancy: "People say that Saray has fallen". Olmo contrasts these vignettes with three dark vignettes below of different sizes and wavy borders that represent the protagonist's thoughts and imagination. The left-hand side of the

Fig. 11.2   Page 9 of *No quiero ser mamá*

page shows the girl falling into a dark space with an expression of horror on her face. As she falls, we see her losing her Walkman and headphones that represent her leisure, entertainment, and possibly even her youth and encountering skulls, worms, and bones, symbolising darkness, loneliness, decay, and death. In the imagination of the protagonist, unplanned pregnancy is equated with a kind of social death that exiles her from her wider social sphere, represented at the top of the page with white vignettes. On the right-hand side, we have two equally sized superposed images, both framed by black backgrounds and wavy borders. Their spatial settings, one wide-open but lonely and barren, the other enclosed and empty, unadorned, with a spot of outdoor light on the floor to emphasise the woman's prison-like confinement and separation from light, depict what ostracism means from an individual and experiential point of view. Ostracism here is also marked visually by body language: the sweaty fatigue of working a field alone, the slouching in the middle of the couch which itself, because it was designed to be shared, subtly accentuates her isolation. The clothes, hair, and bodies of these characters are represented as having lost the femininity that characterised the figures in previous images; they are dressed in either working clothes or religious attire. The cross on the wall beside the couch mirrors the cross in the window bars (repeated on the floor) and suggests that Olmo has configured the internal space to evoke a chapel, a religious retreat, that reminds us of the religious orders who remove children from the non-normative mothers as mentioned above. Olmo places one of the images above the other and makes them similar in size, tone, and shape so that it feels that we are looking at mental images that belong to the protagonist, as if Olmo wants to present the images as part of the protagonist's imagination. With these similarities and their proximity to one another, Olmo invites us to compare them, to see them as variations of a theme: different ways of experiencing misery in isolation. It presents two different ways to imagine the misery of isolation that normative culture wants women to fear as a consequence for not being a mother in the right way, or not being a mother at all.

The second occasion in the story when the protagonists encounter pregnancy as a patriarchal trap, that is, one that encourages little girls to perform and desire motherhood and ostracises them when they become mothers outside the normative patriarchal system, is at university. The protagonist meets Mireia, another variation of María, the ultimate benchmark of idealised, perfect motherhood. Mireia is a pregnant engineering student who dreams of becoming a pilot. Mireia tells her friends about her

personal journey, her family's initial rejection of her pregnancy, their eventual acceptance, and her firm decision to carry on studying after giving
birth. However, it is soon revealed that Mireia left university a month
later. This discovery makes the protagonist wonder: "what kind of mother
Mireia would become after that sacrifice" (32).

Once again, we are invited to enter the protagonist's thoughts and
worries that are made visual for us on the page. The page is divided into
the three usual parts (see Fig. 11.3). The top part has three vignettes. In
the first one Mireia appears clearly in the centre, pregnant and wearing a
green dress against a red background. The second vignette shows her
image fading as she begins to lose sight of her dream of becoming a pilot,
and in the last vignette she has almost completely disappeared along with
her dream. Interestingly, in this final image, Mireia's dress has turned red,
and blends in with the background. In the second section, placed just
underneath the first, we see the inverse process. In contrast to the steady
fading of Mireia, this protagonist initially appears within a fading green
backdrop that increases in intensity to reach a clear image while she says
she never considered becoming a mother. As she never considered that
possibility, red has faded, and her desires and thoughts are highlighted in
green. To support this, she is surrounded by green fish-like creatures that
appeared before in the story and will return later as a representation of her
consciousness or rationale. In this sequence, the protagonist is holding a
paintbrush suggesting the protagonist's agency as she is the one who
chooses the colour on the page. The use of colour is very meaningful in
the novel, although the palette is limited to those used on the front cover:
red, a primary colour, to represent biology and fluids but also the social
construction of motherhood attached to it, and green, a secondary colour
that represents the protagonist's thoughts, experiences, desires, and hopes.
Both colours interact and blend throughout the story, suggesting the difficulty of distinguishing what we want from what we are. In this way,
diQuinzio's (1999) words regarding essential motherhood constructed as
natural and inevitable are contested by giving motherhood the red colour,
associated with biology but not with nature that appears in green. We see
this clearly in the final vignette of this series. Mireia is drowning in a red
kind of see being swelled by her biology with the last bit of her green dress
disappearing beneath the solemn caption: "She would not only bury who
she was, but who she wanted to be" (Olmo 2020, 32). The combination
of image and text here also underscores the troubling endurance of De
Beauvoir's claim that motherhood keeps women enslaved to immanence,

Fig. 11.3 Page 32 from *No quiero ser mamá*

depriving them of the possibility of transcendence (quoted in Bettagglio 2020: 216).

In another book with the same title *No quiero ser mamá* ('I do not want to be a mother') (2021), by the Chilean psychologist and writer Liza Alejandra Toro Soto, the author explores the decision-making process of motherhood with women from different backgrounds interviewed online during the COVID-19 pandemic. Toro Soto (2021) emphasises the universal importance of the study by stating that "one of the very few things that are fundamental in every woman's adult life is the relationship with motherhood whether it happens not" (127). Equally, the Spanish journalist and writer María Fernández Miranda in *No madres. Mujeres sin hijos contra los tópicos* ('No-mothers. Childless women against clichés', 2017) explores the issue of non-motherhood in Spain by interviewing women in the public eye who made the decision not to become mothers and the difficulties they experienced in arriving at and maintaining this decision. While these qualitative studies do the very important work of narrativising the lived experiences of women, the graphic narrative of *NQSM* has the unique ability to show *and* tell; Olmo's work encourages us to think about the contentious issue of motherhood from a personal and imaginative perspective, making the narrative more compelling to a certain extent and also more accessible. Other graphic narratives that have appeared in recent years illustrate journeys into motherhood and the maternal experience (Bettagglio 2020, 212) in part by drawing on other forms of communication like blogs, maternal chronicles, novels, movies, or intertextual associations like *Malas madres*. For example, Henar Álvarez's *La mala leche* ('The bad milk' or 'bad temper', 2020) explores sexuality and motherhood from a feminist perspective. As a comedian, Álvarez uses humour to discuss insecurities and fears surrounding sexuality after giving birth. Similarly, Raquel Riba Rossy criticises society through her famous character Lola Vendetta. She talks about the invisibility of women and the issue of motherhood in *¿Qué pacha mama?* ('Hey mum', 2018) where Lola explains the process of becoming independent and validating her mother. However, despite the foregrounding of maternal experiences in these texts, the issue of deciding to become a mother or not constitutes relatively unexplored territory in graphic narratives. In *Materniyá. Cuando la naturaleza te pisa los talones* ('Maternity already? When nature is at your heels', 2021), Marta Piedra recounts in a humorous tone the adventures of Greta Vinagreta who evaluates the pros and cons of becoming pregnant with her brain, Ce, and her uterus, Gina. In this text, however, the struggle to decide between brain and uterus does not present a solution as the last vignette shows Greta with the pregnancy test in her hand, and Ce and Gina expecting an answer. Equally, Raquel Córcoles (aka Moderna de Pueblo) discusses, in one of her daily Instagram strips, the reasons for women not to become mothers, such as precocity, anti-natalism, infertility, single-motherhood, or *tocofobia* which she describes as "irrational fear about something happening to the baby, fear that something goes wrong during the pregnancy". Among these narratives, Olmo's approach to the issue of motherhood stands out as it shows the process as a subjective experience, drawing attention to the specific conjunctions of visual and verbal texts in autobiography (Whitlock 2006, 966), and visually arranging the relationships of the protagonist with other people in social situations and spatial environments. Unlike Marta Piedra who seems to present a very strict either-or choice between brain and uterus, Olmo's blending and combining of colour suggest her embrace of that which is ambiguous, taking a both/and rather than an either/or approach.

The Decision, a Free Choice?

In the previous section we have traced the protagonist's efforts to subvert the link between femininity and motherhood. At the end of Chapter 2, we see the protagonist appearing in green colours while Mireia fades in red. The differing levels of clarity of these images, paired with the distinct use of colour, suggest that the protagonist sees herself as a woman but not so much as a mother. This seems to imply that the protagonist has reached a freely made choice, but in this section, we will interrogate the attitudes of Spanish people towards the idea of free choice with regard to motherhood. The protagonist's experience will reveal that maternal free choice is compromised in Spain due to cultural expectations of women and the isolation that women experience when they fail to meet these expectations. This is another important insight that Olmo brings to our attention through her graphic novel. In this section we will examine the concept and the challenge of free choice as it relates to the protagonist and her encounters with other people. Similar to the previous chapter, certain elements of fantasy start to emerge as we are invited to enter her imagination and feelings. Chapter 3, entitled "Un tiempo para cada cosa" ('Everything at a time'), starts with the protagonist trying to establish herself professionally. Very soon, the fish-like creatures re-appear, this time combining both colours to remind her that her biological clock is ticking. On page 37, we see a horrified protagonist running away from her green fish in quite a humorous scene. We see humour coming into play as part of her imagination, something that is going to increasingly appear in the next pages. The use of humour has a long tradition in Spanish graphic narratives by women starting with Núria Pompeia (1931–2016), whose foundational work inspired a wave of women's graphic work in Spain. She adapted the humoristic comic style previously colonised by male artists by strategically utilising a minimal, almost child-like technique which did not incite suspicion in spite of its important vindicating content. Like Pompeia, Olmo uses a child-like drawing style to convey a provocative socio-political message. However, for Olmo, humour is more related to the role of fantasy and imagination in her novel. Page 45 presents the reader with a portrait of the protagonist with closed eyes in the centre. Around her, four vignettes with wavy edges imagine her in the future as a mother. Through the use of humour, we see an exhausted and angry woman at different moments of the children's upbringing, including a vignette with an obnoxious teenager: "the more I imagine the time passing, I could not see the positive side of it" (Olmo 2020, 45). Interestingly, the fourth vignette acknowledges the potential for positive interaction between mother and child although the mother in the image does not look like the dark-haired protagonist, but like Mireia: blond and dressed in green. On this page, we see Marianne Hirsch's (2004) concept of "biocularity" at play, or the capacity that comics and vignettes have to bring together verbal and visual elements in the same text so we can "read images as words and words as images" (1212). We also clearly see how Olmo situates the reader at the centre of the protagonist's experience of emotions. The only way she can envision a positive future as a mother is to think outside of herself, placing another woman, a surrogate mother figure, in her own place. This idea of her as non-mother in the imagined future is supported with the first and only inclusion of a name: Irene, as if the protagonist has become a surrogate of the author at this point.

As the protagonist struggles to visualise positive moments as a mother, she decides to ask other women about their motherhood experiences. We see the usual structure of six vignettes per page, when twelve different women make positive statements about the reasons for becoming a mother, reasons that resemble those that she has heard before in social and family gatherings. This journey frames the protagonist as "a killjoy" (Ahmed 2010, 50–88). For Sarah Ahmed, the image of the happy housewife, which could also apply to a happy mother, is "a fantasy figure that erases the signs of labour under the sign of happiness" (50). For her, the claim that women's happiness is behind the work they do rather than being a product of nature, law or duty is "an expression of collective wish and desire" (50). By analysing *Émile* by Rousseau (1762), Ahmed focuses on the figure of Sophy who is educated to be a good wife, to "keep happiness in the house" (55). Sophie can only be happy if she makes her parents happy regardless of what she wants: "the daughter has the duty to reproduce the form of the family, which means taking up the cause of parental happiness as her own" (58). Everybody around the protagonist of *NQSM* wants her to be happy by becoming a mother, but it is in fact their own desire as for them happiness comes with motherhood. As Ahmed asserts, the history of feminism is a history of "women who refuse to become Sophy by refusing to allow other people's goods, or by refusing to make others happy" (60). As we will see later, the protagonist's feminist readings help her to make her final decision, but for now, she becomes a troublemaker because she gets in the way of the happiness of her friends and family. Like Maggie Tulliver, in George Elliot's *The Mill on the Floss* (1860), the protagonist of *NQSM* gets into trouble with her desire to live a childfree life. According to Ahmed, the association between imagination and trouble is powerful because it teaches us how the happiness duty for women is about the narrowing of horizons, as it happened with Mireia, about giving up an interest in what lies beyond the familiar (61). This is one of the most striking points of *NQSM,* as it provides us access to the imaginative process of the protagonist to see how she imagines a different life for herself.

As a troublemaker, the protagonist becomes a feminist killjoy as she "kills" the happiness of others by disturbing the assumption that motherhood equals happiness. We see this very clearly on pages 64 to 71 when she is accused of being a sad and selfish person because she does not agree that the path (or the only path) to happiness for women is motherhood. One of her friends says that "a life without children is incomplete, they give sense to women's lives" (Olmo 2020, 66); while another one states that having children "is an act of generosity that on top makes a woman grow up as a person" (67). The protagonist becomes increasingly angry, disturbing the peace by showing that these stereotypes are wrongly projected onto non-mothers, and that free choice does not exist: "I could also give an opinion and judge your decision to become parents, but I do not. I respect it. Please, respect mine fucking hell" (71). The protagonist becomes uneasy and difficult to be with. As Ahmed states, the protagonist shows that although the happiness of those with children makes her happy, her happiness by not having them makes others unhappy. Her parents, her grandparents, and her friends want her to have a child that would make them happy even if she does not share in that happiness. They project their own assumptions and desires on to her, and experience disappointment when she expresses herself in any way that is at odds with their idealised projection, demonstrating how these constructed cultural ideals are socially policed and maintained. She is represented as a troublemaker because she violates the fragile conditions of peace.

These tensions that make her tired of being questioned and that leave her with a sense of being bullied, attacked, isolated and unhappy drive her to turn into herself and dialogue with her own body. In a foetal position, swimming in an imagined kind of red sea, tied up by what seems to be internal organs (Olmo 2020, 50), the author shows us once again how colour articulates the protagonist's relationship with her own body. There are no greens here, only a red pool where she floats while asking important questions: "am I less of a woman for not wanting children? ", "am I defective for feeling that way"? "Why if my destiny is to conceive, my mind says the opposite?" (50).

This dialogue moves to a fantastic imaginative level when the protagonist makes her final decision of not to become a mother (51) [Fig. 11.4]. Appearing naked in the centre of the page, eyes closed and floating upwards in the red bloody background, she breaks the biological ties that hold her, and in a close shot of her face that looks at the reader with big open eyes, makes the statement: "no quiero ser mamá".

The protagonist's final attempt to validate her decision is by reaching out to other women to hear their views on the prospect of motherhood. This shows how Olmo takes good care to impress readers with a sense of the protagonist's experience of the hollowness of the neoliberal idea of 'choice' as it pertains to the question of mothering. Catherine Rottenberg (2020) discusses the importance of reproduction in the neoliberal ideology: "maintaining reproduction as part of middle-class or so-called aspirational women's normative trajectory and positing balance as its normative frame and ultimate ideal, neoliberal feminism helps to maintain a discourse of reproduction and care work while at the same time ensuring that all responsibility for these forms of labour—but not necessarily all of the labour itself—falls squarely on the shoulders of so-called aspirational women" (7).

Our middle-class, white, heteronormative protagonist struggles to reconcile her own private, personal choice with the aspirational women's

Fig. 11.4 Page 52 from *No quiero ser mamá*

normative trajectory, hence her isolation. So far, we have only partially glimpsed the isolating effects of the protagonist's decision to assume the position of non-motherhood. In the next section, we will trace the additional layers of isolation that Olmo adds to the experience, and we will explore how *No quiero ser mamá* also reveals a positive and profoundly liberating dimension to the protagonist's social exclusion.

ISOLATION AND NEW COLLECTIVITY

In this section, we will discuss how Olmo uses the graphic narrative form to express some quite powerful points about non-motherhood, namely that even when the isolation seems absolute, there is a hidden reality wherein voluntarily childless women can find community, self-acceptance, freedom, and even alternate forms of fertile life. We will see how Olmo's graphic narrative works against the culture of invisibility by taking on the risk of representation (Chute and DeKoven 2006, 772). Chapter 5, entitled "Una isla en un océano" ('An island in an ocean'), exemplifies the protagonist's relationships with others in social gatherings. At this stage of her life, most of her friends have created a heteronormative family unit, and she feels alone, like an island in the middle of the ocean of families with children. We meet her partner, who has sporadically appeared before, socialising with her. In the first vignette, she steps out of the domestic, heteronormative space of her friend's house where actual or aspirational mothers are having what she feels are seemingly endless conversations about children, pregnancies, education and behaviours, and heads towards the garden where men gather around the barbecue to talk about sports. This shows a clear, gendered division of space but interestingly, it seems that is not just that women who occupy and dominate the interior, domestic spaces, but it is specifically mothers. Her femininity alone is not enough to grant her access to this maternal space. To get access, she would have to feign interest in the conversations about children, pregnancies, etc. and she is unwilling to do that, so she feels, in her own words, like an alien.

She feels odd, *rara* ('weird', 'odd', 'queer'), a concept developed by Carmen Martín Gaite in her essay *Desde la ventana* ('From the window', 1987). Martín Gaite bases her concept on Andrea, the main character of Carmen Laforet's (2010) novel *Nada* ('Nothing', 1945), a pioneering figure of the non-conformist woman who "questions the normality of amatory and domestic behaviour that (francoist) society ordered to comply with" (Gaite 1987, 99). In *NQSM*, on their way home from the social event described above, the protagonist tries to establish a dialogue with her partner, questioning the role of motherhood and the illusion of equality. In her view, women's education is still based on domesticity, alluding to Rottenberg's claim that all responsibility for forms of reproductive labour falls on women and to the main argument of Rousseau's *Émile* about the importance of education to maintain social order. In her unwillingness to shoulder these responsibilities, she feels like a troublemaker, a killjoy, and *a chica rara*, totally isolated, even more so when she realises that her partner has fallen asleep mid-conversation. Incapable of sleep herself, she decides to watch television, but she does not find any comfort there either as there is not a single channel where the story does not involve women with children: "and when they did not have them, the roles they represented were of women with serious mental health problems, unbalanced, cold, manipulative and heartless" (Olmo 2020, 93). On this page, we clearly see how graphic narratives express with images what words cannot. Building on Moix's claim about the benefits of the comic genre, the advantage of the graphic novel is that the image dethrones the primacy of the text. The graphic novel creates and maintains a democratising balance between visual and literary that confronts traditional ideas of literary superiority. We see what happens before we read it. On this page, we see a sequence of images against a green background with the word "zap" in the middle, alternating between images of childless women who either are drug addicts or self-harm. Before the black vignette that shows the switching off the television, we see a cute family of lions, alluding to the natural/biological/primal nature of motherhood. The very last vignette of this chapter shows the protagonist completely alone, in the enclosed space of her bed, next to a snoring partner, feeling angry, sad, unable to sleep, and wondering: "Is it so difficult to represent a happy woman without children?" (94). The choice to present popular culture as sympathetic to or even supportive of mainstream attitudes towards motherhood could be a metafictional reflection of Olmos's own use of graphic novel to explore the experience of non-motherhood. By exposing popular culture's misrepresentations of childless women, *No quiero ser mamá* implies the author's self-awareness in her choice of medium and audience. Through the frustration of the protagonist, Olmo accentuates the need for more positive images of childless women in popular culture.

In Chapter 6, entitled *Otros planetas* ('Other Planets'), Olmo's fantastic, imaginative style is fully implemented. Olmo uses imaginative elements to visualise the protagonist's fantasies. For example, we saw in Section 1 the protagonist imagining a dark future for women who become pregnant outside of patriarchal norms. In Section 2, the imaginative elements appear as she delves into herself and initiates a conversation with her own body in relation to the decision not to become a mother. So, while elements of fantasy emerge sporadically in the early chapters of the novel, it is in this section when those elements are fully developed. The first page of this chapter is a one-page vignette of a barren, dark planet where the protagonist is naked inside a bubble that resembles a kind of protective womb against the threatening troglodytes outside the bubble who are trying to attack her with children in their arms. Recalling Ahmed's words, the protagonist feels that her decision to remain childfree is perceived as an attack on other people's happiness. She kills that happiness by disturbing the assumption that fulfilment is achieved exclusively through becoming a mother. We then see her rising up from that planet of threatening normative patriarchal motherhood and flying away in search of other isolated bubbles of women who think like her. She discovers that there are more *chicas raras* like her *no estaba sola. Había más bichos raros* ('I was not alone, there were other weird creatures') (99) and they start connecting with each other. These connections are fostered by her feminist readings of de Beauvoir, Corinne Maier, and Élisabeth Badinter (100). She draws excerpts from each theorist to illustrate the process of making the bubble and allowing fresh water inside. The space inside the bubble becomes increasingly bigger until the bubble finally bursts, allowing her to swim into a free space, which can be interpreted as a re-birth and/or a moment of liberation: "Suddenly everything made sense and the conscious of how women are pressurized to be mothers liberated me" (104).

Once the bubble is finally burst, the black background turns into green/aquamarine water where she freely swims. Once again, colours are part of the narrative. Red has disappeared and the use of the colour of water reminds us of the unhelpful association of biology and nature, of femininity and motherhood.

Using a similar page structure of Fig. 11.2, where a terrified young woman falls inside a dark, barren place, here [Fig. 11.5] we see the protagonist in the left-hand side of the page naked falling into clear water, unafraid and finally liberated. On the right-hand side of the page, three equally sized vignettes show no barren space, no enclosed rooms but a protagonist who gradually looks at us with big open eyes of surprise as she realises how the social construction of motherhood has influenced society: "From that moment I was aware of that manipulation, and could leave my resentment, my fear to disappoint and my guilt behind" (104).

On page 105 [Fig. 11.6], the protagonist slowly emerges from the water: "And a new feeling of peace and safety [...] emerged from that

Fig. 11.5 Page 103 of *No quiero ser mamá*

Fig. 11.6 Page 105 from *No quiero ser mamá*

conscience", having grown an alligator's tale: "I still felt from a different planet but now I liked it". As Martín Gaite suggested, *chicas raras* "dare to be off pitch, to install themselves on the margins and think from there, they are women conscious of their exceptionality and who will live it with a mixture of helplessness and pride" (100). Those feelings are part of her fantasy, a fantasy that continues to develop both on the level of the worlds she imagines (the space and the bubbles) and at a personal level with the growing of an alligator tale. Her association with the powerful creature represents her re-birth and re-imagining but also her newfound embrace of hybridity. The choice of an alligator, a water and land-based reptile with the ability to re-grow its tail, may suggest that she has acquired a regenerative ability that does not centre on producing babies. From this point on, we see the protagonist moving through a range of new environments in the last four pages of the novel. She embraces a fertile space full of vegetation, fauna, cascades, and art where she proclaims a new hope for her life, suggesting that fecundity and creativity do not lie exclusively in motherhood.

Conclusion

It is only recently that non-motherhood has received some attention from scholars and writers in Spain. We have already mentioned two interesting graphic publications about deciding to become a mother or not: *Materniyá* (2021) and the work of Moderna de Pueblo in her daily Instagram strips. However, there is little international awareness of Spanish-language graphic novels about childlessness since comics and scholarly work on graphic narratives are limited in terms of visibility beyond Spanish borders (Magnussen 2018, 2). The last vignette of Moderna de Pueblo's strip about non-motherhood is of important relevance here as it summarises some of the points made in *No quiero ser mamá*. The vignette shows a group of eight women, only one of them with a baby. At the top of the drawing, highlighted in black, it reads: "**Women have not stopped having children because of feminist ideas**", and then, highlighted in red: "but it has helped us to reach peace if we cannot or we do not want to". Moderna de Pueblo, as a writer and illustrator, creates her own stories. The fact that she chooses to highlight both sentences underscores the importance of feminist awareness in making the decision, something that the protagonist of NQSM acknowledges also in the novel.

Unlike Moderna's format, *No quiero ser mamá* is an autographic, self-reflective graphic novel that blends high and mass forms of artistic production (Chute 2011, 354). It has the potential to be more culturally impactful than other forms of engagement with the issue of voluntary non-motherhood and this is due to several important factors. First and foremost, the graphic novel is more publicly accessible with a more immediate appeal. The visual elements of the form appeal to younger generations or "digital natives" who are arguably more comfortable with and accustomed to processing visual information. Olmo chooses the graphic novel as a popular form to discuss the issue of non-motherhood, perhaps due to her awareness of popular culture's misrepresentations of childfree women. Verbal prose, such as scholarship, essays, or novels, struggles to make the same kind contribution as the graphic novel because it does not speak a visual language that can place the reader in memorable spaces of psychological struggle and transcendence. *No quiero ser mamá* shows us the value that the graphic narrative can have in guiding audiences' minds out of regressive notions of compulsory motherhood and towards liberating possibilities like finding fecundity beyond it. Olmo seems to use this autographic form to present herself as a popular storyteller and to open a venue to express vital issues in a non-traditional way, with visuals upfront.

Ultimately, Olmo uses her graphic novel as a feminist tool to explore the choice of voluntary childlessness. As Chute observes, "Some of today's most riveting feminist cultural production is in the form of accessible yet edgy graphic narratives" (2010, 2). *NQSM* responds to social attitudes towards motherhood and non-motherhood that have emerged from repressive regimes and culturally sanctified religious ideologies. The text makes overt references to Catholicism like the cross on the wall, window, and floor. Moreover, the two characters that become pregnant are named with variations of Mary, the ultimate benchmark of idealised, perfect motherhood. Reminders of Mary are everywhere and serve as painful reminders of women own shortcomings as mothers or non-mothers; reminders that are even encoded in the characters' identity and sense of self (via their name). Graphic humour became an important tool during Franco's regime as it was used to criticise the many contradictions of the time (Martín Gaite 1994, 74), and young women's comics (*TBOs*) were very important because they were the only way of permitting unsupervised reading by the Regime: "Before you read a book consult your priest" as it states in n. 224 of the women's comic *Mis chicas* (Ramírez 1975, 38). Contemporary Spanish graphic novels carry the weight of this repressive legacy, but they are simultaneously charged with the potential for transgression. Thus, Olmo's decision to utilise the graphic novel form can itself be interpreted as a political statement, part of a well-established, subversive female tradition that is sure to resonate with Spanish reader-ship. *NQSM* helps us to understand the emotional and psychological jour-ney from being a killjoy and a troublemaker to exceptionality. Olmo's graphic powers have worked to light up the path of the protagonist, a path where she does not only need to do things, but also to think and imagine in order to get to her destination. The protagonist, that at times appears as a surrogate for the author, turns herself into a subject of representation by mapping her development through childhood/girlhood, adolescence, and adulthood. This chapter has demonstrated how this textual and visual mapping creates new discursive spaces in which the naturalisation of moth-erhood can be challenged, the silence surrounding this experience can be broken, the importance of claiming a non-maternal identity outside socially prescribed moulds can be fully appreciated. *NQSM* ultimately demonstrates how non-motherhood can be imbued with the potential for enlightenment, community, self-realisation, and exceptionality.

REFERENCES

Ahmed, Sarah. 2010. *The Promise of Happiness*. Duke University Press.
Álvarez, Henar. 2020. *La mala leche*. Barcelona: Planeta.
Bechdel, Alison. 2006. *Fun home. A Family Tragicomic*. London: Jonathan Cape.
Betagglio, Marina. 2020. Maternal Life Writing in Contemporary Spanish Graphic Narratives: From Blog to Book. In *Spanish Graphic Narratives. Recent Developments in Sequential Art*, ed. Colin McKinney and David Ritchter, 211–233. London: Palgrave.
Blanco, Leticia. 2022. La cara oscura de la maternidad sale a la luz. El Mundo, 19 July. https://www.elmundo.es/cultura/literatura/2022/07/19/62d578a72 1efa044618bef96.html. Accessed 24 Jan 2023.
Chute, Hillary. 2008. Comics as Literature? Reading Graphic Narrative. *PMLA* 123 (2): 452–465.
———. 2010. *Graphic Women*. New York: Columbia University Press.
———. 2011. Form and Narrating Lives. *Profession*: 107–117.
Chute, Hillary, and Marianne DeKoven. 2006. Introduction. *Graphic Narrative*. *MFS Modern Fiction Studies* 52 (4): 767–782. https://doi.org/10.1353/ mfs.2007.0002.
diQuinzio, Patrice. 1999. *The Impossibility of Motherhood: Feminism, Individualism and the Problem of Mothering*. New York: Routledge.
Fernández Miranda, María. 2017. *No madres. Mujeres in hijos contra los tópicos*. Barcelona: Penguin Random House.
García del Cid Guerra, Consuelo. 2012. *Las desterradas hijas de Eva*. Algón: Granada.

Hirsch, Marianne. 2004. Editor's Column. Collateral Damage. *PMLA* 119: 1209–1215.

Laforet, Carmen. 2010. *Nada*. Barcelona: Destino.

Magnussen, Anne. 2018. Introduction. *European Comic Art* 11 (1): 1–7. https://doi.org/10.3167/eca.2018.110101.

Martín Gaite, Carmen. 1987. *Desde la ventana. Enfoque femenino de la literatura española*. 2nd ed. Madrid: Espasa-Calpe.

———. 1994. *Usos amorosos de la postguerra española*. Barcelona: Anagrama.

McKinney, Colin, and David Richter, eds. 2020. *Spanish Graphic Narratives. Recent Developments in Sequential Art*. London: Palgrave.

Moix, Terenci. 2007. *Historia social del comic*. Barcelona: Bruguera.

Oliver, Diana. 2022. *Maternidades precarias*. Barcelona: Arpa.

Olmo, Irene. 2020. *No quiero ser mamá*. Barcelona: Bang.

Piedra, Marta. 2021. *¿Materniyá? Cuando la naturaleza te pisa los talones*. Barcelona: Planeta.

Power, Paola. 2011. *Virus Tropical*. Random House Mondadori.

Ramírez, Juan Antonio. 1975. *El "comic" femenino en España*. Madrid: Cuadernos para el Diálogo.

Riba Rossy, Raquel. 2018. *¿Qué pacha, mama?* Barcelona: Penguin Random House.

Toro Soto, Liza Alejandra. 2021. *No quiero ser mamá*. Digital edition. Independently Published.

Whitlock, Gillian. 2006. Autographics: The Seeing "I" of the Comics. *Modern Fiction Studies* 52 (4): 965–979.

CHAPTER 12

Adapting (to) Non-Motherhood: Ulrike Kofler's Film *What We Wanted* (2020)

Valerie Heffernan

In 2020, Ulrike Kofler's debut film *What We Wanted* (Kofler 2020a) was chosen as Austria's submission for the Academy Award for Best International Feature Film.[1] Though the film was not ultimately nominated for the prestigious prize, its submission nevertheless marks a defining moment in European cinema. Kofler's film foregrounds the problem of involuntary childlessness and non-motherhood and sheds light on the profound grief and distress that the inability to conceive can cause for a

[1] The original German title of Kofler's film is *Was wir wollten* (Kofler 2020a).

This project has received funding from the European Union's Horizon 2020 research and innovation programme under grant agreement No 952366.

V. Heffernan (✉)
Maynooth University, Maynooth, Ireland
e-mail: valerie.heffernan@mu.ie

© The Author(s) 2025   221
J. Björklund et al. (eds.), *Negotiating Non-Motherhood*,
Palgrave Macmillan Studies in Family and Intimate Life,
https://doi.org/10.1007/978-3-031-66697-1_12

couple. The pain of infertility is not often the subject of filmic representation, and certainly not in mainstream cinema. The fact that Kofler's feature film was selected to be put forward for consideration for this prestigious international award demonstrates the extent to which involuntary childlessness is increasingly seen as an important social issue that is worthy of public attention and discussion.

The screenplay for the film, which was written by Kofler and Austrian producer Sandra Bohle in collaboration with Austrian director and screenwriter Marie Kreutzer, is based on a short story by Swiss writer Peter Stamm entitled "The Natural Way of Things".[2] In many ways, the plotline of the Kofler's film remains the same as that of Stamm's short story: Niklas and Alice are a childless couple whose tranquil holiday is disrupted by the arrival of the family next door, whose boisterous interaction gets under their skin and ultimately causes them to question their relationship and the choices they have made about children. However, as this chapter will show, Kofler's film builds on and departs from Stamm's narrative in some interesting ways. In particular, I argue here that in adapting Stamm's short story for the big screen, Kofler places particular emphasis on non-motherhood. She also amplifies an ambivalence inherent in the short story to demonstrate that reproductive decision-making is seldom as simple or as stable as conventional notions of voluntary and involuntary childlessness might cause us to assume.

Until relatively recently, the success or failure of an adaptation was judged in terms of its fidelity to the original; a good adaptation was one that stuck closely to the source text, and when an artist or director inserted him- or herself into the work, modifying the text or changing its meaning or context, this was often viewed negatively by readers of the original. This is especially true of film adaptations of novels, which, as theorist Robert Stam (2000) points out, are often discussed in moralistic terms that assume that the film version represents a "vulgarization" or even "desecration" of the prose original (54). Stam argues that this prioritisation of the written word over visual representation reinscribes a classical hierarchy between literature as a form of 'high' culture and cinema as a form of popular or 'low' culture: "Much of the discussion of film adaptation quietly reinscribes the axiomatic superiority of literary art to film, an assumption

---

[2] Stamm's short story was originally published in German in 2008 as 'Der Lauf der Dinge' in the anthology *Wir fliegen* (Stamm 2008). The collection was translated into English and published as *We're Flying* in 2012.

derived from a number of superimposed prejudices" (58). Against this traditional and rather reductive view, adaptation has in recent years begun to be understood as a creative practice, where the content and form of the source text are re-created and re-imagined from a different point of view. As Adrienne Rich (1972) contends, every adaptation is a "re-vision—the act of looking back, of seeing with fresh eyes, of entering an old text from a new critical direction" (18). Contrary to the idea that an adaptation can only ever represent an impoverished version of the source text, critics such as Rich argue that reworking an existing text for a new medium or a new audience can represent an enriching process that can produce new readings and new meanings.

Drawing on Rich's approach, this chapter considers the creative potential of Kofler's cinematic 're-vision' of Stamm's short story. This chapter explores some of the similarities and differences between the film and its narrative inspiration and relates the changes made in the process of adaptation to the different media chosen, as well as to the conventional depiction and perception of childlessness and non-motherhood in the contemporary moment. Specifically, this chapter 'looks back' at some of the assumptions underlying Stamm's short story and considers how they are re-imagined in the transition from written text to a filmic representation. In particular, I explore how, in both texts, the main characters vacillate between wanting and not wanting to have children of their own, and how this ambivalence is represented both in narrative and in visual form.

MOVING BETWEEN CHILDFREEDOM AND CHILDLESSNESS

One of the strengths of Kofler's film *What We Wanted* is its sensitive depiction of the deep pain of infertility, as well as the cruel reality of Assisted Reproductive Technology (ART). In one of the opening scenes of the film, we watch as Niklas and Alice wait in their doctor's office to be told that their fourth attempt to conceive via In Vitro Fertilisation (IVF) has been unsuccessful. We observe the couple's tense silence as they wait to be called into the office and Alice's vulnerability as she lies, legs splayed, while her specialist carries out a vaginal ultrasound; we eavesdrop on the jargon-peppered conversation as the specialist informs the couple that the fertilised egg has failed to develop into a viable embryo; and we witness Alice pause and take a deep breath as she struggles to compose herself before emerging from behind the curtain after the scan. Later, we are privy to a conversation between Alice and Niklas and the receptionist as they negotiate how to cover the substantial shortfall in the cost of the treatment that is not covered by their insurance. This opening scene is key; apart from providing the impetus for the trip to Sardinia that is the central location of the family drama that will follow—their specialist has advised them to take a break from the treatment and do something nice, perhaps take a vacation together—it also offers viewers insight into the couple's profound desire to have a child and the difficulties they face in trying to make their desire a reality. These short scenes lay bare the discomfort, helplessness, vulnerability, humiliation, and disappointment that accompany the couple on their quest to conceive, where what is left unsaid is often far more powerful than the words that are spoken.

The fact that we, as viewers, are given a window into Alice and Niklas's failure to conceive means that we immediately understand how distressing it must be, and how unfair it must seem, when they find themselves holidaying next to the quintessential nuclear family, complete with sporty nouveau-riche dad Romed, yoga-practising yummy mummy Christl, and their good-looking, if somewhat sulky, teenaged son David and uber-cute blonde daughter Denise. The extent to which this alternate reality clashes with their own unfulfilled desire for family is evident when they arrive to find their villa kitted out with the toddler bed and teddy intended for the family next door. This cruel form of confrontation therapy, as Niklas jokingly refers to it, sets the scene for their everyday interaction while on holiday. When they want to enjoy a meal in their garden or lie in the sun on the sandy beach, the family next door is always close by to remind them of what's missing from their life. Despite their attempts to keep their distance from their neighbours, they repeatedly find their paths crossing, and Alice and Niklas see an image of how their lives might have been if they had been able to have the children they so desperately want.

Given the centrality of the infertility plotline to Kofler's film, it is perhaps surprising to note that the short story that served as its inspiration rests on an entirely different premise: in Stamm's narrative, Alice and Niklaus are childless by choice.[3] Their leisurely holiday—in Italy, in this case—is one of many that they, unconstrained by children, have been able to enjoy, and according to Niklaus, from whose perspective the short story is told, this lifestyle-choice is one they agreed upon early:

---

[3] While Stamm's short story names the male protagonist Niklaus, he is called Niklas in Kofler's film. In this essay, I use the name as given in the chosen medium, though they are variations of the same character.

Alice had never wanted children. When Niklaus found that out, his first reaction had been relief, and he saw that it was only convention in him that had assumed he would one day start a family. On the occasions they had talked about it, it had been to assure each other that they had come to the right decision. Perhaps there's something wrong with me, said Alice with a complacent expression, but I find children boring and annoying. Perhaps I have a wrong gene somewhere. They both worked hard and enjoyed their work, Alice in customer service at a bank, and Niklaus as an engineer. If they had had children, one of them would have had to sacrifice his career, and that was something neither of them was prepared to do. They travelled to exotic countries, had been on a trekking holiday in Nepal, and a cruise in the Antarctic. They often went to concerts and plays, and they went out a lot. All that would have been impossible with children. (Stamm 2012, 220–1)

As this passage elucidates, Niklaus and Alice have decided on a childfree life, and have enjoyed the freedom and autonomy that this choice has afforded them. Their unfettered life of travel and career success is premised on their commitment to their agreed position of not wanting children, even as they recognise that this stance flies in the face of convention.

Unlike the couple in Kofler's cinematic rendition, the arrival of the family next door is—initially, at least—more of an inconvenience to Stamm's Alice and Niklaus than a source of heartache. They react with dismay as they watch the father of the family unloading a kid's bicycle and a toddler's tricycle from his shiny black SUV, recognising that their relaxing sojourn has likely come to an abrupt end. Indeed, they soon find that their quiet afternoons reading in the garden are interrupted by the sounds of the couple's six-year-old daughter screaming or their three-year-old son banging his toys together incessantly, and their peaceful al fresco dinners are spoiled by the noise of the children squabbling or their parents berating them for said squabbling. Seen through Niklaus's eyes, Alice grows increasingly frustrated with the unwelcome disturbance caused by the family next door and increasingly impatient with her husband that he cannot or will not do anything to prevent their noisy neighbours from disturbing their peaceful holiday.

The fact that Kofler has turned Stamm's story of a voluntarily childless couple into a drama that revolves around infertility is a crucial variation from the plot line of the source text and one that has a significant impact on the way in which the characters and their stories are depicted. Indeed, at first glance, it seems as though the two couples are depicted in very stereotypical ways. As Gayle Letherby (2002) argues, individuals and couples who cannot have children are often portrayed in culture and the media as "desperate and unfulfilled", while those who choose not to have children tend to be presented as "selfish and deviant" (10). In many ways, the different depictions of the couple in Stamm's short story and Kofler's film correspond to this timeworn pattern. In the short story, the primary reasons given for the couple's decision to remain childfree relate to their unwillingness to sacrifice the lifestyle they've created for themselves; having children would prevent them from going out whenever they want and from travelling to exotic locations, and it might mean that one of them would have to make compromises in their career. The couple in Stamm's short story are thus depicted in quite unsympathetic terms, and their decision not to have children comes across as selfish and uncompromising. Niklaus's depiction of Alice and her apparent indifference to children suggests that she is cold and unfeeling, traits that are often attributed to women who are childless by choice. On the other hand, the same stereotypical representation of childlessness identified by Letherby is also discernible in the depiction of the childless couple in Kofler's film. The main part of the film focuses on their grief and despondency at their inability to conceive a child, even with the help of IVF. Alice's desperation is so noticeable that even little Denise picks up on it, drawing a picture of her in the sand and telling her, "Das bist du, die traurige Frau". ["That's you, the sad woman".] The melancholy of the childless woman follows her everywhere, it seems, even on her luxury vacation.

In their screenplay, Kofler, Bohle, and Kreutzer imagine a very different backstory for Niklas and Alice than that which is offered in the short story that served as its inspiration. Indeed, this difference may well have influenced the reception of the filmic story, as there is some evidence to suggest that the audience is more likely to be sympathetic to a childless couple who wishes to have a family than to a couple who has chosen not to have children. Leslie Ashburn-Nardo's (2017) recent survey of a large number of studies into perceptions of childless men and women in the United States since the 1970s finds that "reactions to people who choose to be childfree, relative to those who choose to have children, have remained consistently negative" (394). Despite the growing rates of childlessness in Western societies, and especially in European countries, in recent years (Kreyenfeld and Konietzka 2017, 3), and the increasing prevalence of voluntary childlessness, there is still a social expectation that individuals and couples will want to have children and a corresponding lack of understanding when that is not the case. It is easier for an audience to understand and relate to a couple who cannot have children than a couple who have chosen not to. The decision to re-envision the story of Alice and Niklaus as one of involuntary childlessness probably contributed to the popularity of the film and its appeal to a broad audience.

GENDERED PERSPECTIVES ON CHILDLESSNESS

Reading Peter Stamm's "The Natural Way of Things", it is striking that the short story is written entirely from Niklaus's perspective. Our image of Alice, the non-mother, is mediated entirely through her husband, and she is at times presented quite negatively when seen from Niklaus's eyes. In Stamm's short story, the holiday starts off badly from the outset. Alice is grumpy because their Italian country villa isn't as nice as the travel agent's brochures had led her to expect. Though Niklaus does his best to distract her with leisurely walks to the beach and a daytrip to nearby Siena, Alice is irritated by the other travellers, who seem to her to have no appreciation for the cultural richness of the area and make no effort to respect the local language and customs. The arrival of the family next door is especially upsetting for Alice though, and Niklaus describes her uneasiness and dis-comfort from the moment they pull into the driveway. She seems hyper-aware of their comings and goings; even when they are not home, Niklaus remarks upon how frequently Alice glances over to their villa. It seems clear from Niklaus's observations of his wife's actions and his interpreta-tion of her reactions that the family represents a particularly unwelcome intrusion on her restful vacation. He describes her extreme irritation at the noise the children make and her impatience with him that he is not willing or able to do anything about it. In all this, Alice's behaviour and words are filtered through her husband and interpreted from his point of view.

It is also important to note that it is Niklaus who tells us about the couple's decision not to have children. While he himself admits to the occasional twinge of regret—or more specifically, we are told, "he had never regretted not having children, but sometimes he regretted that he had never even felt the desire to have any" (Stamm 2012, 221)—he seems convinced that Alice has never had a moment's doubt about her lifestyle choices. He insinuates that she is unwavering in the position she evidently articulated to him early in their relationship, namely that she "had never wanted children" (220). Whilst Niklaus does not criticise his wife overtly for her professed commitment to non-motherhood, there is an implied criticism in his description of the flippancy with which she dismisses her lack of interest in children and the way she jokes that she must "have a wrong gene somewhere" (220). In particular, Niklaus's description of Alice's facial expression as "complacent" when she passes this offhand remark presents an image of her as smug and self-satisfied.

However, the reality is that this partial narrative perspective means that we never gain any real insight into Alice's thoughts or emotions, and certain events in the narrative cause us to doubt Niklaus's reliability as a narrator. His partiality is revealed in his description of Alice's extreme sensitivity to the goings-on next door; this is particularly evident on one occasion, when a loud quarrel between the neighbours' children brings Alice to tears:

> Alice lowered her newspaper and looked up at the sky. Niklaus pretended to be engrossed in his book. After a while, she threw it down, and went inside. Niklaus waited a moment, and followed her. He found her sitting at the living room table, staring into space. He sat down opposite her, but she avoided his gaze. She was breathing fast, and suddenly she fell into a furious sobbing. Niklaus went around the table, and stood behind her. He thought of laying his hand on her shoulder, or stroking her hair, but in the end he only said, just imagine if they were our children. (220)

In this passage, Niklaus describes Alice's crying as "furious sobbing", attributing her extreme emotional reaction thus to anger or frustration at the noise rather than any other kind of distress or discomfort that might be triggered by the situation. Niklaus evidently recognises that the presence of the children has hit a raw nerve with his wife, but his limited understanding of her response is manifest in his hesitation; he is unsure whether her outburst calls for pacification ("laying his hand on her shoulder") or comfort ("stroking her hair"). Similarly, he interprets Alice's sensitivity to the sights and sounds of the family next door as infuriation and her unwillingness to leave the house in the days following this interaction as defensiveness: "She was at war, and had to guard the terrain" (223). As the story unfolds, we as readers begin to question Niklaus's assumption that Alice's nigh-on visceral reaction to the family next door is purely due to annoyance. The limited point of view that he offers as narrator also reminds us that in the short story, Alice's experience as non-mother is always mediated from male point of view.

The point of view of a film is generally less easily discernible than that of a narrative text, and in this respect, it might be seen as inevitable that

Kofler departs from the original in adapting Stamm's short story for the screen. Film theorist Robert Stam suggests that in analysing the question of point of view in relation to film adaptations of narrative texts, there are a number of related questions to consider: "Does the film adaptation maintain the point of view and the focalization (Genette)—of the novel? Who tells the story in the novel vis-à-vis the film? Who focalizes the story—that is, who sees within the story?" (2000, 72). As is the case with most films, there is no narrator or narrative instance throughout Kofler's *What We Wanted*; rather, the film tends to focus its depiction on external events, action, and dialogue. This means that we must examine the question of who sees in order to understand how the director has opted to render the characters' point of view in the film.

Like Stamm's short story, Kofler's film also centres on the relationship between Alice and Niklas, but unlike its narrative inspiration, the film tends to privilege Alice's perspective over Niklas's. In many cases, the couple are depicted together in the same shot, eating together in the garden of their villa or lying together on a sunbed on the beach; however, in scenes where they go their separate ways, the camera most often sticks with Alice so that we gain a deeper insight into her world and her experience than that of Niklas. For example, when the couple visit their doctor, the camera follows Alice behind the curtain while Niklas waits in the doctor's office, and while Niklas chats to the couple next door, the camera concentrates on Alice's conversations with their children. On two occasions where the couple argue, the audience gets to see how both Alice and Niklas deal with the aftermath, but on both occasions, the camera spends more time focusing on Alice, as if taking her side in the argument. In this way, the film version tends to give more attention to the female perspective, depicting Alice's view of events and fostering the audience's sympathy for her.

Kofler's film also introduces a narrative element that reveals a clear bias towards Alice's perspective. The film is interspersed with hazy images of Alice and Niklas's first trip to Sardinia right at the beginning of their relationship, of them sleeping in a tent, swimming in the sea, and making love. The first of these, which appears as the opening sequence of the film, gives us a strong steer as to how these sequences should be interpreted: Alice stands on a beach while she tells us in voiceover of her dreams of a child that is hers and Niklas's. Alice's interior monologue in voiceover lets the audience know from the outset that the recurring flashbacks that punctuate the film are her dreamlike memories of a time in their relationship when they were young and carefree as well as her musings on an alternative reality that might have followed. This voiceover picks up on the narrative element of the short story and allows us an insight into Alice's thoughts and feelings that would not otherwise be accessible in a visual medium such as film.

This modification in the move from short story to film means that the two texts differ significantly in their point of view: while Stamm's narrative is told entirely from Niklaus's point of view, and our image of Alice is mediated entirely through him, Kofler's film moves between Niklas and Alice and ultimately privileges her perspective over his. If Stamm's short story tells the story of childlessness and non-motherhood from a male standpoint, Kofler upsets this power dynamic and hands the narrative power over to Alice. She reimagines the experience from Alice's perspective and allows her to tell her own story of childlessness and non-motherhood from her own perspective and on occasion even in her own words.

It is important to note that this shift in gendered perspective is not neutral; on the contrary, research shows that non-mothers often face more pressure than non-fathers to explain their childlessness. Rosemary Gillespie (2000) points out that despite changing social roles and increasing rates of childlessness in many Western countries, the majority of women will still become mothers; in the minority, many childless women then still find their choices questioned, belittled, or disbelieved. Maura Kelly (2009) examines 20 years of scholarship on women's childlessness and finds that many women mention the disapproval they sense from friends and family and the stigma they experience in wider society. Indeed, as Kelly underlines, the women's perception of being viewed negatively is in fact borne out by attitudinal surveys that find that women without children are assumed to be unhappy and their lives less rewarding than women with children (165). The fact that Kofler's film focuses on the situation of the non-mother, on her choices and her emotions, means that it offers insight into an identity that is often disregarded or even denigrated in society and culture.

Approaches to Ambivalence

In the course of the two texts—both the short story and its film adaptation—it gradually becomes clear to readers and viewers that the understanding of childlessness they convey is far more complex than how it is frequently represented in culture and the media or viewed by wider society. All too often, individuals and couples without children are assumed to fall into one of two groups—that is, either they cannot have children or they have chosen a childfree life—but these simple categorisations overlook the myriad ways that fertility intentions can change in accordance with life circumstances and the passage of time. A couple might enter a relationship with no intention to have children but may come to feel differently and decide to try for children; or they might initially want to be parents but find themselves unable to conceive; in this case, they may accept this and even come to embrace a childfree lifestyle, or they might choose to pursue other avenues, seeking fertility treatment or adoption as a route to parenthood. It is for these reasons that James Monach (1993) suggests that "it is probably more helpful to consider childlessness in general as a continuum, on which there are those clearly at either end, but there is a group in the middle whose position is not so simple and might change over time" (5; see also Letherby 2002, 7–8). Indeed, we might well imagine that a substantial proportion of childless individuals and couples belong in this "group in the middle", as fertility decisions are seldom clear-cut or stable.

Focussing specifically on the choices and situations of non-mothers, Letherby (2002) reminds us that many women's positions on the childless/childfree continuum are difficult to pin down, even for themselves: "Whereas some 'voluntarily' childless women define themselves as childfree and some 'involuntarily' childless women feel desperate some of the time, others are more ambivalent" (8). In many respects, it is this ambiguous area between voluntary and involuntary non-motherhood that is explored in Stamm's "The Natural Way of Things" and Kofler's *What We Wanted*. Both the short story and its cinematic adaptation highlight the idea that the identity of non-mother is often far more nuanced than it initially seems, and that it can shift and change over time. Although, as discussed above, the two versions of the figure of Alice may initially seem to signify polar opposites, with Alice in the short story representing the position of childfree woman and Alice in the film denoting the position of childless woman, both texts ultimately emphasise ways in which these apparently stable identities can reveal themselves to be far more complex and ambivalent. This section will explore the ways to which the ambivalence that is present already in Stamm's short story is translated in Kofler's film, as well as the ways in which both texts raise questions about conventional assumptions about voluntary and involuntary childlessness.

There is some evidence in Stamm's short story to suggest that Niklaus and Alice's interaction with the family next door, which seems at first glance to be a source of great irritation to them, also reveals sensitivities in their relationship related to their decision not to have children. Niklaus, from whose perspective the story is told, admits to feeling of ambivalence about the lifestyle that he and Alice have chosen and how they have arranged their life together; in particular, he wonders whether "having a family might entail not just a loss of freedom, but perhaps a certain gain as well, perhaps he and Alice might have been more independent of each other, without the exclusivity of love and irritation" (Stamm 2012, 221). Even as Niklaus recognises that the childfreedom that he and Alice have chosen has afforded them the time and money to take advantage of opportunities that would otherwise not have been available to them, he also acknowledges that the choices they have made have robbed them of certain experiences as well. In this way, the confrontation with the family next door has triggered some soul-searching for Niklaus, and he finds himself pondering the road not taken.

Alice's ambivalence about her non-motherhood is explored in quite different, and much more subtle ways in Stamm's short story. Though, as discussed earlier in this chapter, Niklaus seems unable or unwilling to see it, it gradually becomes clear to the reader that Alice's extreme sensitivity to the goings-on of the parents and children next door, which is rendered most obvious in her fit of "furious sobbing" (220) after one interaction, points to more than mere irritation due to the noise. Her overt interest in the children and her continuous stolen glances over to the villa next door suggest that Alice is not as secure in her life-choices as Niklaus sees to assume and that she, like him, is contemplating another life, one in which they have children. Seen thus, Niklaus's words of comfort to his wife after her tearful outburst—"just imagine if they were our children" (220)—give voice to the uncertainty that she too is experiencing in this moment; on the surface, his words suggest an appeal for empathy for the couple next door, who are probably doing their best to keep their children happy and quiet, but on a deeper level, they can be read as an invitation to Alice to imagine herself into the role of mother to the two children next door, or even to consider an alternative life to the one that they have chosen.

In some respects then, the couple from Stuttgart comes to represent a fantasy counterpoint to the life that Niklaus and Alice have chosen to live. Their fascination with the family next door is tinged with curiosity and even envy about how their lives might have turned out if they had made different choices. Niklaus's fantasy of an alternative life extends to an imagined sexual encounter with the young wife who sunbathes topless in her garden, and that fantasy spills over into reality when his excitement at this daydream inspires him to initiate sex with Alice. Their voyeuristic vision of an alternative life reignites their passion for one another, and this incident marks a change in their holiday. The fantasy is brought to an abrupt end, however, when all goes quiet from one day to the next and the couple stops coming out of their holiday villa. Niklaus and Alice learn to their horror that the sudden silence is due to a tragic event: the father of the family accidentally ran over his son with his car and killed him. Niklaus and Alice stand at their window, watching the father pack up the family car—the tricycle that once pointed metonymically to the presence of a child now serving as a haunting reminder of the absence of that child. Despite this morbid turn of events, the closeness that Alice and Niklaus have regained remains, and after the car has driven away, they make love "urgently" and "more forcefully than a few days before" (232).

Alice and Niklaus's ambivalence regarding the life-choices they have made and their decision not to have children is not explored in explicit terms in the short story, and a reader or viewer might thus be forgiven for wondering why Kofler and Bohle chose to introduce what may seem like a new thread into the story when they wrote the screenplay for the film. However, Kofler asserts that this theme is already evident in Stamm's narrative, albeit in intangible form: "The desire for children is only addressed subtly in the short story", she says; "You can see it if you choose to".[4] The challenge for Kofler is how to portray the ambiguity she perceives in Stamm's text in such a way that it is equally open to personal reading and interpretation. To use Adrienne Rich's terms, how can her "re-vision" of Stamm's short story reimagine the sensitive issues and raw emotions that fuel the tense relationship between Alice and Niklaus in a way that allows viewers to see them "with fresh eyes" (1972, 18)?

There are a number of ways that the couple's uncertain feelings about their desire for family, and the ambivalent emotions that this provokes, are handled in the film adaptation, some overt and some less so. The first and most obvious means by which the simplistic distinction between voluntary and involuntary childlessness is unsettled is through the backstory

---

[4] "Der Kinderwunsch ist in der Kurzgeschichte nur subtil erzählt. Wenn man will, kann man es lesen" (Kofler 2020b).

attributed to the couple in Kohler's film. After Alice discovers that Niklas has confided in the couple next door about their struggles to conceive, she reveals to them—defiantly, as if inviting their criticism—that she fell unexpectedly pregnant early in their relationship but decided not to continue with the pregnancy. This revelation sketches a life trajectory that demonstrates the way in which her desire for children has changed over time and in line with her life circumstances. Alice evokes a memory of herself as a young woman—the same young woman whom we now recognise from the hazy images in the flashbacks that recur throughout the film—who is not ready to be a mother and chooses non-motherhood, opting to terminate her pregnancy. We also recognise that the voiceover in which she tells of her dreams of a child is not mere fancy but rather an alternative reality, another potential life-course in which she continues with her pregnancy and becomes a mother. Alice's disclosure of her confrontation with the possibility of motherhood at a time in her life when she was unable or unwilling to take on the responsibility associated with it stands in sharp contrast to her inability to conceive at a time in her life when she is now ready to be a mother. Moreover, it is clear from her defensive attitude in telling her story that she makes a connection between the two experiences, as though her inability to maintain a pregnancy now is somehow a punishment for her decision not to continue with her pregnancy when she was younger. This moment of painful revelation is one of the most poignant moments in Kofler's film.

A second way in which Kofler translates the ambivalence of Stamm's narrative into her film adaptation is through silence and facial expressions. Just as in the written text, what is not said in the film is often more telling than the action and dialogue. We are repeatedly presented with images of Alice and Niklas sitting beside one another but not looking at or speaking to one another. This is most evident in the scene in which they wait in the doctor's office, not speaking or touching: first Niklas turns to look at Alice, but she does not meet his gaze and so he turns away, then Alice turns to look at Niklas, but he does not return her glance, so she looks away. There is no dialogue or action to interpret this scene for us; we are left to read the emotion on the characters' faces and interpret their silence for ourselves. The same is true of several scenes between Alice and the two children next door, particularly her interactions with six-year-old Denise. Though these scenes usually do involve some dialogue, childish and innocent as it is, Alice's facial expressions and gestures, as well as her many stolen glances at the child, leave it to the viewer to decipher her thoughts and the emotion she feels in these moments. In one scene, which takes place just after Denise has broken her expensive designer sunglasses, it is not quite clear from Alice's demeanour whether she is actually annoyed with Denise or merely feigning irritation to hold the child at a distance. When Denise leans her body against Alice, Alice hesitates and then puts her arm around the little girl, pausing at the top of her head as if to smell her hair. There is no narrator to interpret this scene for us, nor does Alice comment on the gesture or on the emotions it evokes in her, so it falls to the viewer to draw these inferences from her facial expressions and attitude.[5]

Finally, it is noteworthy that the ending of film is left open, and we as viewers are not provided with a clear answer to the question as to whether Alice and Niklas will try again to conceive, explore other routes to parenthood, or come to terms with their inability to have children. On a hike together, Niklas lets Alice know—not for the first time—that he is prepared to consider adoption; he even suggests to her that they deserve to have a nice life even if they don't have children and points out how they could use some of the space in their new house to make their own lives more pleasant and enjoyable. However, Alice won't countenance the idea of giving up on her dream of carrying their biological child, and she stomps off in a temper, leaving Niklas to hike home alone. Later, in a conversation over a drink with the hotel receptionist Sabrina about the physical and emotional toll the IVF has taken on her and on her relationship with Niklas, she admits, "I don't know if we can stop"—and then corrects herself with "I don't know if *I* can stop". As in the novel, however, the film takes tragic turn; when the son of the couple next door, the good-looking but troubled teenager David, attempts suicide, it shatters the illusion of the perfect family and causes Alice and Niklas to forget about what's missing from their life and focus instead on what they have together. Their journey home to Austria is pensive, but their arguments are put aside. In the final scene of the film, Alice tears open the waterproof covering in the loft of their new house to look out at the view across the city and

---

[5] Indeed, this aspect of the film is one that was picked up in some of the reviews of the film. For example, Matthias Hoff (2023) notes that "Director Ulrike Kofler presents *What We Wanted* as a quiet, contemplative drama that gives us ample time to explore the characters' feelings".

asks Niklas how he would feel about putting in a panoramic window. While it is not clear what the future holds for her, this gesture of opening, with its hint of possibility, suggests an openness also to a new perspective on her life—even if it doesn't involve motherhood.

CONCLUSION

Ulrike Kofler's film adaptation of Peter Stamm's "The Natural Way of Things" may at first glance seem to depart significantly from its narrative source text. As this chapter has shown, the move from a story of voluntary childlessness and non-motherhood to one of involuntary childlessness and infertility is, at least on the face of it, a considerable deviation from the original, and the change from a male-centred written text to a female-centred visual text might also be seen as a substantial shift in focus. Against this, this chapter has argued that Kofler's film both brings to the surface undercurrents that were already present in the short story and offers a view of voluntary and involuntary childlessness that shatters the assumed opposition between these two positions. Though in many ways Kofler's cinematic adaptation might be seen as being "unfaithful" to the original, it arguably offers another side of the same story, laying bare the ambivalence and vacillation that underlie many, if not most, fertility decisions.

The figure of Alice—her backstory, her desire for family and her position as non-mother—might be seen as having undergone the most significant adaptation in the transition from short story to film, especially as Stamm's Alice is presented in somewhat negative terms. As this chapter has shown, the difficulty we face as readers of Stamm's short story is that we have no direct access to Alice; her story is mediated through the (subjective) eyes and ears of her husband, Niklaus. In a sense then, Kofler liberates Alice from her role as object of her husband's story and offers a more nuanced view of her story of childlessness and non-motherhood. If Kofler's "re-vision" of Stamm's short story offers a more complex and more ambivalent view of the myriad ways in which an individual's desire for children might change over the life-course and in reaction to different life circumstances, her "re-vision" of Alice is arguably even more powerful. The image of the non-mother that emerges through this adaptation is one that invites us to reconsider conventional notions of childlessness and revisit our own preconceptions "with fresh eyes" and "from a new critical direction" (Rich 1972, 18).

REFERENCES

Ashburn-Nardo, Leslie. 2017. Parenthood as a Moral Imperative? Moral Outrage and the Stigmatization of Voluntarily Childfree Women and Men. *Sex Roles* 76: 393–401. https://doi.org/10.1007/s11199-016-0606-1.

Gillespie, Rosemary. 2000. When No Means No: Disbelief, Disregard and Deviance as Discourses of Voluntary Childlessness. *Women's Studies International Forum* 23 (2): 223–234. https://doi.org/10.1016/S0277-5395(00)00076-5.

Hoff, Matthias. 2023. Netflix hat den besten Film mit Elyas M'Barek, aber kaum jemand kennt ihn. *MoviePilot.* July 15. https://www.moviepilot.de/news/netflix-hat-den-besten-film-mit-elyas-m-barek-aber-kaum-jemand-kennt-ihn-1142262. Accessed 21 Jun 2023.

Kelly, Maura. 2009. Women's Voluntary Childlessness: A Radical Rejection of Motherhood? *Women's Studies Quarterly* 37 (3–4): 157–172. https://doi.org/10.1353/wsq.0.0164.

Kofler, Ulrike. Director. 2020a. *Was wir wollten.* Film AG Produktions GmbH. https://www.netflix.com/watch/81233909

——— 2020b. Warum *Was wir wollten* ein Film über das Loslassen ist. Interview by Julia Schafferhofer, *Kleine Zeitung,* December 21, 2020. https://www.kleinezeitung.at/kultur/kino/5914590/Interview-mit-Ulrike-Kofler_Warum-Was-wir-wollten-ein-Film-ueber

Kreyenfeld, Michaela, and Dirk Konietzka. 2017. Analyzing Childlessness. In *Childlessness in Europe: Contexts, Causes, and Consequences,* ed. Michaela Kreyenfeld and Dirk Konietzka, 3–15. Cham: Springer. https://doi.org/10.1007/978-3-319-44667-7_1.

Letherby, Gayle. 2002. Childless and Bereft?: Stereotypes and Realities in Relation to 'Voluntary' and 'Involuntary' Childlessness and Womanhood. *Sociological Inquiry* 72 (1): 7–20. https://doi.org/10.1111/1475-682X.00003.

Monach, James H. 1993. *Childless: No Choice: The Experience of Involuntary Childlessness.* London: Routledge.

Rich, Adrienne. 1972. When we dead awaken: Writing as re-vision. *College English* 34 (1): 18–30. https://doi.org/10.2307/375215.

Stam, Robert. 2000. Beyond Fidelity: The Dialogics of Adaptation. In *Film Adaptation,* ed. James Naremore, 54–76. New Brunswick: Rutgers.

Stamm, Peter. 2008. *Wir Fliegen.* Frankfurt: S. Fischer.

———. 2012. *We're Flying.* London: Granta.

Index[1]

[1] Note: Page numbers followed by 'n' refer to notes.

© The Author(s) 2025   239
J. Björklund et al. (eds.), *Negotiating Non-Motherhood*,
Palgrave Macmillan Studies in Family and Intimate Life,
https://doi.org/10.1007/978-3-031-66697-1

Puberty, 51, 186
Purity, 144, 163, 186, 191

Q
Queerness, 188
Questione di biglie (Zerbini), 123

R
Rabe, Annina, 30
Race
  blackness, 143, 166
  transracial adoption, 158, 160n4
  in *Une poupée en chocolat*,
    12, 158–173
Rahimi, Faranak, 37
Rainey, Sarah, 190
Rank, Mark R., 91
Rape, 12, 169
Raque-Bodgen, T.L., 104
Religion, *see* Bible; Catholicism
Renewal and degradation, 32, 38
Reproduction, 4, 12, 37, 46, 48–51,
  55, 61, 85, 86, 88, 89, 97, 98,
  118, 158, 160–163, 190, 210
Reproductive justice, 158–160,
  172, 173
Reproductive temporality, 86, 89, 97
Repro-lit, 23
Rhizome, 165
Riba Rossy, Raquel, 206
  ¿Qué pacha mama?, 206
Rich, Adrienne, 5, 184, 184n6, 223,
  233, 236
Rodgers, Julie, 5, 6, 11, 30, 129
Rottenberg, Catherine, 189–190,
  210, 213
Rousseau, Jean-Jacques, 209, 213
  Émile, 209, 213
Roy, Arundhati, 193
Ruddick, Sara, 5, 189

S
Safer, Jeanne, 82
Sandberg, Sheryl, 189n7
  Lean In, 189n7
Scholz, Sally J., 158, 160, 161
Sebastià-Sáez, Maria, 12
Secondary infertility
  agency, loss of, 109
  awareness of, 117
  emotions, 105, 109
  in general, 104
  invisibility, 105, 110–114
  and primary infertility, 104–106,
    112, 113
  See also Davies, Helen, *More
    Love to Give*
The Second Sex (de Beauvoir), 4, 52
Sembrava una promessa (Zerbini), 123
Sexual intercourse, 32
Shakespeare, William, 13, 177–179,
  178n1, 187, 190, 192
  Coriolanus, 190
  King Lear, 13, 177, 178
Sharpe, Christina, 166, 173
Simons, Harriet Fishman, 104, 106,
  109–112, 114, 115
Single motherhood, 5, 207
Single women, 29, 89, 97, 158, 160
Sinthomosexuality, 189
Sisterhood, 124, 133
Sita (Hindu goddess), 179, 180, 183,
  184, 189, 191, 192, 192n8, 194
Sonograms, 125–127, 131, 131n8
Spain
  abortion in, 43, 199
  Basque Country, 140
  Catholicism, 218
  family norms, 31
  feminism, 9, 10, 43
  fertility rates, 9, 43
  Francoist regime, 42, 43
  free choice in, 200, 207